Revolutionary Writers

Revolutionary Writers

LITERATURE AND AUTHORITY
IN THE NEW REPUBLIC
1725–1810

EMORY ELLIOTT

New York   Oxford
OXFORD UNIVERSITY PRESS
1982

Library of Congress Cataloging in Publication Data
Elliott, Emory, 1942–
Revolutionary writers.
Bibliography: p.   Includes index.
1. American literature—1783–1850—History and criticism.
2. American literature—Revolutionary period,
1775–1783—History and criticism.
3. Christianity and literature.   4. Authority in literature.
5. Literature and society—United States.
6. United States—Intellectual life—1783–1865.   I. Title.
PS193.E4   810'.9'002   81-4016
ISBN 0-19-502999-2   AACR2

Printing (last digit): 9 8 7 6 5 4 3 2 1
Printed in the United States of America

For my Mother
and the memory of my Father
For my Children
Scott, Mark, Matthew,
Laura, and Constance
And for Georgia

Acknowledgments

This book began in 1974 when I prepared a paper on the rhetoric of the Revolutionary War for the Third Annual Lawrence Henry Gipson Symposium at Lehigh University. Since that time I have received the assistance of many individuals and institutions. A leave of absence and a Bicentennial Preceptorship from Princeton University allowed me time to complete a considerable portion of the reading and research. A fellowship from the John Simon Guggenheim Memorial Fellowship Foundation enabled me to travel to several research libraries, and a fellowship from the National Endowment for the Humanities and a second leave from Princeton permitted me to spend a year at the National Humanities Center in Research Triangle Park, North Carolina, for final research and writing. I am most grateful to these institutions for their support.

Along the way it has been my very good fortune to have the help of many people who have given their time, learning, and encouragement to this work. Most important of these has been Professor Sacvan Bercovitch. From his support, advice, and careful reading of the manuscript I have gained immeasurably. The friendship and counsel of this remarkable scholar are valuable treasures indeed. I am also indebted to several other important scholars who have read the final manuscript: Michael Davitt Bell, Giles Gunn, Richard Beale Davis, William L. Hedges, Lewis Leary, Jay Martin, Russel B. Nye, and Kenneth Silverman. My former student, Mark Patterson, and a number of my colleagues at Princeton have also read all or part of the work and made useful suggestions: Margaret A. Doody, Ulrich C. Knoepflmacher, A. Walton Litz, Jr., and Thomas P. Roche. The work also improved by the careful copyediting of Ms. Kim Lewis at Oxford University Press. Again, I am pleased to thank Edward H. Davidson who encouraged the project from the start and gave the final draft a careful reading.

Small portions of Chapter I were published in a different form in articles that first appeared as "The Dove and Serpent: The Clergy in the American Revolution," *American Quarterly*, Vol. XXXI, No. 2 (Summer 1979), pp. 192–97; and "The Development of the Puritan Sermon and Elegy: 1660–1750," *Early American Literature*, Vol. XV, No. 2 (Fall 1980), pp. 151–64. They are reprinted with permission of those journals. Segments of Chapter IV were excerpted from my essays on Charles Brockden Brown in *American Writers: A Collection of Literary Biographies*, Supplement I, Part 1 edited by Leonard Unger (Copyright © 1979 Charles Scribner's Sons), reprinted by permission of the publishers, and in *Critical Essays on Charles Brockden Brown*, edited by Bernard Rosenthal (Copyright © 1981 by Twayne Publishers) and reprinted with the permission of Twayne Publishers, a division of G. K. Hall & Co., Boston. I am also grateful to The New American Library, Inc., for allowing me to quote from Norman Mailer's *The Armies of the Night* (1968), and to Atheneum Publishers for permission to quote from James Merrill's *Mirabell: Books of Number, A Poem* (Copyright © 1979 by James Merrill [New York: Atheneum, 1979]), reprinted with permission of Atheneum Publishers.

The staffs of several libraries have been kind and helpful: The American Antiquarian Society, The Huntington Library, the Massachusetts Historical Society, the New Jersey Historical Society, the New York Public Library, the Pennsylvania Historical Society; and the libraries of the following universities: California at Los Angeles, California at Santa Barbara, Carolina at Chapel Hill, Duke, Harvard, North Carolina State, Pennsylvania, Princeton, Rutgers, and Yale. At the Huntington Library I also benefited from the advice of Professors J.A. Leo Lemay and Paul M. Zall.

During my year in residence at the National Humanities Center (1979–80), the staff was splendid in every way. I am especially grateful to Alan Tuttle, the librarian, and to those in the manuscript division who patiently typed barely legible drafts: Marie Long, Jan Paxton, Cynthia Edwards, and Madoline Moyer. From discussions and seminars with my colleagues at the Center, I derived knowledge, encouragement, and useful advice, especially from Quentin Anderson, Yehoshua Arieli, Harold Berman, Richard Beale Davis, Robert Magliola, John Moline, Cynthia Russett, Elaine Scarry, and Madolene Stone. It was particularly generous of Professor Arieli to read and criticize early drafts of my first two chapters. While at the Center, I also learned much from Robert Bain, Wesley Kort, Richard Rust, and especially from Paul Ricouer, and I benefited from the administrative support of William J. Bennett, Kent Mullikan, and John Agresto. It was a special honor to spend that year with Richard Beale Davis; all of us who knew him will cherish the memory of that fine scholar and gentleman.

Closer to home, I have depended upon the diligence and proficiency of Francisco Rivero, my research assistant, of

Annette Cafarelli, who read proof, and of Mrs. Helen Wright, who typed the final draft with her usual expertness. Professor Willard Thorp has given enthusiastic encouragement and advice and allowed me to draw upon his impressive collection of Americana.

As all in this profession well know, a work of scholarship is never the result of the efforts and sacrifices of one person. Most important have been the contributions of Georgia Carroll Elliott, my wife, who listened to and challenged early versions of the argument, cheerfully accompanied me on the relocations necessary for my research, and edited my writing with care and intelligence. This book is dedicated to those who have given most to it from their own lives, through their trust, understanding, and love.

Princeton, N.J.   E.E.
October 1981

Contents

Revolutionary Writers

INTRODUCTION

> For in this world of lies, Truth is forced to fly like a scared
> white doe in the woodlands; and only by cunning glimpses will
> she reveal herself, as in Shakespeare and other masters of the
> great Art of Telling the Truth—even though it be covertly,
> and by snatches.
>
> HERMAN MELVILLE
> "Hawthorne and His Mosses," 1850

In 1977, shortly after he was awarded the Nobel Prize, Saul
Bellow considered the relation between the artist and society
in America: "American society likes its artists and writers,
certainly, it's proud of them, it rewards them, but it doesn't
know what the hell they're all about—and there's a sort of
vulgar cheerfulness in its relation to them." Other Western
nations take their writers more seriously; heads of state sometimes even consult them on public issues. In the United States,
however, it would not occur to the President or the secretary
of state to consult with a novelist about the mood of the
American people or features of the American character. The
artist is regarded as having nothing of importance to say
about matters of public affairs, and the suggestion that the
country's greatest novelist might hold an honorary public
office would be rejected as a joke. This situation has obviously
fostered in Bellow a rather ironic attitude toward himself as
a social guardian, for on another recent occasion he seemed
resigned to American attitudes: "Occasionally I worry about
what's happening to culture in the United States, but on
other days I think there is no culture in the United States,
and there's no point in worrying about it."[1]

This oscillating attitude may also be seen as typical of the ambivalence that American writers often display regarding their place in our society. During the two decades after the Revolution the struggle for power and authority in the new nation involved much more than the competition of political parties over states' rights, checks and balances, and the federal Constitution. Because of new opportunities for exerting financial and personal influence upon government and society, those bred and educated in traditional colonial culture found themselves competing with upstarts and entrepreneurs for rank and status in the new social order. By the time the battle for power had temporarily subsided and the nation had entered that period of the early nineteenth century known as the "era of good feelings," profound changes had occurred in the social hierarchy of America.

Most significantly, but perhaps not surprisingly, the greatest number of casualties occurred among the intellectuals. The learned clergy and the cultured men of letters, those who had exercised the greatest degree of intellectual and cultural influence in the prewar society, were left with little or no authority in America. Individual ministers, like Charles Finney or Billy Graham, might again spring up to captivate millions and speak with Presidents, but as a class the learned clergy no longer could command respect or attention. The same rejection of intellectual complexity and serious reflection that doomed the clergy also reduced the position of writers and men of letters, a point upon which even the old adversaries John Adams and Thomas Jefferson concurred. Although Jefferson was usually more optimistic than Adams, he agreed with Adams's assessment that virtue and genius would have difficulty attaining supremacy over the powers of wealth and political manipulation. Adams predicted that "all will depend on the Progress of Knowledge. But how shall Knowledge Advance? Independent of Temporal and Spiritual Power, the Course of Science and Literature is obstructed and discouraged by so many Causes that it is to be feared, their motions will be slow. . . . slow rises Genius by Poverty and Envy oppressed."[2] Drawing out the implications of the Adams–Jefferson *Letters* for the cultural situation in America, Ezra Pound proposed that they marked a turning point in American literature. Never again, Pound declared, would there be political leaders in America who would possess such learning and who would recognize the value of literature to the society as a whole:

> In 170 years the United States have at no time contained a more civilized "world" than that comprised by the men to whom Adams and Jefferson wrote. . . . Neither of these two men would have thought of literature as something having nothing to do with life, the nation, the organization of government. Of course, no first-rate writer ever did think of his books in that manner. . . . I do not believe that either public men or American writers for the past forty years have dared to face the implications of the Adams–Jefferson volumes. . . . Jefferson specifically wanted [to build] a civilization in Virginia . . . [but his desire was shared only by] a very few professional writers and an ineffective minority of the electorate. You have a definite opposition between public life and such men as H[enry] James and H[enry] Adams which you cannot ascribe *wholly* to their individual temperaments.[3]

Many readers of American literature assume such carping on the part of writers toward American society or the extreme sequestration of artists like Thomas Pynchon or J. D. Salinger to be the products of modern disillusionment and alienation. Some scholars have traced this uncertainty to the disappointments of Hawthorne and Melville when they could not match the impressive sales of the "scribbling women."[4] Others find the source of the American writer's curious position in society in the personal eccentricities of figures like Whitman, Poe, or Thoreau.[5] But the dissatisfaction of American authors, usually justified, began almost at the moment the republic was formed and has actually changed very little since the 1780s. The limited sphere of influence of which writers complain today is not simply the result of twentieth-century malaise or nineteenth-century philistinism.

Until recently, however, Pound was one of the few rigorous students of American literature to recognize the crisis of culture that occurred during the early national period. Only in the last ten to fifteen years has there been a serious challenge to the long-prevailing argument about the formation of American literature alleging that it all really started with Emerson. Although a condescending nod was always given in American literature courses and in book introductions to a few Puritan writers and to the importance of Benjamin Franklin, only exceptional scholars such as Perry Miller and Richard Chase have insisted that an understanding of Emerson, Thoreau, Hawthorne, and Melville requires thorough study of their precursors: those unsung poets and novelists of the late eighteenth century such as Joel Barlow, Hugh Henry Brackenridge, Charles Brockden Brown, Timothy Dwight, and Philip Freneau. Anthologies sometimes exposed students to a few unrepresentative poems of Freneau, but the novels of Brown and Brackenridge were largely unread and the long major poems of Dwight and Barlow were seldom mentioned.[6]

Of course, it must be said at the outset that if the only motive for examining the literature of the past is to appreciate great literary achievement and reap aesthetic pleasure, then the teachers of American literature have been right not to assign *The Columbiad* for study. It is the assumption of this study, however, that aesthetic pleasure is only one of many things to be gained from the study of our literary heritage and that from literary works we may learn of the human experience of those who wrote and the world in which they lived. From the study of the careers of our first national writers and close examination of some of their major works, we may gain a clearer understanding of many formative elements of American literature. In the poetry and fiction produced during the critical decades after the Revolution are the earliest signs of the ironies, narrative manipulations, and multileveled ambiguities that would characterize the works of Poe, Hawthorne, and Melville. In the experiences of writers like Freneau and Brown are the seeds of the peculiar relationship between the writer and his audience in American society. By the time Emerson composed his famous essays on the American scholar and the poet, the struggle to establish a role for the man of letters in America had already been fought by this first generation of American writers.

Yet there are many reasons that writers of the Revolution have received so little attention. Not only does the critic have to search for the jewels, but the standards of taste of modern readers have been fashioned by post-Romantic forms and styles. For the most part the first American writers were adhering to literary standards established in the neoclassical period of the eighteenth century. As a result, many of their writings appear antiquated and their subjects and styles are easy marks for ridicule. For this reason the poems of that time that do get anthologized have often been unrepresentative: those few pre-Romantic gems that the editor mined out of volumes of heroic-couplet verse.

Another barrier separating modern readers from the eighteenth-century writers is the intimate relationship between literature and religion that prevailed well beyond the Revolution. Because the clergy and men of letters were striving for similar goals, used many of the same verbal devices, and were sometimes even the same people, the study of the literature of this period involves the reader in matters of theology and religious history as well—a prospect that has not always excited literary critics. Yet the intricate and changing connection between religion and belles lettres is one of the most fascinating aspects of that period, and the moral and spiritual role the American writers inherited became a significant characteristic of those writers and their works.

So fundamental is this connection in American literature that on a deeper level the bond between religious belief and serious literature has remained strong until our own time. In his recent study of American fiction after 1945, *A Literature Without Qualities*, Warner Berthoff has recognized the remarkable persistence of this religious element and has even suggested that the American novelist still sees himself in a clerical role: "In American writing this convergence of secular literary ambition upon essentially religious imperatives runs deep. It is, in one central respect, a *pastoral* model —and by this I do not mean the special set of poetic and mythological conventions descending in western literature from Theocritus and the Virgilian eclogues, but the ministerial pastoralism of the reformed regathered Protestant churches (churches or priesthoods of the single believer, if necessary)."[7]

The continuing debate and confusion over the importance of religious ideas and language upon the formation of an American nationalist ideology has increased the need for a better understanding of the literary works of post-Revolutionary War America. The question of the role of religion in the formation of the republic's ideals is a hotly contested issue that remains unresolved. A provocative and widely respected thesis, elaborated recently by Sacvan Bercovitch, is that religious language and religiously grounded myths about America played a significant role in shaping an ideology of the "American Way of Life." Bercovitch argues that a set of beliefs originally expounded in New England Puritan rhetoric formed the superstructure that encloses virtually all American political and social ideas, even those that appear to be in conflict with one another.[8] Thus, American identity is necessarily a religious identity. Other scholars such as Henry Steele Commager point to the importance of the rules of law, of reason, of political liberalism, which stem from a distinctly non-religious, indeed even anti-religious, tradition of the eighteenth-century Enlightenment from which, in their view, American political and social ideals have derived. For them, religious influences in the last decades of the founding century were quite subordinate to those of classical and modern philosophy, particularly for the leaders who framed the Constitution.[9]

In an attempt to reconcile this debate, Henry May concluded that the function of religion in the minds of the framers was best expressed in *The Federalist* #10. Madison held that a consensus belief in God would be the essential glue binding all Americans together, while a wide variety of denominations would ensure the general weakness of religion in the realms of politics and society. May's compromise does not succeed, however, because the clash is really between two extremely different methods of historical analysis. Bercovitch and the literary scholars who follow him believe that we can understand the deeper structures of a culture through close study of verbal symbols—image, rhetoric, sermons, fictions, and poems.[10] Incisive readings of these products of the imagination will provide insight into the substratum of our society. At the other extreme, historians trusting direct discourse and the non-symbolic language of official documents and records believe that all we may really know of the past is what people said they did, believed, and intended.

The difficulty with both lines of argument and the evidence for them is that they generalize so broadly about a relatively long period of history in which the lives of individuals and the progress of their ideas underwent many changes and even complete reversals of direction. When we begin to look closely at individual lives and the evolution of particular careers or intellectual activities, the generalizations begin to break down. Religious feeling and unconscious ad-

herence to religious beliefs may exist in an individual who
consciously advocates the deistical assumptions of his contemporaries. Or, one person's deepest conviction in the rule
of law and reason may be expressed to an audience through
symbols of religious expression and myths, as in Thomas
Paine's *Common Sense*. Put quite simply, people did not
always say what they meant or felt; nor did they always mean
what they said. And during this time, called the "Age of
Contradictions" by Leon Howard, even poets and preachers
contradicted themselves.[11]

The achievement of our first writers has been slighted as
well because readers often are not aware of the enormous
obstacles these writers faced in creating a literature for the
rapidly changing audience of a revolutionary society. Since
historians of this period are usually interested in demon-
strating those factors that led to stabilization and the containment of the radical tendencies of the Revolution, Americans
possess perhaps too limited a sense of the actual ferment of
the last decades of the century. Some critics have even argued
that Americans have been so obsessed with denying the revolutionary character of the Revolution that they have blinded
themselves to its truly rebellious nature.[12]

To understand the conditions in which the writers were
working, we need to recognize that the immediate social and
psychological effects of the Revolutionary War had all the
potential for creating an internal social calamity of the kind
that has since occurred in so many revolutionary societies. To
say a catastrophe was prevented here because of wise leadership or the rule of law is to identify only one piece of a
complex social picture puzzle. Even before the war was over,
Americans convinced themselves that the Revolution was not
really a revolt but was merely necessary reform, or an inevitable separation or a sacred fulfillment. These myths were
consciously created within the rhetoric of the Founding
Fathers, who wisely employed such terms to mollify the

people's desire for continued changes in social and economic conditions. Once aware of the truly volatile conditions of identity confusion, religious turmoil, and social misdirection that followed upon the war, we may see how easily America could have slipped into the sociological condition of massive despair, cynicism, and anger that has destroyed other post-revolutionary societies.

But containment did occur, and it was furthered by a generation of word-makers—not just the framers of the Constitution but the shapers of the metaphors, articulators of the visions, and the creators of the imaginative projections of America as a nation and of the nature and identity of the American people. The clergymen and poets—the masters of symbolic language—played a role every bit as important, if not more so, as the lawyers and statesmen who crafted the political documents. Writers like Dwight and Freneau approached literature with a sense of religious mission and strove to give America a vision of herself as a promised, New World utopia.

Under the pressures of the changing conditions of the 1780s and 1790s, however, the intimate relationship between religion and literature began to crumble. As religion lost its power to sway people to reform and the ability of the clergy to influence political leaders diminished, some writers, like Brackenridge and Freneau, were less inclined to infuse their works with religious themes and language. In their search for new explanations of the human situation, Freneau, Barlow, and Brown were drawn to the same serious currents of philosophical ideas that would soon inflame the early poetry of Wordsworth and Coleridge. There was even a brief period in the 1780s when the Romantic age of literature as a new religion and the poet as priest might have dawned in America.

With all the moral fervor of eighteenth-century American Calvinism behind them and the expanse of an open cultural horizon before them, these writers saw an opportunity to "make it new" in the fullest sense of the phrase. American writers could confidently dismiss the great classics of literature as secondary and dated because there had been no epoch in history like the present. The classics seemed to have been written on another planet and transmitted to America through eons of time and space; they might provide enjoyment, but the social structure and values they reflected were viewed as completely foreign to the American experience. No subject more important, no theme more sublime, no material more grandiose could be imagined than American life in the present. It seemed only fitting that the mantle of moral preceptor and intellectual leader now be passed from the clergy to the artists and poets.

The premature and temporary termination of the Romantic fusion of art and religious zeal in these decades occurred for a number of complex reasons. The rapid shift of allegiance of the people from religious and intellectual authorities to the military and political leadership, symbolized in the reverence for George Washington as sage and moral exemplar, undermined the last vestiges of social influence of the literary figures. In addition, business and governmental leaders found it to be in their best interests to discredit the intellectuals and ministers because theology and art often challenged the emergent precapitalist ideology upon which the new economy would be founded. Contrary to the basic truth of the Weber–Tawney thesis that ultimately Protestantism and capitalism were mutually reinforcing, individual clergymen frequently annoyed ambitious merchants with sermons denouncing acquisitiveness and self-interest. To make matters worse, book dealers and buyers remained prejudiced in favor of the literary products from abroad because English books were cheaper and considered more fashionable and entertaining.[13]

In spite of these discouragements, the best writers still fought with religious fervor to save their society from peril.

Recognizing the threat of the incipient materialism to all forms of humanistic endeavor, writers such as Barlow, Freneau, Brackenridge, Dwight, and Brown sought to preserve the advances of the Revolution and prevent the slide into moral and cultural degeneracy. While they were in favor of the destruction of the old monarchical order, they each saw, though dimly at first, the weaknesses and flaws of the new republic—consensus, ideology, blind conformity were all to serve the new god of materialism. There would be little place for the expression of genuine human feeling, for passionate commitment to spiritual values, for full dedication to human rights, or for the pleasures of the imagination or aesthetic feelings. As one historian of the period has observed, "This was a society in which nobody played."[14] Fearing that America might become a sterile society which worshiped only the status quo, the writers remained committed to a common goal: to bring art into the marketplace and to use literature to reveal the spiritual meaning and human interests in the practical affairs of life.

Although they were united in their dedication to literature and the life of the mind, these writers also lived in a political world in which they often found themselves at odds with one another over current issues. A questioner of authority from his youth, Freneau spent much of his literary energy and his public life defending the republican policies of Jefferson and attacking the aristocratic inclinations of the Federalists. Joel Barlow underwent a complete change of mind which led him from his early conservatism at Yale to the radicalism of Thomas Paine and William Godwin. The political ideas of Brackenridge and Brockden Brown vacillated between the poles of republican liberalism and the Federalist fear of mobocracy, and these shiftings may be charted in their lives and writings. Those who remained steady on the right throughout their lives or were moved permanently to that position by fears of social decay have

been identified as the Connecticut Wits. The members of
this group, which included Timothy Dwight, John Trumbull, David Humphreys, Noah Webster, and Lemuel Hop-
kins, collaborated on or endorsed the anti-republican satire
The Anarchiad (1786–87).

No writer could be aloof or detached from politics because
the parties themselves were expressions of the deeper identity
crisis and divided consciousness of the new nation. On the
one side, guilt over rejecting the old culture and fear of freedom led many to serious doubts about the American experiment and toward an impulse to make amends for the slaying
of the father and to embrace the old values of the fatherland
with even more zeal than during the years before the Revolution. On the other side, the fervor for expansion, growth,
unlimited opportunity, and utopian liberty had many yearning to cast off all tethers, certainly those imposed from afar
by the federal government. As natural human selfishness of
individuals led to exploitation of the political and economic
confusion and to rampant land-grabbing schemes, the intellectuals and writers of both persuasions began to search for
some means to temper the drive for power and wealth.

Still, opinions differed on the value of religion as a force
for inspiring or enforcing social order. At one extreme, the
Puritan Old Lights like Dwight were clinging more tightly
than ever to the idea that the more political freedom a
people possessed the more they required strict religious controls. Without rigid controls human depravity would run
wild, and the republic would be destroyed from within by
demagogues and criminals. At the other extreme, there were
those sons of the Revolution, such as Paine and later Barlow,
who believed that religion was superfluous. For the Enlightenment had ushered in an era of reasoned judgment in which
persuasion rather than fear would offset human behavior. As
corruption and profligacy actually did increase during the
postwar years, the shrewd leaders on all sides, even confirmed

Deists, began to recognize the desirability of moderate religious strictures to control the rapaciousness of the people and to further systems of benevolence and philanthropy that might serve as means of distributing the wealth that would naturally come into the hands of the few. Although some resisted, most writers came to share the position that, at least during this period of transition, religion was a social and moral necessity, even if intellectually suspect.

With the possible exception of Dwight, each of these writers studied here was aware, though perhaps vaguely, that current philosophical developments were already challenging the notions of free will and moral choice upon which the new American system was founded. The growing importance of empirical science and materialism was accompanied by a growing skepticism about traditional ideals of morality. There is a remarkable tendency toward naturalism and determinism in the writings of the 1780s and 1790s, especially in the work of Freneau and Brown. They recognized that such skepticism even called into question the legitimacy of the very activity in which they themselves were engaged, for the idea that a literary work could cause people to be moral would soon seem absurd to philosophers and most reflective artists. The role of the public man, whether poet, clergyman, or war hero, would be diminished, for forces rather than people would be perceived as the prime movers of history.[15] It was in reaction to this very denial of human interests that Hawthorne and Melville wrote their great moral romances in the 1850s.

During the period after the Revolution, Charles Brockden Brown was the writer who best understood the psychological consequences and literary implications of the collapse of the Enlightenment epistemology. He saw how the cultural schizophrenia would affect the minds of individuals and how impossible it might become for certain people to live with the irrationality of old religion in a political world that stressed

reason and pragmatism. He also recognized how some individuals would react to the fluid economy, which placed only
moral restraints on exploitation and used guilt as the only
probe to keep men honest. He understood the emotional
consequences for the disillusioned individual who discovered
the contradiction between the religious and national ideals
of benevolence and philanthropy expounded in rhetoric and
the realities of disease, crime, and slavery. In his complex
psychological fictions Brown expressed the terror of uncertainty that resulted from this new distrust of reason, a theme
that was to be at the center of Poe's best fiction and the works
of many later American authors.

By 1785, serious writers of both political parties felt that
the new order of the republic would be one of fragmentation.
As Madison argued in *The Federalist* #10, order would
spring from a consensus that would emerge from a plurality
of opinions. Accordingly, the writers realized that traditional
literary forms would have to be replaced by structures that
could encompass a society of discord and competing voices.
The fitting literary embodiment of this disorder would be a
form that was more formless. The narrative strategy that
Brackenridge used in *Modern Chivalry* with its rambling,
picaresque quality was absolutely appropriate to the chaotic
and ever-changing conditions of American life, as Mark
Twain later recognized when he composed *Huck Finn* and
Walt Whitman the many-sectioned *Leaves of Grass*. Indeed,
the shifting, accumulating narrative is reflective of the westward movement itself and of the meandering if not un-
systematic way that American government and society seemed
to many to be organized. Similarly, the several sections and
various speakers of Dwight's *Greenfield Hill* reflect a sense
of social disjunction within the idyllic frame of a pastoral
setting. In both works it is only the voice of the narrator-
author (in Dwight's case his voice speaks in the footnotes)

that provides reassurance that a mind is in control of the events of the narrative.

For all their failures and disappointments, the poets of this age were poets of vision. It fell to them, regardless of their political or social views, to try to imagine the needs of America in the future. Reared in the Protestant churches and trained for the ministry, these writers carried throughout their lives the conviction that authorship was to a degree a sacred calling. This social mission was so burdensome, however, that it weighed down their poetry with meanings and purposes, duties and moral obligations. Rarely could they find the artistic strength to lift their lines to the heights of fancy. The artistry drowned in the social and political messages they included in an effort to achieve the proper didactic effect.

The writers of the new republic were engaged in a task more difficult than they were capable of understanding: the negotiation of an uncharted intellectual and artistic path from a dominant religious vision of America to a new nationalist ideology. They felt it their duty to express the symbolic meaning of America and the social message of how to live and succeed in American society—how to be an American. Yet they had no literary precedents to help them. As they tried to mediate these difficult problems of identity and national inner conflict, they were also trying to understand their own changing identities. Like a person trying to help a friend through a psychological trauma, who accepts the risk of losing his own grasp on reality, these individual poets were striving to gain mastery over their own inner confusion as they preached to others of their duties.

For each of the writers studied here, the changing attitude toward religion in their society created genuine personal crises. As new philosophical and social theories made traditional religion appear irrelevant for the new society, some writers rejected religion on an intellectual level yet at the same time clung to religion, sometimes unconsciously, on a personal psychological level. Artistically, much of their poetic langauge was rooted in religious traditions, and when they tried to strip it of religious associations, as Freneau and Barlow did, or to find new symbols to express human experience, they found themselves flailing about in a verbal vacuum.

The story of these writers remains important for understanding the problem of the writer in America ever since. The social and political demands upon the artist in a democratic society are much greater than those in an aristocratic culture where the nobility and a system of patronage ensure the continuation of the arts. The poets who lived through the American Revolution felt an obligation to use their talents to fill the moral and spiritual void left by a declining clergy, to present the social and political ideals of their nation, and to enlighten and inspire their readers with visions of the human condition in a new age and new world. Perhaps a Milton, the poet they all admired, might have been up to the task, but it must be admitted that there were no Miltons in America in the late eighteenth century.

Although they labored heroically, all of the writers examined here finally fell short of the victory they desired, some for lack of talent and some for lack of courage. It would be forty years before the ground lost would be regained, and even then the artist in America would continue to be regarded as an outsider, and sometimes as a nuisance, whose interests were most often irrelevant or antagonistic to the ongoing concerns of the commercial society. Given the conditions they faced, the achievement of our early national writers is quite remarkable and demands detailed, sympathetic study.

I

THE CRISIS OF AUTHORITY
IN THE REVOLUTIONARY AGE

The poet has a new thought; he has a whole new experience
to unfold; he will tell us how it was with him, and all men will
be richer in his fortune. For the experience of each new age
requires a new confession, and the world seems always waiting
for its poet.

RALPH WALDO EMERSON
"The Poet," 1843

In 1774, at the call of the Burgesses of Virginia, pulpits
throughout the provinces sounded the alarm: the situation
in America was desperate; the moral and religious decay
among God's people was widespread; God was using the
English oppressors to chastise his chosen; awake, reform,
thrust out the evil ones, and purify this sacred land once
more! As the political crisis worsened, men as different in
their religious beliefs as Jefferson, Franklin, and Adams
looked to the clergy to carry the message of resistance to the
people in language and forms that would make it compelling.
Respected clergymen of all denominations, including such
prominent Anglicans as William Smith and Jacob Duché of
Philadelphia, joined voices in urging separation from England, in part because they believed that independence
would allow for a flourishing of religion and learning in
America. From the pulpits the ministers urged the people to
wear homespun and, if needed, take up arms to defend their
freedom while in the colleges they encouraged students to
devote their intellectual gifts to the progress of America.

The results of their efforts were dramatic. Of the fast day
held in protest of the Parliament's passage of the Port bill,

Jefferson exclaimed, "This day of fasting and humiliation was like a shock of electricity throughout the colonies, placing every man erect."[1] So impressed were the political leaders that John Adams sent a message to Abigail to urge their minister at home to preach on the typological parallels between America and Israel in their times of trial.[2] Some ministers, like the Reverend Samuel Sherwood, used every rhetorical device perfected by the Puritans to attack the British "Satan" who had unleashed "the great Whore of Babylon" to ride her "great red dragon" upon the American continent.[3] The powerful impact these patriot preachers had upon the people is attested to by Tories like Peter Oliver and Thomas Hutchinson, who attributed the success of the Revolution to the work of this black regiment. The call to the preachers to participate actively in the American protest seemed propitious for the American clergy. At a time when religious spirit appeared to have cooled and the presence of Roman Catholicism in Canada was a new threatening reality, ministers saw the hand of God at work in this revival of the fast day and recognized a superb opportunity to bring mutual benefit to the separate but intertwined causes of religion and politics in America.[4]

The war years also generated a need for propaganda and patriotic literature, and the best-known secular writers came to be held in the same high regard as the most famous preachers and political leaders. The attention captured by such works as John Dickinson's *Letters* (1767–68) and Francis Hopkinson's fictional satire *A Pretty Story* (1774) was strong encouragement to would-be writers. The prominence of James Otis, Sam Adams, Thomas Paine, and the Whig clergy seemed to ensure that the profession of authorship was firmly established in America. Thus, college students in the early 1770s were preparing to enter a new culture in which the prominent forces shaping America's destiny appeared to be controlled not only by the political leaders and time-honored preachers but also by the newly arrived political writers.

Inspired by this climate of opportunity and guided by a recent shift of focus in the college curricula toward literature and the arts, a generation of talented young men set out to become the moral and cultural leaders of their emerging republic. While some with high ambitions, such as Madison and Hamilton, were headed for the din of politics, several of their classmates entered the world confident that poems and sermons were just as important to their countrymen as debates over taxation and arms. They believed that the "revolution of mind" of the American people which John Adams said had preceded the political revolt would form a foundation for a cultural and religious rebirth as well.[5]

In the excitement of the times commencement poems and speeches of the early seventies were charged with millennial hope and filled with biblical imagery. Because of the Great Awakening that had swept the colonies in the 1740s and 1750s, many Americans of the Revolutionary generation had been exposed to the religious rhetoric and typological habit of mind that the revivalist preachers had absorbed from the Calvinist sermon tradition. The vision of America's millennial role; the emphasis upon guilt and corruption, purgation and perfectionism; the Calvinist stress upon contending and irreconcilable opposites, such as God versus Satan, saint versus sinner, freedom versus slavery: these themes and images, when used to define America's relationship to English authority, still possessed great emotional power.

In their *The Rising Glory of America* of 1772, Freneau and Brackenridge envisioned America as "a new Jerusalem, sent down from heaven" where "Myriads of saints . . ./[shall] live and reign on earth a thousand years,/Thence called millennium." No less confidently than the Puritans John Cotton and Cotton Mather had proclaimed America's sacred mission in the previous century, the American patriots predicted that a "Paradise anew/Shall flourish, by no second Adam lost,/. . . Another Canaan shall excel the old," a time would soon arrive when "Greece and Rome [will] no more/Detain the Muses," and America would produce "glorious works/Of high invention and wondrous art/Which not the ravages of time shall waste."[6] Embodying aspects of the Puritan idiom and didacticism, the "rising glory" poems and the biblical-nationalistic epics of the 1770s and 1780s allowed the poets to demonstrate their patriotic fervor, social usefulness, and commitment to the future glory of American industry, religion, and arts. These poems were born of the assumption that the poet was a respected and manly participant in the intellectual community, whose works could make a significant contribution and were thus worthy of popular acclaim and the respect of political and religious leaders.

The writers had reason for optimism in the new culture. As Kenneth Lockridge has shown, the literacy rate among the colonists by the 1760s boded well for American writers. "In the years leading up to the Revolution," Lockridge finds that "new causal forces . . . made virtually all men literate" and that "the rise carried to the very doorstep of universal literacy."[7] Lockridge identifies the major factors in this remarkable achievement as the educational ethos which prevailed in mid-eighteenth-century America and the influence of religion. Before the Revolution, "the focus of literacy remains essentially religious." As for the actual numbers of people who might purchase literary works, he proposes that about one-fourth of the generation born around 1730 was totally literate; among merchants, gentry, and professionals the figure was around 90 per cent, artisans close to 75 per cent, and farmers near 50 per cent.[8]

Joseph Ellis has argued that economic and demographic conditions were also conducive to the expected flourishing of the arts. The phenomenal increase of the total population of the colonies from about 240,000 in 1700 to about 1,200,000 by 1750 and the growth of economic productivity in the decades before the Revolution created conditions that favored not only political and economic separation from England but a flowering of all aspects of American culture.[9] Thus, with a potential market of between two and four hundred thousand readers, Joel Barlow was not a fool in thinking that he might be able to earn a substantial income as a poet, nor is it surprising that the English sentimental novels which captured the public interest in the 1790s were so financially successful. It was no delusion that led the first American writers to expect a full and favorable response from the American reading public.[10] But finding the proper forms, language, and subjects that would appeal to that audience was to prove far more challenging than any of these writers anticipated.

I

Throughout the seventeenth and eighteenth centuries in New England and in most of the American colonies there existed a bond between poetry and religion. In Puritan New England, poets were often ministers, with some exceptions such as Anne Bradstreet, and the sermon was regarded as the major literary form. Well into the eighteenth century, poetry and fiction were still considered a branch of oratory and public rhetoric, and patriotism strengthened the connection between literary works and public events.[11] By mid-century that pattern began to change with the prominence of a few non-clerical poets such as Benjamin Wadsworth and Samuel Danforth, yet the aims of most poetry remained didactic and religious. In fact, by the 1750s in New England there was greater harmony between the purposes of literature and religion than there had been in the 1680s when Edward

Taylor was secreting away his famous manuscripts of poetical meditations. Poets and ministers frequently worked closely in the preparation and joint publication of funeral sermons and elegies. Of course, there developed in the mid-eighteenth century a secular poetry as well, particularly in the South and the middle colonies where Ebenezer Cooke, Robert Bolling, and Richard Lewis produced lively satires and lyrics free of the moralizing and didacticism of the Puritans. In the New England colleges two young sprites managed to produce witty verse which appeared anonymously in James Rivington's "Poet Corner." But the main tradition of colonial poetry in the eighteenth century was of the kind best illustrated by the work of the Reverend Mather Byles, nephew of Cotton Mather, whose volume of religious verse in heroic couplets appeared in 1744.[12]

Evidence of this close association between religion and literature may also be found in the South in the 1750s. During the Great Awakening of the 1740s and 1750s, Samuel Davies, a Presbyterian and one of the founders of the College of New Jersey, became one of the most influential literary and religious leaders in Virginia. Davies drew his poetic forms from the Bible, Milton, and the hymns of Isaac Watts and Philip Doddridge, and he adhered to the religious view of the sublime that pervaded Calvinist oratory. Through his poetry Davies sought to inspire readers to a realization of God's beauty and power, just as he did in his forceful evangelical sermons. He was fond of quoting Herbert's line, "A Verse may hit him whom a sermon flies./And turn Delight into a Sacrifice," and he often composed poems to accompany sermons on the same subject. With poems that were read from South Carolina to New Hampshire, Davies brought to the South the fusion of poetic and pietistic impulses that critics have long hailed in the prose of Jonathan Edwards, Davies's predecessor as president of Princeton. Richard Beale Davis has suggested that in spite of the strong classical and pastoral tradition in the poetry of the South, it was the sacred poetry of Davies that commanded the literary scene: "Davies' Anglican adversaries wrote too, usually on such frivolous subjects as a lady's appearance, or in satires ridiculing men and manners of the community. But none of their poetry ever received the attention his did."[13]

The poetic successor to Davies was the Scottish Presbyterian James Reid, whose moral essays and religious poetry appeared in the 1760s in England and America. In his poem "To His Pen," Reid declared "religious tenets [are the] constant care" of poetry. Although he did produce a few lighter poems, Reid's works strengthened the bond between religion and literature later inherited by the first generation of republican writers. Professor Davis has said of Reid's work, "Like the great Presbyterian Samuel Davies in two earlier decades, Reid's prose and his verse represent a tradition outside the political which has persisted throughout the South. . . . Reid's temper was closer to Faulkner or Robert Penn Warren's than it was to Jefferson's. . . . For he was a southern puritan."[14]

The continuing influence of Puritanism, which spread throughout the colonies during the Great Awakening, was only one of the many reasons poetry took this direction in the mid-eighteenth century. If American poetry had merely derived from the Puritans, it would have been easy for Benjamin Franklin to laugh it off the stage. Indeed, in a 1722 Silence Dogood paper Franklin had tried to mock and ridicule the most ponderous religious poetry into oblivion with his recipe for a typical funeral elegy of the day: take some borrowed virtues, mix them with the dying words of the deceased, and put them into "the empty skull of a young Harvard to ferment for a fortnight." The results, he said, were such consistent failures that many people were constrained from living good lives for fear of having such poems written about them when they died. Protest as Franklin might, however, the influence of religion upon literature only grew stronger during his time, gaining theoretical legitimacy from the lecture halls at Oxford and Cambridge.[15]

Fortunately for those of Franklin's taste, there did begin to emerge in the colonies by mid-century another mode of literary work which stemmed from the intermingling of the classical, pastoral, and biblical traditions. The most interesting examples reveal a concern with social and moral issues but escape overt religious imagery or themes. The best is William Livingston's "Philosophical Solitude" (1747). Livingston was an influential lawyer, community leader, delegate to the first and second Continental Congresses, and governor of New Jersey from 1776 until his death in 1790. That he was writing poetry at all while so actively engaged in social affairs illustrates the point, often ignored or misunderstood today, that before the Revolution poetry was not thought an improper occupation for practical men. An austere Presbyterian in his own life, Livingston also stressed the social and moral value of poetry in his eulogy for the Reverend Aaron Burr in which he argued that a philosophical man of poetic talent is as essential to the joy and happiness of his people as the astute military or political leader.[16]

In "Philosophical Solitude" Livingston borrowed from the Englishman John Pomfret's "The Choice," but he treated the theme of the intellectual's yearning for solitude and escape from a viewpoint quite opposed to that of Pomfret. Whereas "The Choice" presents the man of letters as one seeking retreat from the world in the comforts of the arts, Livingston depicts the poet-scholar as a hero who takes temporary refuge from society in order to restore his intellectual powers which he then employs for the moral and social improvement of his fellow man. In Livingston's view, strongly influenced by Locke's idea of personal power, it is the imagination of the poet that creates attainable goals of happiness and moral perfection, which in turn lead others to action.

Livingston's poem illustrates that the idea of the moral power of poetry, which the generation of the Revolution would inherit, remained strong even in poetry that was not overtly religious.[17]

II

One of the most important reasons for the persistence of the bond between religion and literature in eighteenth-century America was the tight control the colonial clergy continued to exercise over the arts and letters. In spite of the awakening of religion in the 1740s, throughout the eighteenth century there continued to be a gradual decline in the status of the clergy and in the influence of religion in public affairs. As this gradual secularization occurred, the clergymen suffered a crisis of identity, as David Hall has suggested, and the definition of the minister underwent important changes. While ministers had always been the acknowledged intellectuals in their communities, especially in New England where Increase Mather had kept his twelve-hour "scholar's day," they began to emphasize their importance to the society as men of learning.[18]

Throughout the eighteenth century, in funeral sermons and in prefaces to published writings, the ministers stressed the value of a learned clergy for the welfare of the community and for the image of America abroad. In his 1712 sermon on the death of John Wally, Ebenezer Pemberton explained the religious and social dividends of letters and substituted the words "literature and learning" in the places previously held in such sermons by the words "zeal and true religion":

> To promote good literature is to serve one's generation.
> This is necessary for the true prosperity and happiness
> of a People. Greece and Rome are more renowned for
> the flourishing State of learning in them, than for their
> Arms. This has for ever been the highest esteem among

the Civilized Nations. Hence, the Roman Emperors and
Generals were ambitious to be celebrated for their Perfection in Letters as for their Achievements in Arms.
Learning makes men capable of being a great blessing in
their day. . . . A Learned Ruler makes a happy City. The
more good literature Civil Rulers are furnished with,
the more capable they are to discharge their trust to the
honour and safety of their People.[19]

Pemberton explained that the rank and order in heaven
would be determined by *learning* as well as by good works,
and that, as protectors and promoters of literature and culture, the clergy had a special obligation to encourage not
only true religion but also learning and letters. In this context clergymen such as Mather Byles and Samuel Davies were
proud to be recognized as poet-preachers.[20]

Still, as new fashions of thought and opinion were im-
ported from abroad, the ministers faced a constant challenge
to their control over arts and letters in America. Indeed, the
religious foundation of American culture might have under-
gone severe deterioration during the eighteenth century had
it not been for two powerful events: the Great Awakening
and the French and Indian Wars. With the resurgence of
religious enthusiasm in the 1740s, the language and ideas
of the Puritan sermon took on new vitality, and the techniques of preaching and conversion spread throughout the
colonies. When the American conflict with the French and
Indians broke out in the 1750s, clergymen and political
orators infused religious rhetoric with military language to
give expression to the patriotic unity and the incipient na-
tionalistic feelings of the colonists. When the Stamp Act
crisis occurred in 1765, the political writers found in the
Puritan idiom a ready tool for castigating the enemies of
America, as would Sam Adams and Tom Paine in the early
1770s.

Though kept alive by repeated use, the Puritan images and sacred myths were altered by the intellectual developments of the century. As Sacvan Bercovitch has argued, the Puritan typology and vision of providential mission remained a major element in the formation of an American ideology, but a fundamental evolution occurred from the myth of the sacred errand of the Puritan eschatology to the formation of a national ideology.[21] This transformation involved a shift to a new image of America, which drew upon the Puritan myth of the New Jerusalem for its force while importing other ideas as well. An important new feature in the emerging national self-portrait was supplied by Bishop Berkeley in his "Verses on the Prospect of Planting Arts and Learning in America" (1725). Building upon the long existent idea of *translatio studii*—that the seat of culture was constantly moving westward—Berkeley foresaw a time when America would represent the pinnacle of the arts. In the 1770s when the task of arousing a nationalist spirit fell to the clergy in the pulpits and in the universities, they were quick to seize upon the opportunity of projecting America as at once a new Zion and a new Athens.[22]

During the Revolution, American writers and orators fused the old Puritan image of America with Berkeley's projection of America as a cultural "city on a hill" to create a new type: the "Genius of America." The Genius of America would be apparent in every aspect of American life: in the boldness and political wisdom of its leaders; in the shrewdness and courage of its soldiers; in its crafts, inventions, industry, and commerce; and in its moral purity, artistic excellence, and devotion to the Christian God who had ordained its creation. This people of genius would lead mankind into the future in every branch of human endeavor. This symbol, repeated in sermons, speeches, and poetry throughout the 1770s and 1780s, fused the political conviction and religious belief that the providential union of history and geography had engendered a national equivalent of the individual genius who possessed the best of ancient and modern political thought, art, and culture.

III

Nowhere in the colonies did such conviction in the Genius and geniuses of America take shape more conspicuously during the years before the Revolution than in the colleges of Philadelphia, New Jersey, and New Haven. Young men who felt they were living in the most important of times spent their college years engaged in public demonstrations, debating political and legal issues in forensic societies, and preparing for what promised to be exciting careers. The clergymen-professors of the most important institutions, who gave direction to this enthusiasm, were also engaged in a revolution —academic reform that involved a total revamping of the curricula and the introduction of new theological and literary theories, which can be broadly defined as the tenets of Scottish Common Sense philosophy. Those who would become the first writers in the United States were profoundly and permanently affected by the moral and literary assumptions of the Scottish school.[23]

When the liberal Anglican minister William Smith arrived from the University of Aberdeen to become provost of the College of Philadelphia in 1755, America gained an important intellectual and cultural leader. Kenneth Silverman has said of him, "By profession a politician, preacher, and educator, Smith was by disposition a literary man."[24] Smith introduced in America the first courses in rhetoric, literature, and criticism, which provided terms for expressing the vague difficulties American poets had been experiencing and a full-blown theory of literature for solving those problems. Put quite simply, the issue troubling American poets was this: how could poetry be morally and spiritually useful for American readers and yet good enough to win the praise of critics at home and especially abroad? Poems like those of Byles, Reid, and Davies, which pleased the ministers and inspired colonial readers to thoughts of God, good deeds, and grace, were usually scorned by respected intellectuals, while the kind of poetry admired by Augustan critics was considered by most Americans to be frivolous if not immoral. But the critical theories of Lord Henry Home Kames which Smith brought to Philadelphia offered a resolution of these seemingly contradictory purposes and thereby provided a new understanding of the function of literature and the role of the artist.[25]

As elaborated in the works of those writers most widely read in America, notably Kames and later Thomas Reid, James Beattie, and Hugh Blair, the critical theories of the Scottish Common Sense philosophy proposed that all thoughtful men could use their reason and good sense to resolve the moral and intellectual problems they confronted, and that those of superior intelligence and training had the power and duty to lead the less enlightened toward truth and improvement. This philosophy seemed thereby to articulate an ideal of democratic intellectual equality while assuming a reality of intellectual hierarchy. The particular doctrine of this system that held the most promise for establishing the authority of the man of letters was the idea of associationism, which enjoyed great popularity in American thought.

This theory proposed that all aspects of thought and action are interrelated. An alteration in one area results in parallel changes in other aspects of life. If an individual or a society were to experience a change in government or religion, parallel developments would occur in law, morality, and the arts. Thus, it would be reasonable to try to improve the morals and character of a people by raising the level of literary taste through good writing. Similarly, a heightening of religious devotion in a society could be expected to lead to an improvement in its literature. When critics today write about the connection between the debasement of language and the moral corruption of society, it is apparent that such ideas are still current. Similar assumptions about the impact of taste upon politics and society underlay the principles and motives of the New Critics of the mid-twentieth century. For American poets and ministers of the 1760s and 1770s, the ideas of psychological associationism also served to reassert the assumed relationship between religion and literature and between the poet and the social leader.[26]

So enlivening did this set of ideas prove for Smith's students in Philadelphia that his first graduates included the painter Benjamin West and three important poets, Thomas Godfrey, Nathaniel Evans, and Francis Hopkinson. Godfrey's *The Prince of Parthia* is considered the first play ever written by an American, and the published collections of Evans's poems show him to have been a writer of great promise. Unfortunately, both young men died within a few years of leaving college, Godfrey suffering heatstroke in Carolina while Evans succumbed to illness in New Jersey where he was a New Light missionary. Hopkinson went on to become an influential poet and writer of propaganda and fiction during the Revolution.[27]

Meanwhile, during the late 1760s and throughout the following two decades, Princeton's Scottish Presbyterian President John Witherspoon inspired and challenged young men of literary talent to achieve the moral and literary standards set by the Common Sense doctrines. Poetry and preaching, Witherspoon argued, were "like two colors" that "melt into one another by almost imperceptible shades till the distinction is entirely lost."[28] Witherspoon taught his students that the man of literary talent has a divine duty to use his pen to further the cultural and moral progress of his fellows. If he does not join the ministry, the man of letters may exercise a high degree of moral authority and thereby share many of the obligations of the minister. Because the secular writer delves into the mysterious realm of the imagination and passions once considered the special domain of the clergyman, he must be a person of superior moral character if his writing is to be useful to the society and critically successful. Like the preacher, too, the writer must strive for simplicity of style so that he may affect audiences of every social and educational level.

In his influential lectures on poetry, Witherspoon took care to distinguish the role of the secular writer from that of the clergy and established for the first time in America a definition of the role of the American literary artist and the criteria by which to measure his achievement in letters. Using the theory of associationism, he proposed the new argument that the writer need not feel an obligation to use his imaginative works for the specific purpose of teaching morals. If he were a good man and wrote well, the writer could be confident that his works would create in his audiences the proper moral as well as aesthetic result. Thus, Witherspoon gave the poet a degree of religiously sanctioned freedom unheard of previously.

However, this liberation in subject and literary method placed formidable demands upon the individual writer. To achieve true greatness in literature a writer had to possess what Witherspoon called "greatness of mind" or "genius." "The true genius is of a nobler nature than servilely to submit to the corruption or vitiated taste of any age or place; . . . he knows he will not swerve from the truth of art; he will produce what is noble and excellent in its kind; he will refine the public ear, and teach them to admire in the right place." Modern readers may be inclined to hear in this statement the seeds of Emerson's arrogant assertion of his power to make "the great world come round [to him] at last," or Whitman's call to his readers at the end of *Leaves of Grass*

"failing to fetch me at first keep encouraged," or Wallace
Stevens's jar which stands upon a hill in Tennessee and
brings all nature to worship man's achievement. What the
young poets at Witherspoon's feet heard in 1770 was the
American formula for expressing the Genius of America
through the genius of the individual poetic imagination.
Witherspoon continued with a confident prophecy of America's cultural future: "The great poet and the great orator,
though, through the prevalence of bad taste, they may find
it difficult at first to procure attention, yet they will procure
it at last; and when they are heard, they carry the prize from
all inferior pretenders; and indeed, their doing so is the very
touchstone and trial of their art itself."[29] As much as he
later rebelled against the theological doctrines of Witherspoon's Presbyterianism, Philip Freneau was never able to
erase from his mind the challenge to poetic greatness that
his teacher presented, especially when his poems failed to
sell or were critically condemned.[30]

At Yale, President Thomas Clapp and the popular tutor
Ezra Stiles introduced budding writers like Dwight, Trumbull, and Barlow to the critical principles of the Common
Sense thought. Lord Kames's *Elements of Criticism* and
James Beattie's *Essay on the Nature and Immutability of
Truth* (1770) were both in use at Yale in the early seventies,
and Hugh Blair's *Rhetoric* was adopted as a text in 1785. As
with all new critical theories, however, the Scottish doctrines
could be variously interpreted, and the faculty at politically
conservative Yale avoided the degree of poetic freedom which
Witherspoon expounded. While the Yale poets drew from
the doctrines a heightened conviction of their moral and
literary authority among the mass of men, they held much
more firmly to the idea of the blending of poetic and religious vocations in one man, the poet-preacher, which both
Dwight and Trumbull became. Barlow struggled throughout
his career to escape these political and literary strictures, and

his efforts finally resulted in complete rejection of his early beliefs—religious, political, as well as philosophical. His dramatic turnabout of thought made him notorious in New Haven and led Dwight, his former teacher and friend, to remove Barlow's portrait at Yale.[31] But that event belongs to the later days of gloom.

As they left their respective colleges in the early 1770s, the young men of literary talent and social ambition had good reason to be eager and optimistic. From their teachers they had learned the secret to becoming the moral and intellectual leaders of their generation. While their contemporaries would ply the trades of law, business, and government, they would be the beacons of light, preaching the sacred truths of scripture in the pulpit and depicting the eternal verities of human nature in their literary works. Whatever their political or theological inclinations, young talents as different in temperament as Dwight and Freneau shared a set of accepted beliefs about the role of the man of letters.

Not since the time of Virgil, perhaps with the exception of the brief period in which Milton flourished, had there been an age so right for the production of great works of genius. The rebirth of the classics had established the forms, the movement of history was providing the material, and the preservation of pure Christianity had allowed for the proper foundation of beliefs and the appropriate moral climate. A generation was trained, the historical stage was set, and events would shortly witness the emergence of the Genius of America.

IV

What soon became apparent, however, was that the revolution of mind taking place in America was conducive neither to the arts nor to religion. Even before the fighting was over, the ministers and the poets began to comprehend the emergent threat to their social status and intellectual authority. Politicians and patrons who had been so encouraging to the arts turned cool; congregations grew sullen and rebellious; literary journals failed; literary works by Americans sold poorly. For many of the clergy and for most of the men of letters who lived in America during the last decades of the eighteenth century, the American Revolution seemed to involve a betrayal. As the more perceptive writers and the ministers realized, the changes being brought about were only signs of a radical shift of attitude within the American populace that could constitute a serious threat to traditional religious and intellectual authority. Unless the men of letters could establish new grounds for asserting their intellectual leadership in the society, they would find themselves at the mercy of public favor on the one hand and the power of political and economic interests on the other. The writers and ministers who had entered the Revolution with such optimism and high hopes for America found themselves in a struggle for the survival of values and traditions which only a few years before they had assumed to be permanent. At worst they feared that the new nation would become a cultural and spiritual wasteland, a new Sodom where social anarchy and moral corruption reigned. At the least they foresaw a diminishing of the role of the clergy and men of letters to positions of social insignificance. The initial results of the "shock of recognition," which came during the turmoil of the postwar period, were a severing of the relationship between religion and belles lettres, the formation of newly defined roles for the poet and the minister, and a complete reevaluation of the social use and function of religious and literary activity.

Two facts of American religious and literary history have made it difficult to recognize the seriousness of the crisis that occurred between 1776 and 1815. First, religion did survive.

By the early 1800s a revival of religious feeling was again upon the land and by the 1830s the status of the clergy, though drastically altered and diminished, was reestablished so firmly that it would not be seriously altered again until the twentieth century. Thus, modern interpreters regard the claims of Timothy Dwight and his contemporaries that America was on the verge of becoming a nation of heathens as only ritualistic laments of backsliding which actually signaled all was normal. However, the decline of the clergy's authority in eighteenth-century America was real, and the transformation of religious belief into political ideology was so rapid and sweeping that it nearly left the religionists without a domain. At no point in our history was religion in such danger of being cast off as obsolete, if not dangerous.[32]

The second fact is that literature also endured, but until very recently American critics, for similar reasons, tended to overlook the plight and accomplishments of those writers who kept imaginative literature alive during the darkest decades for the arts in American history.[33] While the barriers encountered by those first American writers have been faced by every generation of authors since, it fell to Freneau, Brackenridge, Barlow, and their contemporaries to face them for the first time. It was their unique task to forge a new identity for the American writer and to establish the fundamental techniques for overcoming the formidable obstacles to artistic expression. In his study of the influence of Milton in America, George Sensabaugh has observed that American literature seems "to have taken a wrong turn someplace during the Revolution."[34] Indeed, whether right or wrong, turns taken by both religion and literature were to have permanent consequences for American culture. Though time may have obscured these events and struggles, for the writers and ministers who lived during the Revolutionary epoch, the issues were immediate and genuine.

V

As the war neared a close, it became clear to the Congregational and Presbyterian clergy that the Revolution had altered relationships between the churches and the people in ways that could be detrimental to the churches. The immediate results were a sharp reduction of the status and power of established clergy and a rapid increase in the number of untrained ministers who were free to teach any number of heresies. Having counted on a rise of religious feeling in the nation, resulting from the people's gratitude to God for their victory, the established clergy encountered a populace that seemed concerned only with land, goods, and politics. The ministers found themselves more vulnerable to insolent church members ready to dismiss their ministers on various charges. Frequently, ministers were accused of having shown a lack of militancy for the revolutionary cause or of preaching doctrines that were inappropriate for an independent people. As the Treaty of Paris was being signed in 1783, many ministers found themselves being paid in worthless Revolutionary War currency and being told, when they complained, to move on to another church.[35]

The most resounding public announcement of ministerial discontent with post-Revolutionary America came in the widely circulated pamphlet by Reverend Peter Thacher titled *Observations upon the Present State of the Clergy of New England, with Strictures upon the Power of Dismissing Them, Usurped by Some Churches.* Thacher states the issue boldly and rather bitterly: "The late contest with Great Britain, glorious as it hath been for their country, hath been peculiarly unfortunate for the clergy. Perhaps no set of men, whose hearts were so thoroughly engaged in it, or who contributed in so great a degree to its success, have suffered more by it."[36] Thacher went on to explain at length that the central problem for the clergy was the remarkable presumptuous-

ness of the citizens: "The people, having emancipated themselves from the British government, and felt their competence
to carry every point they chose, have, in some places at least,
forgotten that they could never be emancipated from the
bonds of justice. They have been too ready to suppose that
their declaration and authority were sufficient to dissolve the
most solemn engagements, and that *the people could do no
wrong*" (p. 4).

While it is certainly not unusual in the annals of preaching in the seventeenth and eighteenth centuries to hear
ministers complain about the religious indifference and par-
simoniousness of their congregations, there are two aspects of
Thacher's protest that set it quite apart from the grumblings
of preachers in earlier years. First, there was a notable increase in such cases of dismissals of clergy by their churches
during and after the war. The issue of national loyalty and
the theological disagreements resulting from the new diversity of opinions were causing rifts in churches throughout
the colonies. The second unusual feature of Thacher's pamphlet is the angry answer that it sparked from a layman.
Identifying himself only as "J. S.—A Layman," James Sullivan, the commissioner of laws for the state of Massachusetts,
published a detailed response to Thacher's pamphlet. Sullivan, who soon became attorney general of the state and later
governor, explained the new secularized process for dismissing pastors from their churches and vigorously defended the
procedure as befitting a republican people.

In what may have been the first assertion that an act of
criticism of the American people may involve a violation of
national security, Sullivan began by warning Thacher that
a public attack upon the American people by a man of influence could constitute treason, for some unfriendly nation
could use his allegations to embarrass or undermine the
country. Sullivan then went on to point out that, under the
newly created United States legal system, Thacher and his

fellow clergymen occupied their pulpits and parsonages at the pleasure of the town officials and church members. Should the members of a church wish to withdraw their support, they need only notify town officials to suspend payments. If the clergyman wished to appeal this action, he could bring suit against the town, and his case would be heard by a judge and jury of the townspeople. Whereas Thacher had protested that ministers were being denied the traditional right to have an ecclesiastical council of their reverend peers be brought in to decide matters, Sullivan explained that such councils were now powerless and therefore superfluous, for in a republic, a minister's peers are his fellow citizens: "It is vain for a clergyman to seek another mode of justice in a popular government."[37]

In an apologetic reply Thacher said he regretted appearing to humiliate the American people, but he expressed some concern over the direction that religion would be likely to take in America if the clergy were indeed at the mercy of their congregations. In what turned out to be a keen prophecy of the path that the threatened clergy were to follow in the closing decades of the century, Thacher warned that America would soon lack the social and moral criticism and the intellectual tempering that are the practical benefits of a strong clergy:

> It is not in the interest of the people to keep their ministers in this state of poverty and dependence. They will not derive that benefit from their councils and instructions which they would probably do, were their ministers more independent; for poverty and dependency agree not well with instruction. Ministers are under temptations to be less plain, less pungent in their reproofs and testimonies against vice, when these testimonies expose them to the displeasure of those whose bread they eat. [p. 8]

This exchange between Thacher and Sullivan indicates clearly the position of the clergy in society during and after the Revolution. It explains why the ministers of the time complained of religious apathy even though modern historians point to the early stirrings of the second Great Awakening as a sign of religious health. When the old-guard ministers berated "apathy," they really referred to the people's defiance of the ancient authority of the clergy and ecclesiastical councils and to their objections to the long-standing requirements for baptism and church membership. The people now demanded that their ministers be more responsive to their particular religious opinions. Many churches searched for new ministers with new ideas or chose to leave the pastorate empty because the diverse religious views of the community precluded a selection.

Ironically, the long association of the clergy with poetry may have also worked to the detriment of some ministers during this period of trial, for, as Rev. Moses Welch of New Haven observed: "Many people expected every minister to be an accomplished essayist and the pulpit to be a theater for oratorical display."[38] Others, who considered literature to be a frivolous activity, attacked the clergy for self-indulgence in the pursuit of letters. When the clergy of the established churches looked back upon the prewar years, they may well have silently agreed with the Anglican loyalist, Jonathan Boucher, who believed the ministers had been victimized: "We were compelled to become in some degree subservient to insurgency. We were inextricably entrapped, before we were well aware that a net had been spread for us. . . . Some clergymen indeed saw through the flimsy veil; but thinking it neither wise nor safe to set themselves directly against the current of the time, as no particular services were prescribed, they judged it best upon the whole to attend their churches."[39]

The ministers' response to the crisis of authority was so imaginative and successful that it is difficult today to appreciate the severity of their situation. Of course, the originality of style, doctrine, and preaching of the itinerant Baptist, Methodist, and Universalist ministers, the "wandering stars" as they were called, enabled them to make gains in new geographical areas and among people who had wearied of the old disciplines or who had not yet been exposed to the word. But in the long-settled areas and for well-established denominations, drastic measures were needed. As Douglas Sweet has recently argued, the creation of new ecclesiastical harmony among Congregational and Presbyterian clergymen enabled them to consider their common problems and devise new solutions.[40] Anticipating Madison's reasoning in *The Federalist* #10 regarding republican diversity, ministers like Jeremy Belknap and Samuel Langdon argued in the 1780s that religious pluralism might be a source of strength and that the clergy should cease their sectarian bickering and prejudice and strive to preserve the precious metal of true Christianity even if the wood and stubble of the various superstructures of separate churches had to be burned. Most importantly, as the sermons and biographical information of the two decades following the Revolution reveal, there was a rebuilding of the relationship between individual ministers and the leaders of the society upon a new social foundation, a redefinition of the function of the clergy, and an enlivening of the language of the sermons with imagery designed to appeal to the Revolutionary War generation.[41]

As they searched for a new language and forms in those critical decades, the American clergy of all denominations helped to formulate new roles for the minister of God in a republic. To the social elite, the clergy reasserted the social benefits of religion. By persuading the leaders of government and business that religion was the most effective tool for exacting docility from a democratic-minded people, the ministers became the first leaders of what would later be known as the "benevolent empire."[42] Ministers like Benjamin Stillmann organized philanthropic societies designed to demonstrate the virtue and public interest of the economic elect and to assuage the disgruntlement of the poor. The biography of Stillmann, published in 1808, announced proudly: "We find his name amongst the first members of the Humane Society of his Commonwealth. Of the Massachusetts Fire Society he was a useful officer, and the Boston Dispensary a member from the beginning, and President at his death. The Boston Female Asylum is likewise much indebted to his exertions."[43] Addresses to the Masonic lodges and Society of the Cincinnati clubs quickly began to replace election sermons as the most prestigious forums for clerical wisdom. The messages of these sermons usually flattered the wealthy for their generosity and suggested that the organizations were an essential part of the structure of a democracy because they provided a way for the wealthy to get to heaven and the less materially fortunate to be pacified. By associating themselves with these societies, the clergy provided them an aura of divine approval while gaining in return a measure of social status and respect.[44]

When the ministers turned their attention to the common people, they searched for ways of instilling into the language of their sermons the kind of imagery and metaphors that would make emotionally appealing the key postwar message of docility and obedience to authority. Perhaps they took their cue from the pronouncements of the Society of the Cincinnati and the boastings of former soldiers, for they played upon the military camaraderie and nostalgia that formed a common bond among those who had lived through the war.

The central image used in presenting this message was the figure of Christ as an obedient soldier in his Father's army. In a 1785 sermon on *The Doctrine of the Cross of Christ,*

John Mellen explained to the people of Wellfleet, Massachusetts, the importance of Christ's example of militarylike
discipline: "If ever the world afforded an instance of real
heroism and genuine greatness of soul, it is this of our Lord
Jesus Christ, freely and nobly facing death, from no motive
of fame and glory, but in obedience to his Father's will."[45]
Mellen went on to associate the sacrifice of Christ with those
of American soldiers who had recently displayed similar heroism: "And such Christian heroes in great multitude there
have been, who being supported by their Lord and Captain,
and animated by the same spirit have braved all dangers and
encountered death in all its most shocking and dreadful
forms, as their Lord had done before them" (p. 28). Once
he established the glory of these former soldiers in war,
Mellen needed only to transfer that situation to peacetime
and substitute a new set of clerical leaders for recent military
ones. He said that those who are God's envoys on earth "hold
a Commission" from the Almighty and should receive proper
respect and obedience: "The ministers of Christ who hold
office under so intrepid a leader [should] be brave and valiant
like their great Lord and Master enduring hardness like good
soldiers." They are holy commanders "equipt for the higher
stages of Christian warfare" and thus are able "to lead others
on to victory and glory who themselves shrink at every danger and prospect of worldly inconvenience" (p. 29).

Just as their seventeenth-century predecessors had done
during the trials of the 1670s and 1680s, the ministers
adapted the Christian message and symbols to the needs of
the new republic. By 1791 the ministers had succeeded in
convincing most political leaders of the importance of religion as the foundation of justice and a tool for social order,
a point not lost on George Washington, who in his 1796
Farewell Address asked, "Where is the security of property,
for reputation, for life, if the sense of religious obligation

deserts the oaths which are the instrument of investigation in courts of justice? . . . Let us with caution indulge the supposition that morality can be maintained without religion . . . that national morality can prevail in the absence of religious principle." With faith in the ultimate fulfillment of the American errand, the ministers formulated and nurtured the rituals and organizations that would serve the national interest in the decades that followed.[46]

VI

For the writers, the prospects for success were also radically altered by the Revolution. At first, as the war ended, the familiar call for American letters was given a new republican emphasis, and the literary activity of the early 1780s suggests that optimism prevailed. Robert Bell, the Philadelphia printer, declared that the best literary works should be made available to "every Son of Adam, farmer, Mechanic, or Merchant," especially the members of the "middle class."[47] George Washington himself endorsed the arts in his letter of encouragement to Mathew Carey who founded *The Columbia Magazine* and *The American Museum*: "I consider such vehicles of knowledge more happily calculated than any other, to preserve the liberty, stimulate the industry and meliorate the morals of an enlightened and free people."[48] However, just as the clergy had begun to experience resistance by the mid-1780s, so too the writers discovered that the promise of prosperity for the arts was very short-lived. Patriotic American poems were left unbought in the bookstores, magazines began to fold after only a few issues, and critics grew impatient and condemned American literary works as weak imitations of English or classical models or as unpolished products of the forest. In the Pennsylvania Assembly, self-appointed spokesmen for the arts such as the

Philadelphia magnate Robert Morris quoted the Comte de Buffon when he declared: "America has produced nothing yet like a poet."[49]

Throughout the next two decades American writers responded to such difficulties and demands in a number of ways that would have a decisive bearing upon the position of belles lettres in American society and upon the themes, forms, and techniques that would characterize much of our imaginative literature. The developments of this period resulted in many changes that are best examined in individual writers and texts: new relationships between writer and audience; a movement away from poetry and toward various forms of prose fiction; and a shift in attention from man in society to man in nature—the individual, sometimes the artist, isolated from the community. The pressures also resulted in a break between the interests of religion and those of literature that led writers to seek a new ground for establishing their own moral authority. In spite of the best efforts of the clergy to cling to literature as their tool, there even emerged during the postwar period an antagonism between art and religion as debate ensued over the function of the imagination. As Lewis Simpson has argued, some American writers even began to embrace the long-standing notion of literature as a "Third Realm" of intellectual activity, quite separate from the realm of government and that of religion. This concept, well established in England and Europe by the late eighteenth century, was especially appealing to conservatives and those of Federalist political persuasion who wanted to set themselves apart from the affairs of the society in order to perfect their art. But this impulse would prevail only after 1805 and only among some writers.[50]

Reinforcing this tendency toward isolation was a crude notion of republican manliness, which flourished just after the Revolution. Although Brackenridge was a robust pioneer, Freneau a seaman, Barlow a shrewd businessman and politician, and although many members of the clergy had fought in the Revolution or braved harsh conditions as front-line chaplains, an attitude emerged that literary and religious activity belonged to the domestic world of women. The stereotype of the minister or poet as a weak, effeminate, and impractical person became so firmly established during these years that when Barlow returned from France in 1805 and sought political office, a member of Congress protested that it would be dangerous to allow a poet to hold office. Of course, the popularity of novels among women readers, the physical weakness of writers like Charles Brockden Brown, and the utopian social ideals of others only strengthened the stereotype. But works such as Livingston's "Philosophical Solitude" or the sermon orations and biographies of ministers before the Revolution, which describe religious, literary, and military achievement in the same terms, reveal that such attitudes were not commonly held before the Revolution.[51]

During the critical period of the 1780s and 1790s, the most interesting writers continued to search for some way to be men of letters and moral leaders in the society. Writers of quite different temperaments and political views, such as Dwight, Freneau, and Brackenridge, and later William Dunlap and Charles Brockden Brown, attempted to create a place for the American writer in society in spite of the resistance of both the financial elite and the common people. As they struggled to gain a popular audience, these writers recognized an important feature of their republican readers: they were inclined to resent anyone, whether preacher, politician, or poet, who presented himself as an authority figure. Through trial and error the writers discovered that the relationship between the American writer and his readers would have to be one in which the author appeared to have no lesson to teach, indeed in which he seemed not even to be speaking for himself. Only from a position of seeming detachment and distance could the writer in a democracy reach the mass of readers. To instruct his audience without alienating them, he would, above all, have to communicate a sense of sincerity and humility, even as he gave his insights the force of authority and conviction.[52]

Some, like Brackenridge, discovered early that prose narrative provided a form by which readers might be instructed through the voices of characters and narrators who are clearly distinguishable from the author himself. Freneau and Dwight, who turned increasingly to the prose essay as the proper medium for moral instruction, discovered that the traditional devices of pseudonyms and personae had special value in America. These fictional speakers allowed the writer to present personal convictions as though they were really the thoughts of people more socially acceptable to the common readers than to the author himself. The favorite mask of Freneau, Brackenridge, and Dwight was that of the philosopher in the forest—Freneau often called him the hermit or the pilgrim. In their writings, the character of the hermit-pilgrim is a wise and learned but humble man who loves his countrymen and wishes to instruct them through his example of simple living and his moral observations. Neither a misanthrope nor a romantic idealist, he has withdrawn to the forest because he is aware that his ideas might seem threatening to others, and he wishes to avoid needless contentions. He is also accessible to those who seek him out for conversation and sage counsel; occasionally, significant public events provoke him to send his thoughts to newspapers and magazines for publication.[53] In many ways this figure is a forerunner of Cooper's Natty Bumpo.

In the character of the hermit-pilgrim, the writers also found an apt metaphor for describing their understanding of the relationship of the American writer to his society. The literary calling in the new republic would require the writer to hold himself somewhat *apart* from his countrymen in order to pursue his own pilgrimage to truth. But in order to communicate his insights to a wide audience, he would have to be careful not to appear to hold himself *above* his fellows, even if that should require him to engage in forms of literary masquerade. In the fictions of Charles Brockden Brown, Poe, and Melville, the authorial mask would itself become material for literature. But even as Melville probed the theme of literary duplicity in his novels, he still advised would-be writers that in order to aspire to "the great art of telling the Truth," they must learn "to insinuate the truth craftily."[54]

In their efforts to achieve such subtle effects, the early writers fashioned intricate devices for addressing two levels of readers at once, such as ironic disjunctions between the surface moral and deeper meaning of a novel or poem. In so doing, the writers were adhering to two accepted literary dictates of the Common Sense school. First, the writer had an artistic obligation to compose works that would appeal to those of the most refined taste. Second, he also had a moral obligation to instruct the widest possible audience. The true genius, it was assumed, could achieve this double aim with creations that would raise the aesthetic sensibilities of all readers to his own level. But, despite two decades of determined effort, this dual objective proved unattainable for the first generation of American writers. No matter how well crafted, books can only speak to those who will listen, and readers at both ends of the spectrum were inclined to see in American literary works only what they were predisposed to see. The English critics carped of banality while the common people in America complained of highfalutin imitative style. The frustration of the American writers increased as the taste of the American reading public seemed to decline and English reviewers began to ignore American productions. Faced with such disappointments, the writers blamed themselves rather than the outmoded literary principles that limited their possibilities and stifled true originality.

Also inhibiting was the doctrine that insisted the imagination of the true poet was not only the moral beacon of society but that the poet's flights of fancy should serve the religious needs of the people as well. Because the churches themselves were suffering troubled times, intellectual ministers like John Blair Linn and Witherspoon recognized that they needed more than ever to keep literature at the service of religion. In his *The Powers of Genius* (1802) Lynn said, "Literature, next to religion, is the foundation of our greatest consolation and delight . . . literature renders men more eminently useful, opens wider their intellects to the reception of divine light, banishes religious superstition and bows the knee with purer adoration, before the throne of God."[55] As Coleridge became known in America, the ministers were full of praise for his rejuvenation of the imagination because they believed that heightened aesthetic sensitivity would lead to greater piety and generate much religious poetry and prose. When Elijah Fitch, a Massachusetts clergyman, published his didactic epic titled *The Beauties of Religion*, which aimed "to give just views on religion, and to persuade the love and practice of it," he was both upholding tradition and laying a new foundation for the sentimentalized moralistic writing that would enjoy great success in the nineteenth century, much to the dismay of Hawthorne and Melville.[56] Twain's parody in *Huckleberry Finn* of Julian Moore's funeral elegies illustrates both the persistence of such poetry and the scorn it aroused among serious artists.

But the concept of the function of the imagination that led clergymen to praise Wordsworth and Coleridge was limited by a religious notion of the sublime that prevailed against unchained flights of fancy. Novels were held to be particularly dangerous, and verbal attacks on fiction were sometimes reinforced by censure. Because, with the exception of Timothy Dwight, serious writers sought "to enchain the attention and ravish the souls of those who study and reflect,[57] in the words of Charles Brockden Brown, they found that the demands of the artistic imagination and those of religious and moral instruction were often in conflict. As the clergy-men were fond of warning, the indulgence of "the reveries of a perverted imagination" might lead to "fairy visions" of human pleasure and "exhibit such a licentiousness of senti-ment and description, as cannot fail to inflame the passions which they ought to restrain, and to undermine the virtue which they profess to support."[58]

William Hill Brown's moral fiction *The Power of Sympa-thy* (1789) has this tension between religious dictates and artistic passion as its central theme. In the first paragraph, the passionate Harrington writes to the reasonable Worthy, "you call me with some degree of truth, a strange medley of contradiction—the moralist and the amoroso—for these are interwoven in my constitution, so that nature and grace are at continual fisticuffs." The disastrous consequences for Harrington in the novel, which include near-incest, cynicism, and his sister's suicide, suggest the extreme psychological and social pressures that result from these conflicts between morality and feeling within the individual and the artist.[59] Perhaps the underlying theme of this novel is more in accord with Freneau's eventual conviction that the artistic salvation of the American writers would not lie in a close alliance with religion but in the release of the imagination from the strictures of piety, and of common sense realism as well. After a long period of religious and philosophical searching, Freneau concluded that only through the free engagement of poetic fancy with American Nature and with the conditions of American life could the American writer produce works of art that would have genuine social usefulness and spiritual value.[60]

A close study of literary works of this period suggests that it was not Puritanism that made it difficult for literature to get started in America; it was not the demand that people cultivate the fields and clear the wilderness; it was not even the materialism of the Protestant ethic that stifled the imagination and made symbolic language appear irrelevant and trivial: it was the moral burden of the Enlightenment. Without the Scottish Common Sense school of philosophy, American literature and the American writers of the late eighteenth century might have led the Western literary world into the Romantic era, but the restrictions on the symbolic imagination of those trained in the eighteenth-century American colleges effectively prevented the young writers from conceiving of the calling of the writer in terms that would free them from the secular priesthood of letters.

VII

Since 1785, American literary critics have declared that the first American writers were unable to solve their problems or to find ways to transcend them. Why, ask the critics, did a nation so eager for world fame and filled with so many ambitious young men fail to produce respectable literary works? In 1809 Barlow's old teacher and adviser Joseph S. Buckminster chose the occasion of the Phi Beta Kappa address at Harvard for the formal pronouncement that America had become a literary wasteland. In his "On the Dangers and Duties of the Men of Letters," which was immediately reprinted in *The Monthly Anthology*, Buckminster explained that the problem was caused by the direct conflict of the notion of equality and the democratic spirit with the highest standards of taste upon which literature and the arts must be established. This "pernicious notion of equality . . . has not only tainted our sentiments, but impaired our vigour, and crippled our literary eminence."[61] Although he could not be precise about how this had occurred, he was certain that its result could be found in all aspects of the culture: "This secret influence of the public opinion, though not easily described, has been felt and

that our early specimens will be sought after with avidity, and
that those who led the way in the rugged discouraging path
will be honoured, as we begin to honour the adventurous
spirits who first sought, explored, and cleared this wilderness."[62] In the literature of these decades we may find a
continuing record of that relationship between literature
and society that existed in America before the Revolution,
the impact of social and political changes upon the role of the
literary artist, and the strategies which writers adopted in
response to their new conditions.

The consequences of these changes involved redefinition
of the callings of clergyman and poet, a reassessment of the
nature of intellectual leadership in the republic, the adaptation of old literary and religious forms to new circumstances
and audiences, and the emergence of new techniques for
communicating with American audiences. Especially interesting are the ways in which particular writers confronted
this crisis of authority and how their material and literary
forms reflect their attempts to accommodate or to change
their new society. Underlying these developments is a reappraisal of the moral purposes of imaginative literature and
of the relationship between art and religion. Yet study of
these first American writers reveals that certain circumstances
they encountered during this seminal period have persisted
in American culture. Thus, in the literary strategies and
methods they devised, we may discover a kind of genetic code
for the role of the artist in America and for the peculiar
nature of American literature.

lamented by many of us who were educated in the pr
generation" (p. 148). Echoing the challenge that John Wi
spoon had presented to his aspiring writers four dec
before and anticipating, in some ways, Emerson's *Amer
Scholar* two decades later, Buckminster insisted that
the men of letters could save the cultural philistines f
themselves: there must be "men of letters who are abl
direct our taste, mold our genius, and inspire our emula
. . . men whose writings are to be the depositories of
national greatness" (p. 148). Yet even as he tried to ins
his audience to pursue with renewed vigor the goal of lite
achievement, Buckminster ended by proposing the same
tradictory aims for the writer in America. In seeking
achieve literary excellence, the poet must not abandon
social and moral obligations to use his talents to instruct
common people: "Learning is not a superfluidity; and uti
must, after all, be the object of your studies" (p. 1
The best writer is one "who makes truth intelligible to
humblest," he declared; and every writer must recognize
close tie between the aims of religion and the purposes
literature. The accomplished artist is one "who imparts
divine warmth of his own soul to the souls of his reade
(p. 155).

What Buckminster was incapable of understanding, ho
ever, was that the writers had succeeded in this better th
he or they knew. Although most of them considered th
compromises of style, accommodations of form, and creatio
of characters and material to have been futile efforts ir
losing struggle, what they had actually achieved was t
necessary adaptation of traditional methods to their n
circumstances and in some instances the creation of origir
solutions to unique aesthetic problems. In a *Salmagun*
essay of 1819, James Kirke Paulding looked back briefly up
the writers who had preceded him and predicted that whe
authors of truly great stature appear in America, "It is the

II

TIMOTHY DWIGHT:
PASTOR, POET, AND POLITICS

If I could put a notion in his head:
"*Why* do they make good neighbors?
. . .

Before I built a wall I'd ask to know
What I was walling in or walling out,
And to whom I was like to give offense.
Something there is that doesn't love a wall,
That wants it down." I could say "Elves" to him,
But it's not elves exactly, and I'd rather
He said it for himself.

ROBERT FROST
"Mending Wall," 1914

Timothy Dwight is often portrayed as a narrow-minded, politically reactionary Puritan because he embraced religious and social traditions and beliefs that extended from the days of Cotton and Increase Mather to his own time and he never strayed from the true path. He greeted the Revolution with the enthusiasm that Cotton Mather had expressed for the overthrow of Edmund Andros a hundred years earlier, and he reacted to the moral decay and social turmoil of the postwar period with the same fiery rhetoric that Increase had poured out upon the recalcitrant children of the Puritan founders. For these reasons, Dwight's writing and the pattern of his career illustrate how an established Calvinist clergyman perceived the new republic and how he used inherited rhetorical forms and religious language to try to guide the nation during and after the Revolution.[1]

Unlike his literary peers, Dwight remained a clergyman to the end. In fact, he became the most influential religious

leader of his time and from his chair and pulpit at Yale set
the direction for American higher education. As a writer, he
employed every available form except prose fiction. In his
efforts to raise the taste and moral standards of his countrymen, he wrote an epic, a mock epic, a long pastoral essay, and
sermons. So attuned was he to the direction that American
writing was taking that he turned in his later years to the
travel narrative, anticipating the great importance of travel
literature in nineteenth-century America. Although he is
usually depicted as rigid in thought and style, Dwight actually
adjusted to the changing society in many ways, altering his
forms, modifying his own public image, and gradually lowering his expectations for the moral progress of the new nation.[2]

Born in Northampton, Massachusetts, in 1752 to a merchant father and a mother who was the third daughter of
Jonathan Edwards, Dwight seems to have had from birth the
credentials to become the formulator of the language of the
emerging capitalist-Christian ideology. In the tradition of
early piety fostered by the Puritans, he was reading the Bible
at the age of four and by age seven was instructing local
Indians in catechism. When he was thirteen, he was admitted
to Yale, and by nineteen, in spite of some non-academic
interruptions, he had been appointed tutor, had composed his
first four poems, and had started work on his epic, *The
Conquest of Canaan*. Recognized as America's rising young
man of letters and religion, Dwight was asked to give the
1772 Yale commencement address, and his lecture, "A
Dissertation on the History, Eloquence, and Poetry of the
Bible," is a brilliant adaptation to the American scene of
the then latest critical thought of English and Scottish
theologians and literary theorists. Although he was continually troubled by health and family problems over the
next ten years, he managed to serve as an Army chaplain,
preach at Weathersfield, marry Mary Woolsey, support his
mother and twelve siblings, complete a draft of *The Conquest*,

and become the pastor of the Congregational church at Greenfield, Connecticut. At Greenfield he also founded an academy for young men and women. He would later celebrate his twelve happy and successful years in this pastoral haven in his 1794 poem, *Greenfield Hill*.[3]

The turbulent decade of the 1780s disturbed the peace of the hermit-philosopher-educator that Dwight had become and had an adverse effect upon his hopes for the new nation. In the face of declining clerical authority in the states and increasing political unrest, Dwight became alarmed. When the publication of *The Conquest of Canaan* met with luke-warm acceptance at home and critical attacks from abroad, the disappointed and angry Dwight employed his poetic skills in a bitter satire on the decay of American morals and religious values, *The Triumph of Infidelity*. Although he had the discretion to publish the invective anonymously, his Federalist opinions drew him into the political arena and won him angry enemies as well as loyal friends over the next two decades. Noah Webster and Jedidiah Morse were among the men of letters who were warm supporters of Dwight's efforts to halt the decline of religion, morals, and public literary taste, and they cheered when he was appointed president of Yale in 1795, following the death of Ezra Stiles.

Until his death in 1817, Dwight used his position at Yale as a foundation for his political and social influence. In his baccalaureate jeremiads Dwight attacked the infidelity of the undergraduates to the church and the general decline of religion in America. Declaring that there were no more than two Yale students who believed in Christ, he called for a revival of religion as the only means to save America from the corruption at home and abroad that threatened destruction. Citing the "XYZ" affair, the atrocities of the French Revolution, the threat of another war with England, the supposed plot of a group of leftist "Illuminati" to overthrow the government, and other calamities, Dwight cried out in

his "The Nature, and Danger, of Infidel Philosophy" (1797)
and in "The Duty of Americans, at the Present Crisis"
(1798) against America's "open and professed war against
God." His political enemies identified him as the "Pope of
Federalism" and "His Holiness Pope Timothy."

Unflagging in his energy and commitment to a Christian
America, Dwight met criticism with renewed efforts. He improved the curriculum and faculty at Yale, increased the
student body three-fold, and led the great religious revival
that began about 1802 and had swept the entire country by
the 1830s. In the meantime, he continued work on a major
work in divinity, his *Theology*, published in 1818; he took
horseback journeys collecting materials for his four-volume
Travels; In New-England and New York, published in 1821;
and he attacked his enemies and defended the American
mission in a number of pamphlets, essays, and books. His
anti-Jefferson, anti-Deism journal, *The New England Palladium*, was Dwight's forum for promoting the values and
traditions of New England, the rights and authority of the
clergy, and the value of religion to the progress of the new
nation.[4]

Because of his training in the doctrines of Common Sense
philosophy, Dwight's literary intentions were similar to those
of Brackenridge, Barlow, and Freneau. Like them, he wanted
to reach the common people with his writing and improve
the morals and culture of Americans through literature.
However, Dwight wanted to establish his authority as a
respected intellectual leader in the society and, at the same
time, to strengthen the authority of the clergy in general.
Freneau and Brackenridge and even Barlow finally despaired
of making the man of letters into a figure of social importance,
and they all developed grave doubts about the contribution
of the clergy and the value of religion in general—certainly,
they were wary of the ministers having power. Dwight, of
course, never admitted doubt and never abandoned his goal,

and all of his writing must be viewed in light of his political ambition.[5]

Although there are signs in his writing that he might have privately questioned whether the emergent capitalist-Christian ideology that his works promoted was really the best foundation for the new nation, his urgent need to create for himself a leadership role in the republic prevented him from pursuing such doubts very far or from exploring them in his art. He suffered disappointments and never attained the kind of eminence he imagined for himself, but he was successful. Perhaps for that reason he never really doubted the essential role of the poet in society as did Freneau and Brackenridge, whose isolation allowed them some opportunity to view the American scene with more detachment and clarity. Dwight was always an insider, and though intelligent and sensitive enough to recognize how things were going wrong, he never would risk his own position to press his criticism beyond the accepted formulas. A New England Jeremiah he was, but a disaffected American critic he would never let himself become. Because Dwight did maintain a consistent Christian vision throughout his life, his work presents a sharply focused view of the nature of his world rather than a prism through which various angles of vision might be reflected and exposed.

To convey his message with force and variety, Dwight was always searching for speakers—voices that could teach the common man and voices that could influence those at the highest level of the social order. Dwight shared the hope of the other writers for unlimited possibilities for literature and learning in America. He felt this enthusiasm when he started writing *The Conquest of Canaan*, but by the mid-1780s, when he finally published the poem, he had lost some of his certainty. Like the writers of republican leaning, Dwight also felt an antagonistic relationship with his audience, but, as a descendant of New England ministers, he had grown up expecting to be resisted, ignored, even scorned. When he encountered the enemy or witnessed backsliding, he was not shocked or discouraged. He was prepared to fight.

When Dwight entered Yale in 1765 at the age of thirteen, he already seemed destined to become an important intellectual figure. Although his progress in school was delayed somewhat by a broken arm and by the political turmoil that followed the Stamp Act crisis, he and the college recovered quickly enough for Dwight to become a tutor and an acknowledged literary leader by 1771. After establishing his reputation with his early patriotic poems "A Song" and "America" and after trying his hand at biblical poems with "The Trial of Faith" and "Ester and Mordecai," Dwight started his biblical epic, *The Conquest of Canaan*. During the twelve years it took him to compose *The Conquest*, he served as a chaplain in Parson's Brigade and as a preacher at Weathersfield and later at West Point. Having employed the Puritan typology in his sermons to justify the war against England, Dwight was well practiced in the use of biblical allegory to portray the tale of America. In *The Conquest of Canaan*, he tried to accomplish an enormous feat of synthesis: to transport the Puritan experience of the seventeenth century across the chasm of the Revolution, to annex the new republican vista, and thus to create a vision of the future that would fuse the Calvinist and Enlightenment world views. To his mind, the biblical epic seemed the proper form for such a monumental task, but he could not yet understand —though his delay in publication may suggest his uneasiness —that the psychic shock of the Revolution had fundamentally altered the way Americans would view themselves and their national purpose. The biblical story of the chosen people led out of bondage to freedom and glory in the wilderness no longer seemed adequate to account for the divided American people of the 1780's and the ambiguity many people felt about the direction of the social experiment.

Thus, there existed a fundamental contradiction between the form of the narrative and the rhetorical purpose of its author and the emerging attitudes of potential readers. By 1786, the American people were losing faith in the vision of a providentially designed, scripturally revealed sacred mission. It had been Dwight's original purpose to set the direction for the future, to urge his countrymen toward the promised land of New World America. But a millennial expectation of ultimate national salvation in some future epoch would not inspire farmers and laborers to sacrifice their energies for the good of all, nor would it help to suppress the problems of corruption, slavery, and economic inequality that were already present among the chosen.

Another barrier was the language itself. Dwight chose Joshua as the central figure of the epic, but military biblical types had been used to excess during the war and were drained of their power. Also, the proliferation of denominations and religious ideas in the 1780s made the poem's typology seem too narrowly Calvinist. Perhaps Dwight realized the types had become suspect, for he always denied any connection between Washington and Joshua. In addition, the implications of the biblical parallels were not all favorable to America. While he was expanding and revising his poem, Dwight was also becoming worried about America. As a result, in the final version the theme of backsliding and possible failure rather than triumph of God's people threatened to emerge as the central meaning. When the epic met with unfavorable reactions from the European critics for its overblown style and weak imitation of Pope and Milton and, even worse, when the American audience seemed indifferent to its message, Dwight tried another approach.[6]

Just as some of his contemporaries, like Freneau and Brackenridge, were turning from poetry to the prose essay and the creation of fictional voices to mask their own public images, Dwight started a series in 1786 for *American Museum*, which he wrote under the pseudonym of "The Friend."[7] In these essays, modeled on the English Augustans, Dwight created two distinct authority figures designed to appeal to the separate prejudices and expectations of his readership. In the case of James Littlejohn, Esq., who is an intellectual and scholar, most like Dwight himself, he concocted an elaborate autobiography tracing Littlejohn's development from a precocious, do-good child to an author and, as Littlejohn immodestly admits, a "great man." The basis of Littlejohn's authority is his learning, intelligence, moral superiority, and aristocratic style. The other speaker, John Homely, is a variant of the hermit-pilgrim figure, a wise farmer whose patriotism and passion for American ideals feeds his prejudice against the English and European influence in America. There is a third voice, too, the "Friend" himself, Dwight's initial persona, whose self-description reveals Dwight's notion of how the audience would perceive a literary spokesman. The Friend's self-effacing yet firm and authoritative tone is similar to that often used by Puritan ministers threatened by congregational unrest:

> The writer wishes his readers to consider him as a friend to each of them, and to the whole human race; as a sincere friend, who would consult their interests rather than their inclinations; who, when those interested require it, would not hesitate to administer an honest reproof, or to communicate advice, which to the ear of prejudice, would sound less loftily than the silver voice of flattery. . . . At the same time, he would wish to be viewed as a familiar friend, who would advise, not dictate; and whose lessons will be communicated in the style of affability, and not of dogmatism. [p. 71]

That Dwight felt the need to assert his modesty and lack of presumption directly indicates how vulnerable he felt as a writer to the cursory rejection of offended republican readers.

In the first number of the series, Dwight leaned markedly toward prose fiction in his detailed presentation of the narrator's account of himself. Dwight developed several themes in this portrait which were to recur throughout *The Friend* series. Ever since childhood, Littlejohn has found his good nature and religious spirit to be in conflict with the materialistic values and pragmatism of young America:

> The first thing by which my character was distinguished, as my grandmother has long since informed me, was that good nature which usually fixes upon children the stigma of wanting good common sense. I always gave up my top to my brother when he cried out for it; and frequently imparted my gingerbread to my sister because she had eaten hers and looked sorry. "O the fool!" exclaimed my mother, upon seeing me so tamely yield up the favor to objects of infantine desire—I fear, said my father, all is not as it should be, with poor James— little did either of them then think that I would not one day become a great man, sometime author, and have my name printed as a writer of essays. [p. 220]

Dwight's point here is that pragmatism that ignores the moral values of charity and virtue also misses the advantages such virtues may have in laying the groundwork for intellectual achievement. Thus, learning and morality are rejected together.

Littlejohn goes on to say that because he was considered "good for nothing to work" his father "sent me to a neighboring college, to see if he could make anything of me." At college he loved his books, but he was viewed by his classmates as a "strange creature." Upon graduation he tried medicine but failed because he was too forgetful in practical matters such as taking the proper pills to patients. Finally, he stumbled into a role which gives him much in common with a great many other observer-narrators in American

literature, including Hawthorne's Coverdale and Fitzgerald's
Nick Caraway: "I became a mere, but not a cool spectator of
human life and separated from every personal concern, soon
made the business of all others my own. I was not indeed
manager or meddler; but I earnestly wished the happiness of
my fellow men; and to promote it, cheerfully tendered my
advice and assistance" (p. 222). This identification of the
author with the role of critical but genial observer of society
would persist in American literature. Just as Dwight speaks
through the displaced Littlejohn, American writers have
often been cast or cast themselves as outsiders.[8]

But the voice of Littlejohn, Dwight recognized, was not
appropriate for all situations. For more rigorous and direct
criticism, he used John Homely. While it is Littlejohn's task
to critique the moral and economic values of Americans and
to comment upon their cultural inadequacies, Homely's
major theme is similar to the one Emerson would pursue
forty years later in the *American Scholar*: the folly of
America's intellectual dependence upon England. In his
effort to arouse national pride and cultural independence,
Homely appeals first to the nostalgia for the fervor, unity,
and idealism of the war years. Just as many of the ministers
hoped to use familiar rhetoric to keep the militancy of the
Revolution alive and direct it toward religion, Homely
employs the jeremiad formula to stir a cultural awakening.
In the opening of *The Friend* III, he complains:

> During the war I enjoyed with supreme satisfaction, the
> era, when men, when freemen, began to feel themselves
> to be men, and realized their equality with the other
> sons of Adam. The entire national glory and importance
> acquired by us, through every stage of the war, and
> especially in its conclusion, secured, to my flattered
> hopes, the future excellence of this manly and becoming
> character. But I have lived to see these hopes disap-

> pointed. . . . But unfortunately we have reaffirmed the
> spirit of colonial depressions, and returned to our
> original babyhood. [p. 446]

This appeal to military pride is not the only tack Homely takes, however. He also touches upon a theme that Charles Brockden Brown would pursue in such novels as *Arthur Mervyn*, the vulnerability of Americans to the con artist who uses his European background to play upon the blind prejudices of Anglophile Americans. Homely relates a tale of a man who had recently arrived from abroad and was immediately taken to be a lawyer and appointed to an office of importance. Fawned upon and admired by all, he is seen to be "a man of genius, or in other words, a European." Then, his wife arrives to expose him as a "tallow chandler."[9]

Dwight's concern about the continued dependence upon Europe was not entirely motivated by nationalism nor was it free of self-interest. He recognized that a continued psychological reverence for the past and for European authority was impeding the transition toward a new state of moral and cultural independence in which he and his fellow American intellectuals could establish standards of taste and values that would be conducive to American productivity and receptive to American literary and artistic products. But thus far, every time the religious, political, and intellectual leaders tried to weave a pattern of American cultural unity, the fabric was rent and twisted by the tug of European dominance. As much as Dwight himself believed in the actual superiority of European arts and literature, he was committed to the idea that America must detach itself in order to get on with the task of designing its own culture from within.

In *The Friend* IV Littlejohn takes up the issue especially close to Dwight in 1787: America's literary dependence. He begins with a general example and an extended metaphor strikingly similar to the central image of Robert Frost's

"Mending Wall." He tells a tale of a man's blind dependence upon an aged father.

> The man, who, upon his shoulders, carried weekly to the mill, a stone of sufficient weight to balance a bushel of wheat, and who refused to rid himself of the burden, because his father and grandfather had carried the same stone, forty years before him, was, in the eye of reason, a less ridiculous object than the person, who is voluntarily burdened with a load of errors and follies, because others, whose shoulders are humped higher than their heads, laughing heartily at the awkward figure, their fellow Hudibrasses make around them. [p. 565]

Having established this symbol of the irrationality of generational and historical dependence, Dwight connects it directly to literary matters. Sounding like a literary radical, he argues that the present system of criticism, inherited from the European past, only serves to stifle creativity and imagination in America where the new environment should inspire new forms and themes for unfettered minds: "To those persons who never questioned the authority of the received system of criticism, these remarks will appear ill-founded; for the prejudice above mentioned, which produced their implicit faith in it, will prevent them from discerning their propriety." In America, however, "criticism will advance towards a higher perfection, as the varieties of the human mind open new views of poetical objects, and peculiarity of genius furnishes new spiritings and meanderings of delight" (pp. 565–66).

With the foundation established, Littlejohn expands his concern about criticism and literature into a theory of culture, politics, and science in America. Borrowing his logic perhaps from Madison's *The Federalist* #10, Littlejohn argues that diversity of ideas and freedom of thought are the keys to the emergence of individual geniuses:

In our open happy state of society, disjointed from the
customs and systems of Europe, commencing a new system of science and politics, it is to be ardently hoped,
that so much independence of mind will be assumed by
us, as to induce us to shake off these rusty shackles,
examine things on the plain of nature and evidence, and
laugh at the grey-bearded decisions of sotting authority.
There is ever a propensity in the mind, when forming a
class, species, or genus to form it from the knowledge of
a few individuals. Hence, it is of necessity imperfectly
formed, and all conclusions based upon it, must be
erroneous. This is the great imperfection of theories and
systems, and the chief cause of their failure in a practical
application; classes ought never to be erected but from
the knowledge of many individuals belonging in them,
and to be accurately just from the knowledge of all.
[p. 567]

In such an ideal pluralistic state, a new form of literary
criticism would also spring forth that would be appropriate
to the values and aspirations of a free-minded people. A
"general and liberal" set of critical principles would encourage experimentation and imagination. Then, "the wings
of genius would be no longer clipped, and its flight, taking
a natural direction, and using the natural strength of opinion,
would be free and elevated; on this plan, the writer who
produced pleasing selections of images and sentiments from
the wisely extended and endlessly diversified paradise of
nature, would be assured of regaling the taste of his readers"
(p. 567). Although Dwight has been accused of constructing
this argument to justify *The Conquest of Canaan* and to
answer his English critics, his statements do constitute a
critical theory for a writer in a free democracy similar to the
ideas that Emerson and Whitman would later articulate.[10]

Dwight ended *The Friend* series with an eloquent piece
of rhetoric in which he used the strategy of the Puritan
jeremiad to assert the wonders of America. Acknowledging

the special design of Providence and then raising the specter
of possible war, plague, and ruin if the people backslide from
the ideals of the Revolution, Homely considers the military
and political brilliance of Americans up to the mid-1780s and
the crossroads of history at which the nation presently stands.
So complete yet concise a statement of the fears and hopes of
Dwight and his learned contemporaries in 1787 is this final
paragraph, that it deserves to be quoted in full.

> "I have, indeed, Mr. Littlejohn, with no small pleasure,
> viewed the American revolution, as a new era of im-
> provement in all things natural and moral. When I see
> all Europe surveying and admiring our military and
> political exertions—when I see princes, and philoso-
> phers, learning from us new views of human rights, and
> blessing nations with new enjoyments, copied from our
> enlightened constitutions of government—when I see
> good men, throughout Europe, as well as America,
> anticipating, from our circumstances, brighter and hap-
> pier days for the enslaved eastern nations—when I see
> gloomy bigotism in the sight of our catholicism, relaxing
> their aspect, and expanding their hearts with charitable
> regards to the once-hated professors of adverse systems
> of religion—when I see then a thousand fetters of
> authority and systems dissolved, as by the fairy touch of
> enchantment, and the mind escaped from prison, begin-
> ning to prune its wings for elevated and daring adven-
> ture—I cannot but persuade myself, that these mighty
> preparations of Providence are designed for advanta-
> geous changes in the affairs of men. I cannot but think,
> arts, policy, science, and virtue will begin to wear a
> brighter aspect, and claim a more extensive influence.
> Judge, then, of the mortification, I must experience, in
> seeing any event begin to overcast this delightful
> prospect, and threaten the return of all those prejudices,
> which through a long and dismal continuance, have
> darkened the horizon of the eastern continent." [p. 156]

For all of the directness of these essays, Dwight still had good reason to feel in 1788 that he was not reaching the American readers, that he had not created the proper voice for asserting his authority, that he had not discovered the appropriate form for appealing to the widest possible audience. This frustration, added to the near panic he began to feel about the declining morality and increasing corruption of the people, moved Dwight to a direct attack upon the conspicuous source of all of America's ills: irreligion. The publication of *The Triumph of Infidelity* in 1788 marks an important turning point in Dwight's literary adjustment. This work illustrates clearly the continuation of an intimate interrelationship between religion and literature in the 1780s. As Dwight became increasingly aware of the serious threat to religion being posed by social changes at home and intellectual influences from abroad, he responded with the same kind of fervor that appears in the most bitter poems of Freneau, the most fiery sermons of a Calvinist divine, and the most pointed barbs of Brackenridge's satire. As in so many of the works of this period, the pressure and confusion of the social and political situation results in a breakdown in the literary form. As Dwight struggled consciously to express his religious, social, and political disagreement, the coherence of his work is repeatedly undermined by his desire to speak to too many kinds of readers on too many levels at the same time. Often claimed by its readers from the time of its publication to the present to be almost totally incomprehensible, *The Triumph of Infidelity* is in its very confusion a literary reflection of the schizophrenic political unconsciousness of Revolutionary America.

Whereas Dwight would later be able to create an idealization of the capitalist-Christian synthesis in *Greenfield Hill* through his theme that industry and "competency" yield morality, *The Triumph of Infidelity* is a cry of outrage at being betrayed. The historical sections, which take up so

much of the beginning of the poem, establish an evolutionary
context for the continuous drift toward religious liberalism
and moral decay that will lead to world ruin. Satan's patient
work has gradually led mankind away from redemption in
Christ toward the fires of a last day and eternal damnation,
and the ideas of Voltaire and Hume and of Charles Chauncy
in America are products and causes of the last stage. In his
anger, however, Dwight became entangled in the dire implications of his apocalyptic logic: If the present time is a
last stage, then there is no hope for the future of America,
and all efforts to save mankind are doomed. Thus, the
leadership of the clergy and the call to reform are futile
efforts against the forces of providential determinism. Dwight
knew he had trapped himself in this, so he corrected his
earlier condemnation and modified Chauncy's crime into an
unfortunate American misdemeanor which could be redressed
by the present generation's reform. He was thereby able to
retreat from his naturalistic prophecy of doom and strike a
balance between fear and hope.[11]

After publishing *The Triumph* and answering some English reviewers of *The Conquest*, Dwight withdrew, like the
figure of the hermit-philosopher, from the American audience
that had rejected his epic and ignored his prose pieces to his
rural home in Greenfield. Ever tireless and determined to be
heard, however, he soon began to work slowly on a completely different sort of poem, which would not see publication until 1794.

Despite his disclaimer in the preface that he wrote *Greenfield Hill* "merely to amuse his own mind and to gain
temporary relief from the pressure of melancholy," Dwight
actually intended the poem to present the local social utopia
he believed he had created in his community at Greenfield
as a model for American society as a whole. At the same time
that he denies serious intentions, Dwight also indicates in the
preface that he is quite conscious of the social implications

of his poem: "Poetry may not, perhaps, produce greater effects in promoting the prosperity of mankind, than philosophy; but the effects which it produces are far from being small. Where truth requires little illustration, and only needs to be set in a strong and affecting light, poetry appears to be as advantageous an instrument of making useful impressions as can be easily conceived" (p. 7). Moreover, Dwight also argues that the kind of audience that poems reach is often different from that touched by other forms of social discourse, and thus it brings the doctrines of progress to new minds. "It will be read by many persons, who would scarcely look at a logical discussion; by most readers it will be more deeply felt, and more lastingly remembered; and to say the least, it will in the present case, be an unusual, and for that reason, may be a forcible method of treating several subjects handled in the poem" (p. 7). While *Greenfield Hill* surely has many flaws, it is by far a more subtle and pleasing piece of moral instruction than Dwight's early works and is certainly his outstanding literary accomplishment.[12]

Borrowing his theme from Oliver Goldsmith's "The Deserted Village," his form from William Manson's *Museus,* and his language from several earlier writers, Dwight had intended to imitate a different English poet in each of the poem's seven sections. Abandoning this plan after the third section, he turned to American voices for the last four parts and reinforced the American heritage of the poem by taking some of his characters from Benjamin Franklin, by rhapsodizing upon the Connecticut landscape, and by dedicating the work to John Adams, lest any reader miss the poem's political slant. In the first section, "The Prospect," the narrator speaks in the blank verse of James Thomson's *The Seasons* as he overlooks the autumn harvest from atop Greenfield Hill. He recounts the story of the American Revolution, sings the glories of America's future peace and prosperity, and concludes with praise for humble rural clergymen. In the second section, "The Flourishing Village," Dwight presents an optimistic American counter to Goldsmith's despairing poem "The Deserted Village." The contrast provides Dwight with ample opportunity to have his narrator develop one of his favorite themes: the decadence of Europe as opposed to the pristine physical and moral beauty of America. Next, in "The Burning of Fairfield" the speaker tells of the recent destruction of that Connecticut town by British troops. This part, which borrows its octosyllabic couplets from the English poet John Dyer, seems to have been designed only as a context for the following section's apologia for the American atrocities against the Pequot. With its Spenserian stanzas, "The Destruction of the Pequods" is modeled upon James Beattie's "The Minstrel," but Dwight shifts voices and gives the narration to a local mother who justifies the destruction of the Indians as necessary and inevitable.

The final parts of *Greenfield Hill* are spoken by a succession of American characters. In section five, "The Clergyman's Advice to the Villagers," a country pastor becomes the speaker. In his deathbed sermon he exhorts his congregation to uphold the renowned American virtues of family worship, public virtue, and self-denial and calls upon future clergymen to earn the respect of their people by following his humble example. In section six, "The Farmer's Advice to His Villagers," Dwight imitates the speech of Father Abraham in Franklin's *The Way to Wealth*. In nice balance with the religious counsel of the previous section, the farmer supplies practical wisdom on husbandry and economy: financial success will be the fruit of social harmony and of wise planning and child-rearing. In the last part, "The Vision," another new character appears, "the Genius of the Sound," who rises from the waters off Connecticut to prophesy America's role in future ages. Besides surpassing all other nations in its social order and judicious government, America will set an example for the world in its advancement of the arts and support for the clergy. From even so brief a summary of the poem, it is not difficult to discern the central theme: to achieve a successful individual life and fulfill the national destiny, every American should subordinate the self to religion, the arts, the clergy, and country. But such a synopsis or statement of theme does not do justice to the internal complexity of this remarkable poem.

In both major poems of his biblical period (1774–88), Dwight manipulated familiar themes and forms in an effort to accommodate the prevailing conditions of the postwar period. During the years that he was experimenting in this Puritan idiom and growing concerned about the larger universe, he was also witnessing the successful application of his New England values in the rural haven of Greenfield. After venting his rage against the infidels in 1788, Dwight sought a new form, language, and narrative method for reasserting the promise of America and found them in his didactic pastoral, *Greenfield Hill*. He finally abandoned the Puritan story of America's errand to formulate a new myth that would incorporate the values of the Puritans with the values of the emergent capitalist-agrarian economy.

In *Greenfield Hill* Dwight held and expressed the deepest values and unconscious desires of the culture in the language of utopian ideology that the culture endorsed. Instead of exposing evils to purge them, in pre-Revolutionary fashion, he tried to accentuate the positive. Although he attacked deception, fraud, and imposture as the worst features of the European stain upon America, he himself engaged in an imaginative act that may be interpreted as a deception. Janus-faced, the poem looks back with Puritan scrutiny upon the mixed record of God's chosen in the wilderness and looks forward with strained optimism to a time of pastoral harmony. Dwight's insistent tone masks fears of failure which had been heard in America before, in John Winthrop's *Journal*, Cotton Mather's *Magnalia*, and Jonathan Edwards's

History of the Work of Redemption, and which would be heard again, in Emerson's *Self-Reliance*, Whitman's *Democratic Vistas*, and Norman Mailer's *The Armies of the Night*. From a literary standpoint, *Greenfield Hill* is really Dwight's most interesting work because it springs from his personal response to these new pressures in postwar America. As with the other writers of his time, Dwight's attempt to unify the traditional literary elements into a form and language reflects the complexities of the American situation.

Dwight moved from a literature of conflict, in which war and victory were central, to a poetry of containment, which stressed conformity and melioration. Appropriately, he exchanged the Puritan New England teleology for a precapitalist ideology that combined Calvinist themes of discipline with mercantile themes of economic progress. Anticipating American middle-class dogmas that would link sexual reward to success, peace to prosperity, and comfort to competency, *Greenfield Hill* stands as an early effort to create a new image of domestic bliss for which men and women of the republic are supposed to labor and sacrifice. Dwight gave symbolic expression to the economic motives and the psychological inclinations of the new nation as they were being formed.[13]

Dwight brilliantly chose as his major symbol for this work organic imagery depicting the slow growth of nature, and he reinforced this imagery with the pastoral form. The imagery of the gradual flourishing and spreading of progress overshadows the social conflict and the competitive economic and political forces underlying this momentum. The social and economic system is a simple one founded upon men's harmony with nature. Dwight does include conflict in the poem by opening with tales of the Pequot War in the seventeenth century and the Revolution in the eighteenth century, but he soon puts these in the past. It is interesting that he felt obligated to put the history of the Pequot War into this poem, for in *The Conquest* he had passed over such trials and negative experiences. Apparently, he believed that for the national errand to go forward the admission and justification of the destruction of the Indians was necessary; continued American progress would require further removal of the Indians.

At the same time that Dwight condoned Indian wars, he condemned slavery as a national evil. This contradiction is indicative of Dwight's sometimes precritical acceptance of his culture's values. As a New Englander, he was not economically dependent on slavery, so he was an abolitionist; but as a white American Christian, he approved the slaughter of the Pequots. In his view, such bloodshed was necessary to create the nation and preserve the land for the spread of republican freedom. But by exposing and disposing of these antagonisms, he sets the stage for a future where good husbandry, wise child-rearing, and divine favor will yield abundance.

Dwight begins the first section with an image of one successful farmer tilling his own garden. Then he expands from this tiny enclosed garden to wide-angle pictures of Greenfield Hill, Connecticut, New England, and finally America in the world.

> Fair is the landscape; but a fairer still
> Shall soon inchant the soul—when harvest full
> Waves wide its bending wealth.
>   . . .
>   Hail, O hail
> My much-lov'd native land! New Albion hail!
>   [I, 30–32, 66–67]

The revolution in consciousness that occurred in America is seen as the beginning of a worldwide social evolution in which other nations will come to imitate the productive pattern of life in America. After contrasting the way that

Europeans have ruined their lands and productivity through selfish policies of aristocracies, Dwight praises the wisdom of the American Founding Fathers whose labors have recently laid the constitutional foundation for social and economic harmony. When other nations witness the success of these institutions and the strivings of individual freemen, they will put aside imaginative visions of utopias and look instead to the real utopia in America.

> Oh, would some faithful, wise, laborious mind,
> Develop all thy springs of bliss to man;
> Soon would politic visions fleet away,
> Before awakening truth! Utopias then,
> Ancient and new, high fraught with fairy good,
> Would catch no more the heart. Philosophy
> Would bow to common-sense; and man, from facts,
> And real life, politic wisdom learn. [I, 225–32]

Of course, there is rich irony in the fact that Dwight, himself embroiled in the bitter debates and party conflicts of these years, projected these images of tranquillity and social concord. To hold up America as a genuine living utopia, Dwight had to suppress many facts about actual American life—facts of economic inequality, slavery, and injustice of which he was painfully aware. Thus, implied in the grand design the poem proposes for America is the suppression of internal conflicts and disregard for any disparity between articulated utopian ideals and present realities in order to speed the growth of the American vine and bring on the day when the great world will come round the garden planted on Greenfield Hill. By concentrating upon the larger panorama of America in the world community, Dwight presents a vision of the forest in which the people and their problems are lost among the trees. He also looks through the forest, past the towns and villages, to focus upon the microcosm of the simple American farmer and his family.

He expands the popular figure of the hermit in the forest into a myth of the wise farmer—practical yet learned, hard working yet brilliant at conversation—the philosopher-freeman upon whom the new nation depends.

Because the farmer is satisfied with taking only what he needs from the general abundance, he is able to remain pure and free of such crimes as tempt the greedy.

> His lot, that wealth, and power, and pride forbids;
> Forbids him to become the tool of fraud,
> Injustice, misery, ruin. [I, 462–64]

Without the urges of consuming ambition, the farmer's life grows naturally from the seedbed of virtue. Content with simple pleasures, he remains at home and instructs his children, avoids temptations, and reaps the constant rewards of his goodness.

> Rarely forc'd from home,
> Around his board, his wife and children smile;
> Communion sweetest, nature here can give,
> Each fond endearment, office of delight,
> With love and duty blending. Such the joy,
> My bosom oft has known. [I, 473–78]

Again, because this portrait of American life may seem too fantastic to be believed, Dwight's narrator stresses the point that in America reality surpasses expectation. The farmer's life expands in goodness to the point that his real life transcends the fancied truth of poetry.

> To him, her choicest pages Truth expands,
> Unceasing, where the soul-intrancing scenes,
> Poetic fiction boasts, are real all:
> Where beauty, novelty, and grandeur, wear
> Superior charms, and moral worlds unfold
> Sublimities, transporting and divine. [I, 530–35]

Dwight adds to this set of utopian themes, however, an important dimension from the Calvinist perspective: the beneficial function of personal guilt. Whereas the old Puritan rhetoric usually placed emphasis upon an opposing force outside the garden, such as Satan or papists, as at least one of the causes of the trials of the chosen, Dwight's pastoral jeremiad places blame for the failure to achieve the ideal on the individual gardener. Success becomes a personal and private issue. The individual planter is solely accountable for his own contribution to the evolution and progress of the society. Because Dwight's farmer is virtuous and thereby successful, he is free of the burden of guilt that can send the failed laborer into a downward spiral of self-destruction: "Sufficient good is his; good, real, pure,/With guilt unmingled" (I, 472–73). Thus, the Puritan connection between self and society remains, but the individual no longer shares his burden of guilt with the congregation or community. The farmer whose children and harvest are good has proved his competence. The unsuccessful farmer knows that he alone has failed in his methods and diligence.[14]

In the second section of the poem, Dwight continues to develop the organic imagery of growth as he focuses upon the individual, the family, and the farm laborer as the sources of strength for the new republic. Now, however, he confronts the larger community of the "flourishing village." At first, he simply carries his utopian rhetoric into his depiction of the social order.

> See the feats of peace, and pleasure, rise,
> And hear the voice of Industry resound,
> And mark the smile of Competence, around!
> Hail, happy village. [II, 709]

The recurrent word "Competence" rises to become a controlling idea of the section: "These humble joys, to competence allied" and "every joy, to Competence allied"

(II, 50, 79). "O Competence, though bless'd by Heaven's decree,/How well exchanged is empty pride for thee!" (II, 91–92). And the quality takes on special importance in regard to women: "But, O sweet Competence! how chang'd the scene,/Where thy soft footsteps lightly print the green!" (II, 157–58). Women play the special role of mediator between the individual family and the community and educate the future generations for competence. But Dwight cannot direct his attention to the society for long without confronting the two most serious threats and contradictions to the capitalist-Christian synthesis: slavery and poverty. With his myths of the ideal nation of model families well established, he prepares to root out the weeds in America's garden.

At the start of his attack on slavery, it appears that Dwight will employ the Manichean imagery of a conflict between the powers of evil who prolong slavery and the virtuous who seek to end it. The initial rhetoric is forceful and the images vivid:

> O slavery! laurel of the Infernal mind,
> Proud Satan's triumph over lost mankind! [II, 259–60]

> Ceaseless I hear the smacking whip resound;
> Hark! that shrill scream! that groan of death-bed sound!
> [II, 285–86]

But then, in the interest of his theme of American progress, Dwight softens this language with the imagery of growth. By juxtaposing his bitter criticism of slavery with his optimistic depiction of the growth of virtue in the first generation of the republic, Dwight suggests that economic and moral progress will naturally erase the evils of slavery and lead to the freedom of all men and the eventual education of every American in a love of virtue and industry. Using imagery of light and darkness as symbols for wisdom and ignorance, Dwight envisions a "modest ray," "Eden's seventh-day light," shining upon America and growing stronger with the additional energy stored in the emerging American society.

> In the clear splendor of thy vernal morn,
> New-quickened man to light, and life, is born;
> The defect of the mind with virtue blooms;
> It's flowers unfold, it's fruits exhale perfumes;
> Proud guilt dissolves beneath the searching ray,
> And low debasement, trembling, creeps away;
> Vice bites the dust; foul Error seeks her den;
> And God, descending, dwells anew with men.
>
> [II, 357–64]

Dwight's next image, however, shows him at his rhetorical best. In a masterful stroke of Calvinist logic upon which struggling clergymen had learned to depend, Dwight resolves the conflict over slavery into the common effort of all men to overcome the real source of poverty and bondage, the unpardonable capitalist sin of sloth. A new character enters in this section to describe a family fallen upon corruption and poverty as a result of "hardy Sloth"; he depicts in detail "the house of Sloth" which "stands hushed in long repose" (II, 396). After a brief picture of the hidden evils of society—the backwoods poverty that results from the private sin of sloth—the speaker turns to a description of the house of Industry:

> "Such, such, my children, is the dismal cot,
> Where drowsy Sloth receives her wretched lot:
> But O how different is the charming cell,
> Where Industry and Virtue love to dwell!"
>
> [II, 467–70]

In this setting the speaker finds the virtuous woman whose example, wisdom, and teaching are the foundation stones of the American future. Slavery and poverty will disappear as soon as Christian virtue, industry, and the American woman stamp out sloth.

In the conclusion of this section, Dwight shifts attention away from social blemishes to the individual happy home on Greenfield Hill. In a single passage, Dwight unites the themes of competence and social and moral progress with the imagery of youth, growth, and light:

> Such, here, the social intercourse is found;
> So slides the year, in smooth enjoyment, round.
> Thrice bless'd the life, in this glad region spent,
> In peace, in competence, and still content;
> Where bright, and brighter, all things daily smile,
> And rare and scanty, flow the streams of ill;
> Where undecaying youth sits blooming round;
> And Spring looks lovely on the happy ground;
> Improvement glows, along life's cheerful way,
> And with soft luster makes the passage gay.
>
> [II, 633–42]

And again, from this image of the private life, Dwight expands to envision America's imperial mission:

> All hail, thou western world! by heaven design'd
> Th' example bright, to renovate mankind.
> Soon shall thy sons across the mainland roam;
> And claim, on far Pacific shores, their home;
> Their rule, religion, manners, arts, convey,
> And spread their freedom to the Asian sea.
>
> [II, 707–12]

> Proud Commerce, mole the western surges lave;
> O'er morn's pellucid main expand their sails,
> And the starr'd ensign court Korean gales.
>
> [II, 718–20]

In an astonishing prophecy of the worldwide Christian missionary movement of the nineteenth and twentieth centuries, Dwight also imagines the central role of the American clergy in this expansionism. As a poet and as a religious leader, Dwight thinks in ecstatic terms of the widening of the audience for Christian truth in American literary productions:

> But peace, and truth, illuminate the twilight mind,
> The gospel's sunshine, and the purpose kind.
>
> [II, 727–28]

> Where slept perennial night, shall science rise,
> And new-born Oxfords cheer the evening skies;
> Miltonic strains the Mexico hills prolong,
> And Louis murmurs to Sicilian song.

> Then to new climes the bliss shall trace its way,
> And Tartar desarts hail the rising day;
> From the long torpor startled China wake;
> Here chains of misery rous'd Peruvia break;
> Man link to man; with bosom bosom twine;
> And one great bond the house of Adam join;
> The sacred promise full completion know,
> And peace, and piety, the world o'erflow. [II, 733–44]

This striking conclusion to the section shows how completely the ideology of capitalist-Christian imperialism had already begun to replace the Puritan vision of the enclosed city on the hill of God's chosen, sealed off from the world. Thus, by 1794 Dwight had yoked the dreams of an international Christian conversion movement and economic expansion in a new version of the national mission—an active errand to the corners of the earth.[15]

Having established the image of stability and the myth of progress surrounding Greenfield Hill, present and future, Dwight turns in sections three and four to the past. The struggles of the original Puritan settlers, the heroism of the revolutionary Founding Fathers: these are the necessary trials through which others had to pass so that the present and future generations could inherit the prosperity and the spiritual benefits designed by Providence for America. These sections recapitulate the formula of the election sermons with a review of the perils and triumphs of the past and an assessment of the present conditions. Sections one and two establish the virtues of the new land and the spirit of industry and competence that are essential to the emergent utopia, while sections three and four rehearse the past. Sections five and six approximate that segment of the Puritan sermon usually labeled "use," in which the preacher introduces the practical application of the doctrines.

When viewed together, sections five and six have the effect of establishing a balance and a bond between the values of the old religion and the new materialism. The dying clergyman's farewell sermon is followed by the farmer's secular homily. The parallelism suggests that the representatives of the churches and the secular community must pool their wisdom in guiding the new generation. Had Dwight's design not been to underplay the authority of his speakers by putting them on the social level of ordinary readers, he might have presented these sections in the voices of Jonathan Edwards and Benjamin Franklin themselves. The opening lines of the farmer's section echo Franklin's Father Abraham and Dwight's own preface with the observation that spokesmen and forums are needed to reach different kinds of audiences: the farmer addresses a "Gathering on a pleasant Monday,/A crowd not always seen on Sunday." Although the advice in section six is similar to that in standard seventeenth-century instruction manuals on child-rearing and domestic life, there is a new blend of traditional religious and materialistic motives for family discipline.[16] For example, whereas the Puritan sermons and guidebooks stress the salvation of parents and children together in eternity as the reward for proper child instruction, Dwight's farmer has a more practical argument: A poorly raised child will grow up to be unproductive, if not economically dependent upon his parents. Unwise or misguided parents who have such children may be breeding their own economic ruin. Such children will not only be unable to provide for their aged parents but will use up the financial resources that the parents accumulated through their own labors. In addition, the most painful punishment the father of such a family will incur is not the chastisement of God but the bitter hatred of his own children, who will grow up to realize that their suffering is the direct result of their parents' failure in training and discipline. Capping his argument with a metaphor, the farmer says that just as the blacksmith labors patiently to shape a piece of metal into a product that does not show signs of the working, so the well-wrought child will not show marks of the parents' labors but will prove to be a perfect instrument for the duties of life. There may be no more concise example of the shift in the fundamental ideology of the country during the postwar period than in this verse epistle to the common man.

Opening with imagery strikingly similar to the verdant dreams of the Dutch sailors in Fitzgerald's *The Great Gatsby*, the last section of *Greenfield Hill* presents a culmination of the themes of the poem in a vision of the American utopia expressed by "the Genius of the Sound." What the Genius sees when emerging from offshore Connecticut is the green breast of new hope for mankind:

> and whitening coast, were seen
> Small isle, around her, wrought in living green;
> The loftier Mainland there allur'd the eye,
> It's margin winding toward the southern sky.
>
> [VII, 35-38]

> And Man once more, self-ruined Phoenix, rise,
> On wings of Eden, to his native skies.
>
> [VII, 81-82]

Repeating the pattern of the poem as a whole, this section begins with assertions about America's promise in contrast to Europe's decay and then turns to the present with specific examples from daily lives, which show the practical results of American policies and virtues.

In the Genius's vision of the future are compressed all the qualities that will flourish in the new Eden: industry, competence, virtue, and truth. In particular, the Genius promotes knowledge as the key to success: "The sun of knowledge light the general mind,/And cheer, through every class, oppress'd mankind" (VII, 75–76). Not only will the spread of knowledge allow the ignorant masses to participate in the great middle-class culture, but through science and invention America will be able to use its vast natural resources to produce goods to be used by other nations, thereby increasing America's wealth. As a richer nation, America will be stronger and better able to defend itself against outside aggression. In sum, knowledge is power.

> "See, in each village, treasur'd volumes stand!
> And spread pure knowledge through th' enlighten'd land"
> Knowledge, the wise Republic's standing force,
> Subjecting all things, with resistless course. [VII, 401–4]

Next, the Genius sets forth a step-by-step program for America's progress: first, Republican policies will encourage productivity; second, nature will provide abundant materials; third, America's secure geographical situation will protect the people from attack and enable them to unite the entire continent to the Pacific under one language, religion, and government; fourth, knowledge will foster efficient use of resources—as evidenced already in the canal system—and yield abundance for all so that poverty and oppression will be eliminated naturally. Once these features of American civilization are established, they can be disseminated to the rest of the world. Having envisioned American expansion to the East in the previous section, Dwight has his Genius now look to Europe, Asia, and Africa as scenes of future American influence.

> Yet there, even there, Columbia's bliss shall spring,
> Roused from dull sleep, astonished Europe sing,
> O'er Asia burst the renovating morn,
> And startled Africa in a day be born. [VII, 303–6]

> Thus, thro' all climes, shall Freedom's bliss extend,
> The world renew, and death, and bondage, end;
> All nations quicken with th' ecstatic power,
> And one redemption reach to every shore.
>   [VII, 311–14]

Once the economic supremacy of the nation is established, the Genius envisions the rise of a generation of poets in America who will combine the literary skills of the greatest writers of the past with the spiritual and religious fervor and correctness of the prophets. Inverting the long-standing theory of England's Bishop Lowth, whose study of the Bible as literature proposed that the writers of the scriptures were poets, Dwight suggests that American poets will be the national religious prophets.

> See rising bards ascend the steep of fame!
> Where truth commends, and virtue gives a name,
> With Homer's life, the Milton's strength, aspire,
> Or catch divine Isaiah's hallo'd fire. [VII, 483–86]

Although not saying so explicitly, the Genius hints that as American poets write their accounts of American progress they may be seen as adding volumes to the sacred scriptures. In his headier moments Dwight might have felt that his *The Conquest of Canaan* would, in fact, serve as one of the first books of this national new testament. The poet will join with the clergy, the "ambassadors of Heaven" to "Spread truth, build virtue, sorrow soothe, and pain,/And rear primaeval piety again' (VII, 556–58).

Perhaps because he felt the need to keep the vision of the Genius grounded in some kind of reality or because he wanted to intrude his own voice to remind the reader of his position, Dwight laced the poem liberally with footnotes. The notes are interesting both for the information they add and for their matter-of-fact tone, which gives the text a dimension of sincerity and authority. The notes keep the reader constantly aware of the non-poetic, actual world of events of which the poem usually speaks in abstractions. Dwight gives precise meanings for social and political terms, as in his conservative interpretation of the term "equal division of property": "Whenever an *equal division of property* is mentioned, in this Work, the reader is requested to remember, that that state of things only is intended, in which every citizen is secured in the avails of his industry and prudence, and in which property descends, by law, in equal shares, to the proprietor's children" (p. 172). Dwight even uses footnotes to comment upon his authorial intentions: "This part of the poem, though designed, in a degree, for persons in most employments of life, is immediately addressed to Farmers" (p. 178). The constant presence of Dwight's voice in the notes also binds together the poem's fragmented form and reminds the reader at every point that the poet is consciously selecting the material and infusing it with his own personal but reasoned convictions. By balancing the verse with the prose notes, Dwight keeps the myth-making function of the poetry separate from the sober commentary and thereby emphasizes his leadership role as scholar, preacher, and man of affairs.

In *Greenfield Hill* Dwight managed to depict the fulfillment of the capitalist and Christian missions under the leadership of the preacher-poets in as effective and complete a vision as can be found anywhere in the literature of the period. In using Greenfield Hill as a microcosm of American life, Dwight stands at the head of a long line of writers, including Emily Dickinson, E. A. Robinson, Sherwood Anderson, John Steinbeck, Edgar Lee Masters, and James Thurber, who were also to find the small community the source and symbol of the American way of life.[17]

Although *Greenfield Hill* was modestly successful and surpassed *The Conquest* in both popularity and critical reception, Dwight still must have wondered in the 1790s if it were possible to reach a truly wide audience in America with any of the available literary forms. He had experimented with the biblical epic, the pastoral, the sermon, the familiar prose essay with fictional speakers. He had created many different voices of humility and authority, soon to include the persona of the *Review of Inchiquin's Letters* who identifies himself as "a Federalist, a New Englander, a Yankee."[18] Yet from 1795 until his death, Dwight labored indefatigably. He worked steadily on his *Theology*, translated Watts's *Psalms*, preached and wrote political tracts and sermons, and contributed attacks against Jefferson to the *Palladium*. During these years he also continued to travel and to collect and record his observations on America. Somehow he found time from all his other duties to shape his notes into his contribution to a new literary form that would soon become a major genre of American letters in the nineteenth century: the travel narrative. Perhaps he knew that in the four travel volumes, he had finally found his proper form and had produced a work that would ultimately win respect as his most lasting contribution to American literature, for when he was asked on his deathbed what of all his manuscripts should be published, Dwight answered *"The Travels."*

After having employed so many personae throughout his writing career, Dwight chose to present his travels through his own character and voice. He confidently opens by asserting his authority as an intellectual leader in the nation: "In the year 1795 I was chosen president of Yale College."[19] Then he elaborates on the nature of his role as president, especially his position as professor of moral theology. Perhaps he felt at this stage in his life that his authority was well enough established that he did not need to mask it beneath a persona, or else he no longer cared to be self-effacing in order to win a popular audience. Another factor affecting this decision could have been that he had aimed this work partly at an English audience with the hope of correcting some of the derogatory reports about Americans rendered by European travelers, and he might have felt that the presidential voice of Yale would most impress the audience abroad.

Yet, for all of the attention he directs to his English readers, those who know his entire lifework will perceive yet another motive in his travels: to persuade Americans that New England clergy are the legitimate source of ideas, religion, culture, and social behavior for the nation. The world he presents is one in which Puritans are heroes and America continues to be shaped on the pattern of New England. His travels are an exercise in the blending of statistics and fiction. The facts are real and give an impression of exactitude to the entire work, yet the intervening interpretations are quite subjective and impose a vision on the landscape as elaborate and mythical as the vision of *The Conquest of Canaan*. Dwight took every opportunity in the *Travels* to argue for religion as the bedrock of a stable society, government, and culture, and for the poet-minister as the intellectual leader.

With this work Dwight takes his place with Cotton Mather in the seventeenth century and George Bancroft in the nineteenth century as the mythic historian of eighteenth-century America. As in the works of Mather and Bancroft, the portrait of America that emerges from Dwight's *Travels* is a blend of personal opinion, even prejudice, and fact. He admits that he is creating a new kind of work, one that uses narration for religious ends. Other ministers might confine their discussion of religion to theological writing, while historians and travel writers ignore religion, but Dwight's objective was to write a book that reflected the blending of religion with culture in America.

In the *Travels* Dwight once more suppresses aspects of the American reality in order to set forth his idealized version of the expected republican perfection that would spring from the fusion of Christian and democratic principles. He asserts that it is the function of the imagination to enable Americans to see the past and future of their country in the same instant that they see the present—to look at a landscape and leave out the imperfections because they will soon be removed: "whatever is rude, broken, and unsightly, on the surface, will within a moderate period, be levelled, smoothed, beautified, by the hand of man. . . . all these perfections must be left out of account, and the country exhibited, either as it is in a state of nature, or as it will soon be in a state of complete cultivation" (II, p. 129). In other words, understanding the glory of America—the genius of America—involves an act of national, religious faith of this highest order of imagination. That is why for Timothy Dwight the creation of a literary work was always a spiritual and political act.

The career of Dwight and his methods for coping with the religious and literary changes that occurred in America after the Revolution may serve as the standard by which to measure the achievement of every other serious writer of his age. Dwight may not have been the best writer of his generation, but he certainly was an acknowledged and influential social leader whose writings were respected, even by those who did not read them. Unlike Freneau and Brown, Dwight never seemed to have serious self-doubts, and unlike Barlow and Brackenridge, he stood at the center rather than at the side of the major public events of his time. Though the others may have known they were better writers than Dwight, they must have envied his social position and prestige and the respect accorded him by the academic establishment. Dwight is the first in a long line of what are sometimes scornfully called "university poets"—writers of modest talent who adopt the traditional forms of their time and live an artistic life that is in fundamental harmony with reality.

III

JOEL BARLOW:
INNOCENCE AND EXPERIENCE ABROAD

> . . . Look at
> what passes for the new.
> You will not find it there but in
> despised poems.
> It is difficult
> to get the news from poems
> yet men die miserably every day
> for lack
> Of what is found there.

> WILLIAM CARLOS WILLIAMS
> "Asphodel, That Greeny Flower," 1925

Army chaplain, lawyer, land broker, statesman, poet, Joel
Barlow was a man of enormous energy and ambition. Many
have questioned whether he used his talent and drive wisely
or even in his own best interests. Most have concluded that
he was a failure, if not at all he attempted, then certainly
at poetry. His modern biographer has condemned his proud-
est literary work as "a dinosaur in the clay pits of literary
history,"[1] and he is usually lumped with the Connecticut
Wits as one of the more gifted wags who mocked the leveling
tendencies of the 1780s in their anonymous *The Anarchiad*.[2]
Some critics have begrudgingly conceded that Barlow had one
good poem, "The Hasty-Pudding," a jeu d'esprit in which he
praised American mush in heroic couplets. For once, it is
said, he stopped taking himself so seriously and gave his
mediocre talent free reign, to produce but one piece of verse
worth preserving.

But again, these are the judgments of political opponents

or of sophisticated modern readers, who consider the involvement in public affairs to which Barlow was so committed to have been an unfortunate diversion from his art. No writer of the period more eagerly and energetically embraced the social and political role of the poet than Joel Barlow. Unlike Freneau, who was a poet trying to become a social philosopher and social reformer, Barlow was at heart a political thinker and social planner who held to the traditional conviction that the authority of the man of letters should be unquestioned and that the proper voice for expressing social ideas was the voice of the poet. Though "The Hasty-Pudding" may be more fun for us to read today, it tells us much less about the poet, his literary efforts, and the situation of American literature in the 1780s and 1790s than do Barlow's major works, *The Vision of Columbus* and *The Columbiad*.[3]

Throughout his life, people tried to persuade Barlow that the life of letters was not for him. His good friend Joseph Buckminster told him to become a clergyman instead of a poet because America would always be a country hostile to poetry: "Enter the ministry if you want to indulge your poetic genius, for a Pope or Milton might starve in America if he looked for support to the few people who are relishing good literature."[4] John Perkins, a Norwich, Connecticut, merchant, advised him to "go into business for a living, and make poetry only an amusement for leisure hours."[5] A member of the United States Senate objected to his nomination as minister to France because a poet and a visionary could not be trusted with serious matters of this world. Barlow had ample reason to abandon his poetic efforts, but he was not easily discouraged. Full of optimism and ambition, he was convinced that he was living at the start of an American golden age. In spite of the lagging sales of his works, the frowns of Timothy Dwight, and the jeers of American critics, Barlow wrote as though there were never a question of his or of America's success. Even when he shocked his friends and countrymen by totally reversing his political position from the conservative federalism of his Yale classmates to the liberalism of Paine, Godwin, and the French Revolution, Barlow did not falter in his poetic calling. An extremist in many other ways, Barlow remained steady in his dedication to literature from the time he composed his "rising glory" poem, "The Prospect of Peace" (1778), until his bitter, deathbed poem, "Advice to a Raven in Russia" (1812).

Because Barlow was so intensely engaged in his own philosophical and political searching and because his poetry expresses this pursuit so vividly, an examination of the development of his ideas through his works provides an excellent study of the literary situation in the 1780s and 1790s. His poetry may not provide abundant passages pleasing to modern tastes, but it does reveal how his remarkable efforts to express new themes in traditional forms and language resulted in innovations in imagery, style, and form that advanced poetry in America. While "The Prospect of Peace" reveals Barlow's early faith in the harmony of religion and literature, *The Vision of Columbus* (1787) is his most interesting poem, for there his confusions are laid bare. In contrast, *The Columbiad* (1807) is a work frozen in time, for it is the product of Barlow's seventeen-year separation from the rapidly evolving American culture. When he returned from France in 1805 and finished the epic, Barlow was out of touch with his American audience. His poem is an anachronism in its own time, trapped in the past by the dizzying pace of change that made the ideas and images of a 1790 mind seem like those of a century past.

Barlow was never a settled individual, either in his intellectual life or in his career. After starting at Dartmouth at age nineteen, he moved to Yale as a sophomore in 1774. After graduation Barlow first, like Freneau, took a position as a schoolmaster, but he soon became discontent and returned to Yale to take a Masters degree in theology. Although he finished a detailed plan of *The Vision of Columbus* by April 1779, his many public activities during the next eight years delayed completion of the poem until 1787. He enlisted as a chaplain for the Third Massachusetts Brigade in 1780, married Ruth Baldwin in 1781, joined with Elisha Babcock to begin publication of *The American Mercury* in 1784, and opened a bookstore in 1785. He had also been preparing himself to take the Connecticut bar examination, and in 1786 he began the law practice that would soon lead him to Paris and to important positions in business and government.

Even with all of these activities, Barlow somehow found time to keep writing. In his early poetry, he showed an awareness of the potentially harmonious relationship between poetry and religion, at least for rhetorical purposes. In his Yale commencement poem, "The Prospect of Peace," he projected a future in which the poets would lead America to her destiny as the holy seat of culture and religion until Judgment Day. The central image is the light of American Genius, produced by the focusing of the rays of nature, religion, and American talent into a single beam. The poem depicts America as a new land which enjoys "Kind Nature's bounty" and is unified by "One friendly Genius [who] fires the numerous whole,/From glowing Georgia to the frozen pole."[6] This American Genius inspired "Fair Science" which soars "with Genius to the radiant stars"; it sparks the "Genius kindling a Franklin's fame" and is the source of the inventive power of "that young Genius" Rittenhouse (pp. 7–8).

At this point in his intellectual development, Barlow still believed in the unity of religion and letters, and he must have pleased Dwight and his Yale colleagues with the theological elements of the poem. He envisions "genius of the rising age" warming a generation of religious poets to lead America into a new era:

> Unnumber'd bards shall string the heavenly lyre,
> To those blest strains which heavenly themes inspire;
> Sing the rich Grace on mortal Man bestow'd,
> The Virgin's Offspring and the *filial God*;
> What love descends from heaven when Jesus dies!
> What shouts attend him rising thro' the skies! [p. 9]

Praising Jonathan Edwards for his soaring metaphysics, which
reached "to the realms of Light," Barlow celebrated the
"blest Religion" and the "pure Church, descending from her
God,/Shall fix on earth her long and last abode" in America
(p. 10). In biblical types long familiar to his Calvinist
audience, he called for the new "Zion arise, in radiant
splendors dres'd,/By Saints admir'd, by Infidels confes'd"
(p. 10).

The role of the poet-minister in this American-Christian
triumph was the same role proclaimed by Edward Johnson
and by Cotton Mather, to sing the glory of the thousand
years of heavens' reign in the New Jerusalem. Though the
images and ideas of Barlow's poetry were to change, the same
spirit of excitement captured in these lines would also characterize the most anti-religious and radical poetry of his later
career:

> Then Love shall rule, and Innocence adore,
> Discord shall cease, and Tyrants be no more;
> 'Till you bright orb, and those celestial spheres,
> In radiant circles, mark a thousand years;
> 'Till the grand fiat burst th' ethereal frames,
> Worlds crush on worlds, and Nature sink in flames!
> The Church elect, from smouldering ruins, rise,
> And fall triumphant thro' the yielding skies,
> Hail'd by the Bridegroom! to the Father given,
> The Joy of Angels, and the Queen of Heaven!
>   [pp. 11–12]

The blending of nationalist aims and Christian vision presented through the Puritan idiom illustrates how closely the

young Barlow was tied to the religious ideas and language he had inherited from his New England ancestors. But the fusion of Puritan and Enlightenment intellectual structures necessary for this revolutionary rhetoric would be sundered within a few years after the war.[7]

Barlow remained remarkably consistent in his almost religious faith in the ultimate triumph of learning and letters in America. In the early days of his career this optimism was part of the Christian belief he derived from his religious training and from his New England Calvinist heritage. Although he realized he was not suited for the ministry, the young Barlow was a serious student of theology and was especially interested in the effect of religious ideas upon the actions and traditions of the American people. After the Revolution, he joined the clergy in berating Americans for their licentiousness, godlessness, and scorn of religious authority. The outlet for this wrath was his contribution to the satiric *The Anarchiad* (1786–87), a product of several "wicked wits." But Barlow knew that America would not retreat from its republican principles. Though deeply concerned about the drift toward social chaos and political anarchy, Barlow began to rethink his position about the direction of America in the larger context of the condition of man in the modern world. His first major poem provides a partial record of his intellectual reassessment.[8]

The Vision of Columbus is by far Barlow's most interesting poem. Although it is full of contradictions, is inconsistent in tone, and is interrupted by digressions and discourses, it remains engaging because it is so evident that the mind shaping the poem is intensely involved in a process of personal and cultural reevaluation. Barlow's philosophical uncertainty and personal search for solutions to the cultural and social problems of America are visible behind the thin veil of Columbus's doubts and his questioning of God's messenger. The very structure, language, and meaning of *The Vision* project Barlow's inner conflicts and his desperate effort to make sense of his evolving world view. As he reworked the poem during the 1780s, Barlow was undergoing a transformation from political and religious conservatism to liberalism and Deism, but had not yet developed his more radical concepts. Thus, for a reader aware of the direction of Barlow's intellectual changes during those years, *The Vision* takes on a dramatic dimension in which the major actor becomes Barlow himself.[9]

The fundamental purpose and organization of *The Vision of Columbus* is fairly simple. Throughout its nine books the speaker is an angel who addresses Columbus as he sits in prison contemplating his wasted life and his rejection and disapproval of the world. In consolation, the Angel takes the explorer to the Mount of Vision from which they view the future of mankind. The image of America that the Angel presents is cast in language that might have been composed by any good seventeenth-century Puritan poet.

> As that great Seer, whose animating rod
> Taught Israel's sons the wonder-working God,
> Who led, thro' dreary wastes, the murmuring band
> To the fair confines of the promised land,
> Oppress'd with years, from Pisgah's beauteous height,
> O'er boundless regions cast the raptured sight;
> . . .
> In nobler pomp another Pisgah rise,
> Beneath whose foot thine own Canaan lies.
>
> [pp. 129–30]

By using the device of the Angel, who informs Columbus that his sacrifice prepared for the future glory of America, Barlow is able to achieve the basic social purpose of the poem: to remind his readers of the importance of the American mission and to inspire them to accept responsibility for fulfilling their sacred destiny. Of course, Barlow's Angel is particularly eager to impress upon Columbus the importance of the arts in America during the period after the Revolution when "genius unconfined/Awakes the arts and bids the Muses soar" (p. 131). Barlow devotes the entire Book VII to the Angel's review of the history of the arts that will be brought to final perfection in America.

> That train of arts, that graced mankind before,
> Warm'd the glad sage or taught the Muse to soar,
> Here with superior sway their progress trace,
> And aid the triumphs of thy filial race. [p. 203]

Not only will new poets arise, but Barlow also sees a new audience for literature and the arts as America fulfills the promise of universal education.

> Great without pomp the modest mansions rise;
> Harvard and Yale and Princeton greet the skies.
> . . .
> With humbler walls unnumber'd schools arise,
> And youths unnumber'd seize the solid prize.
>
> [pp. 203–4]

Although the advancement of the arts is clearly a major preoccupation of the poet and his Angel, the foundation for all progress in *The Vision* remains the flourishing of Christianity. Yet, the peculiar mixture of religious idealism and political sophistication that characterizes the Angel's responses in the poem indicates Barlow's appreciation of the competing attitudes toward religion in his society. At first, the Angel expresses a conviction that might have been shared by John Cotton, or Increase Mather in his happier moods, that "In no blest land had fair Religion shone,/And fix'd so firm her everlasting throne" (p. 204). But then the Angel begins to sound like Madison in *The Federalist* #10. He becomes an apologist for American republicanism as he stresses the practical value of religion to society and the virtue of having so many different sects. Religion is "virtue's animating flame" because religion forms a foundation: "for social compact harmonizes mankind" (p. 204). What may seem to outsiders to be "discordant" religious confusion as "different faiths their various orders show," Americans recognize as sects held together by "one universal flame" of national Protestantism.

Columbus finds this picture of religious diversity very different from his understanding of religion, so the Angel explains that enlightened moderns have a different idea of the Deity now. As Christianity has spread throughout the world, God's "Stern vengeance" has softened, and a new era in God's relationship with man has begun. The Angel assures Columbus of his own lasting role in the divine plan: after He used Christ to establish salvation, God made America the stage for the final act of his sacred drama. The new chosen people will lead all into the millennium in every area of human endeavor:

> Thro' nature's range their ardent souls aspire,
> Or wake to life the canvass and the lyre.
> Fixt in sublimest thought, behold them rise,
> Superior worlds unfolding to their eyes;
> Heaven in their view unveils the eternal plan,
> And gives new guidance to the paths of man.
>
> [p. 207]

As evidence, the Angel follows with a review of the accomplishments of American inventors and artists to date: Franklin, Rittenhouse, Godfrey, West, Copley, Trumbull, and "daring Dwight the Epic Muse sublime" all qualify with "Immortal Washington" as names that might cheer the despondent Columbus.

Now that the poet and his Angel have the attention of their respective audiences, Barlow delves more deeply into some of the theological and epistemological issues troubling him and his contemporaries. Sounding somewhat like Milton's Adam, and perhaps like one of the disgruntled parishioners in the Congregational churches after the Revolution as well, Columbus poses a question to the Angel that touches on the underlying problems of myth and religion and the problem of evil: instead of making mankind endure centuries of slavery, ignorance, and suffering, "Why did not Heaven, with one unclouded ray,/All human arts and reason's powers display?" (p. 215). The Angel's answer abruptly introduces a mixture of Christian millennialism and Lockean empiricism of the evolution of human knowledge, reason, and human progress: "In elder times, when savage tribes began,/A few strong passions sway'd the wayward man," but now "fair Science, of celestial birth . . . leads mankind to reason and to God" (p. 217).

In this chronicle, religion begins to appear as a system of primitive control that is in the process of yielding to the rule of reason. Even the "shadowy types" of scripture point toward a time when "benevolence and truth refined,/Pervade the world and harmonize mankind" (p. 217). But the implication of this history of the progress of reason is that the time will soon arrive when the superstitions and religious myths of the past, which served to tame the savage beast of man, will no longer be needed. Although Barlow does not push the argument that far, and in 1786 may not have even recognized the conclusion to this logic, he has laid the groundwork here for a radical reassessment of the function of religious ideas and language.

In response to Columbus's inquiry about how God will reveal his truths to man in modern times, the Angel explains the epistemological process. First, he offers proof that God's rational plan has always been in operation by pointing to the consistency of basic religious beliefs held among the various peoples of the earth. In spite of the many differences in particulars, the persistence of certain shared notions prove a divine source for religious ideas. From this perspective the proper function of all beneficial religions has been to lead men toward a sense of moral beauty based upon an awareness of the justice and mercy of God. However, because human passions and pride were so great, centuries of history were required to refine man's moral sense and prepare his reason for the truth of the New Testament God of charity and benevolence. At first, this explanation appears to be in accord with traditional Christian dogma, but the new perceptions that Barlow, as an emergent cultural anthropologist, tries to blend with established doctrine create ambiguity in the closing lines of Book VIII. The Angel sings of the coming of Christ in language that echoes Barlow's "The Prospect of Peace," yet close scrutiny reveals that the divine offspring is not the living flesh of Christ but the "great moral Sense" which is to "human sense in earthly form reveal'd."

This forced amalgam of traditional religious imagery and Enlightenment epistemology exposes the internal tension of the poem and of the period. The awkward juxtaposition results from Barlow's attempt to use the poem to prepare his readers for the transition from Christian interpretations of history to a more scientific understanding of the myth-making process that produced those religious stories. The last stanza of Book VIII presents a clear analysis of the evolution from religions of scripture and revelation to scientifically inspired doctrines of universalism and transcendentalism:

> Here all religion rests, and soon thy race
> Her purest lights, by wisdom's eye shall trace.
> Here the last lights of science shall ascend,
> To look thro' heaven, and sense with reason blend;
> View the great source of love, that flows abroad,
> Spreads to all creatures, centers still in God,
> Lives thro' the whole, from nature's compact springs,
> Orders, reverses, fills the sum of things;
> In law contains, in gospel reconciles,
> In judgment frowns, in gentle mercy smiles,
> Commands all sense to feel, all life to prove
> The attracting force of universal love. [p. 235]

Although this is a poem narrated by an angel and contains a subscription page with the names of twenty-five clergymen, *The Vision of Columbus* presents a summary of the progress of religion in world history, which concludes that if all continues to go as planned, religion will soon be unnecessary.[10]

When he composed *The Vision*, Barlow had not yet made the break with organized religion and with theological explanations of history that the next fifteen years of his study, writing, and personal contacts would bring. In *The Vision* he was still trying to hold together the contradictory explanations of science and revelation, but the most conspicuous crack in this amalgam occurs at the point in the poem where Barlow introduces a piece of cultural analysis that stands as bold evidence of his new thinking. In this piece, he not only violated the fragile thematic unity of the poem, but he also temporarily abandoned verse and resorted to a long prose intrusion.

The "Dissertation on the Genius and Institutions of Manco Capac" tacked onto the end of Book I is another case of a republican poet turning to prose as a pedagogical medium when poetry failed him. Although awkwardly interrupting the flow of the epic, the essay provided Barlow with a means of achieving two key goals: the establishment of his own authority as a moral instructor separate from the speaker of the poem, and the presention of a piece of historical evidence to support his implicit argument that religion is a tool of government. In case the reader misses the connections between the Peruvian culture of the "Dissertation" and contemporary America, Barlow later inserts a pertinent digression in Book VIII and a lengthy footnote in Book IX to stress the relevance of Capac's system to the present American situation.

The essay on Manco Capac is concerned with two questions: How might political power be transferred from aristocratic leaders to the people without creating moral dissolution and social anarchy? And during this period of transition, what role should religion play? Barlow recognized that religion could serve to strengthen the leadership of benevolent authority and encourage voluntary compliance of the people to the laws of the state. Until such time that reason would reign supreme and a minimum of law and political authority would be needed, religion would have to serve the social function of evoking obedience and even awe in the people.

In the wisdom and example of Manco Capac, the Peruvian lawgiver, Barlow found what he thought was a useful model for keeping order during the transition of power. If more were known about Capac, Barlow says, he would be respected as one of the great philosopher-kings of history. After comparing him with Moses, Lycurgus, Mahomet, and Peter the Great, Barlow concludes: "Thus far we find the political system of Capac at least equal to those of the most celebrated ancient or modern lawgivers" (p. 187). What most impressed Barlow was Capac's understanding and use of religious ideas and feelings: "his ideas of the Deity were so perfect, as to bear a comparison with the enlightened doctrines of Socrates or Plato" (p. 187). Significantly, Capac was great because he led his people carefully out of the darkness of religious superstition into the rationalist ideas of a benevolent deity: "in one particular, his character is placed beyond all comparisons; I mean for his religious institutions, and the just ideas he had formed, by the unenlightened efforts of human wisdom, of the nature and attributes of the Deity" (p. 187). In particular, Capac's "exploding the worship of evil beings and objects of terror, forbidding human sacrifices, inculcating more rational ideas of the Deity, and accommodating the rites of worship to a God of justice and benevolence, produced a greater change in the national character of his people, than any of the laws of Moses": Like Peter the Great, he provided for "the future improvement of society" (p. 187).

While Barlow himself was shifting from Calvinism to

Deism, he realized that the difficulties of republican society would not be erased by the abolition of religion. But he believed that the leaders and intelligent people needed to understand the function of religion and use it wisely in forming the social system. There were two paths to follow. Control could be maintained by using an image of a wrathful deity to frighten and threaten the people into self-sacrifice and control. Already in America, this had been the function of the Puritan jeremiad which chaplains like Barlow had refurbished to inspire men in battle. But this system of intimidation required that the religious leaders remain powerful, that the people be kept in constant fear of outside attack, or that the political leaders become pseudo-religious figures.

Ancient leaders had had to resort to such manipulations. Moses recognized that "those constitutions of government are best calculated for immediate energy and duration which are interwoven with some religious system" and that "the legislator, who appeared in the character of an inspired person, renders his political institutions sacred, and interests the consciences as well as the judgment in their support" (p. 180). Thus Moses "appeared not in the character of a mere earthly governor, but as an interpreter of the divine will. By enjoining a religious observance of certain rites, he formed his people to habitual obedience" (p. 180). The effect of such a yoking of religious and political power is to maintain order but also to limit the progress of mankind. The people cannot be permitted to advance in knowledge because new ideas will always put them at odds with the established system: "These systems appear to have been formed with an express design to prevent all future improvement in knowledge, or enlargement of the human mind; and to fix those nations forever in a state of ignorance, superstition and barbarism" (p. 181).

For Barlow the beauty of Capac's system is that it offers

a moderate alternative to the social views represented in America by the Federalists and by the radicals. By stressing the benevolent features of the Deity and carefully manipulating his own religious authority, Capac allowed for the progress of the human mind within a system of social and religious controls: "the pretensions of Capac to divine authority were as artfully contrived and as effectual in their consequences as those of Mahomet" (p. 186). As Capac gained control over the people, he gradually shifted the focus of religious attention away from himself and toward a benevolent godhead; according to Barlow, such a Deistical view of the Divinity had been held only by the wisest in history: "The Deity as a God of purity, justice and benevolence . . . a sublime and rational idea of the Parent of the universe!" Capac "taught the nation to consider him as the God of order and regularity; . . . especially attributing to his inspiration the wisdom of their laws and that happy constitution, which was the delight and veneration of the people." As a result, "these humane ideas of religion had a sensible operation upon the manners of the nation" (p. 189). Capac's successful form of government survived for about three hundred years, during which "the arts of society had been carried to a considerable degree of improvement" (p. 190). Religion continued to play a vital role in maintaining of social order, and it was only when the twelfth monarch violated one of the sacred laws by an improper marriage that the social order crumbled.

Barlow gained two important insights from his study of Manco Capac, which would affect his thought and writing in the decades to come and which he would repeatedly attempt to convey to his republican readers: first, that religious ideas are myths—products of the human imagination—which can be manipulated for the good or ill of society, and second, that religion may be an essential element of a successful society. Barlow concluded that the confidence of the people, their strength of will, their willingness to sacrifice self-interest for higher goals, these characteristics could be fostered through a judicious application of religious myths and moral instruction. Once order was established, enlightened leaders, aided by sensible clergymen, scholars of antiquity, and poets, might guide the people through the transition from a society dependent upon religious threats to one founded upon religiously inspired humanitarianism and moral excellence.

Toward the end of *The Vision of Columbus*, however, Barlow seemed to realize that problems remained which neither his "Dissertation" nor his Angel had resolved. Resorting again to a prose intrusion, this time in the form of a footnote of nearly three full pages, he apologized for the digression by saying that "the author first ventured upon these ideas in the course of the Poem, with all the timidity of youth; determining not to risk a serious illustration of the sentiment in prose" (p. 344). He declares that he has been emboldened by a recent essay written by the eminent English philosopher Dr. Richard Price that confirmed his own long-standing conviction that the American Revolution has marked a new stage in the maturity of mankind. With this support Barlow now dares to make explicit his theory of progress, which had been an implicit theme of the poem: "finding that a theory so pleasing to himself has not been unnoticed by others, he feels a greater confidence in the subject, and hopes the importance of it will apologize to the reader for so lengthy a note" (p. 341).[11]

What is immediately evident is that the point of the note is not quite the point that Barlow has announced. Although he deigns to insert the note to cite Price's confirmation of his own ideas, it is clear that Barlow felt compelled to add it because of a nagging issue that threatened to subvert his theory of cultural progress: the superiority of ancient literature and the arts to those of the present. If the political and social millennium is approaching and the Revolution was a preparation for that progress, then why is it that the

literary works of the Greeks and Romans are so far superior
to those of the present? In order to resolve this dilemma,
Barlow does not turn to Promethean images of the untouched
wells of creativity buried in the American soil but borrows
from the logic of theologians like John Witherspoon who
damned the ancients for their pagan ideas.[12] Barlow argues
that the arts of the ancients were aesthetically superior but
were moral and political failures because the artists and
writers performed only for the aristocracy. Had the society
been founded upon republican principles, the writers would
have been addressing a larger, more diverse audience and
their art would have been suitably unrefined: "As the arts
were adapted to gratify the vanity of a prince, to fire the
ambition of a hero, or to gain a point in a popular assembly,
they were carried to a degree of perfection, which prevented
their being relished or understood by barbarians" (pp. 342–
43). Because of this misguided purpose, the cultivation of
the arts was inappropriate for the culture and only hastened
the downfall of society. The deluded leaders, cut off from the
people, began to think of their nation as more advanced
than it really was, and they were unaware of the internal
unrest and external forces that would destroy them. In short,
when learning and the arts serve only the elite, they are not
only misused; they become dangerous.

Thus, Barlow proposes that the leaders who understand
their country's relationship to the history of world progress
will encourage proportionate progress in all areas of development. Under certain circumstances a young person who could
have become a genius in the arts might have to use his talent
in the field of commerce or military service. Until basic social
needs are satisfied, there might not be much opportunity for
the arts to flourish. The Greeks made a serious mistake,
Barlow says, in placing a high premium on the arts when
they really needed their best people to go into other fields:
"Had the expenses of the Egyptian pyramids been employed

in the furnishing of fleets of discovery, to be sent out of the Mediterranean, the civilized world would probably never had been overrun by Barbarians" (p. 342). Had the Greeks encouraged more "navigation and commerce," they might have survived.

From this assessment of the failure of the ancients, Barlow constructs a system of cultural priorities for America. Based upon his own stages of progress, Barlow says that before there can be arts the land must be peopled. Then, different nations must be known to each other through the process of trade and commerce. Next, "imaginary wants must be increased" in order to establish a demand for variety and finer things. Finally, a natural demand for works of the imagination will arise.

Barlow concludes his footnote by disagreeing with Price: the world is not entering its manhood, Barlow says, "We are rather rising out of infancy." He is again caught in a contradiction that undermines his own poem. If the country is only at an early stage of development, then cultivation of the arts may be a dubious activity. Aware of this difficulty, Barlow can only justify his own poem as a piece of moral and political instruction designed to educate people on all levels of society and not simply to delight the highly educated few.[13]

Beginning about 1788, Barlow embraced an entirely new personal philosophy, which resulted in a total reversal of his concepts of social organization. At first, he was caught in a dilemma: from his religious training he knew that democracy carried to extremes would lead to anarchy, but his romantic temperament made him feel that the people should have control of their own destiny. But Barlow also recognized that the emphasis upon law and reason which dominated the thinking of his learned contemporaries was neither imposing discipline upon the masses nor inspiring obedience. Though his colleagues at New Haven favored a stronger social hierarchy as a solution, Barlow was sympathetic to the ideal of democracy. He was deeply troubled by the contradiction between the nation's articulated principles and the drift toward aristocratic rule. Unlike Freneau and Brackenridge who could live with frustration and without a unified system of beliefs and whose philosophical pliancy enabled them to attack errors and folly on all sides and in all parties, Barlow was a man who needed a whole and consistent vision in order to live and write.

Thus, when he sailed for France in 1788, Barlow was well prepared to fall under the influence of those English thinkers who were formulating a comprehensive response to the problem of tyranny and revolution in the modern world. After meeting liberal thinkers like Horne Tooke, Mary Wollstonecraft, and William Godwin and after becoming reacquainted with Thomas Paine and Jefferson in a European setting, Barlow underwent a complete change of philosophy within two years. He concluded that a radical and immediate reorganization of Western societies was necessary—a reform which would depose not only monarchies but the ecclesiastical structures that supported them. In France he found intellectuals who gave voice to his feeling that civilization could not return to the tyranny of the past, that the progress of democracy was inevitable. With these thinkers, Barlow reasoned that social change must be ushered forward as quickly as possible in order to reduce the length of the transition period in which people were being duped by corrupt upstarts grabbing for power. Thus, he embraced the Jeffersonian principles of universal education, widespread availability of land, and broadly representative government.

Barlow went from being a child of the Moderate Enlightenment to become a soldier of the Skeptical Enlightenment, to use Henry May's useful categories. In 1792 he published three important prose works that gave clear evidence of his radical shift: *Advice to the Privileged Orders, The Conspiracy of Kings,* and *A Letter to the National Convention of France.*

In *Advice* Barlow argued that the world was in the process of being transformed by the democratic revolution begun in America and the privileged orders could not resist these changes; therefore, to avoid the spread of violence, they should wisely and willingly yield. When Timothy Dwight, Barlow's mentor and former teacher at Yale, read these works, he was so outraged that he removed Barlow's picture from Yale College. But Barlow possessed a more flexible mind than Dwight, and he responded more imaginatively to the philosophical and social changes of his time.[14]

Perhaps because Barlow remained in Europe for so long and at such a crucial point in the development of early republican culture, he was able to maintain his optimism about the opportunities for literature in his homeland. In France he worked as a representative of a land-selling group, which later turned out to be disreputable, and he served on diplomatic missions to the new French government. Certainly he knew of the scandal which his libertarian ideas had caused among his old friends, but he was too far removed to have any appreciation of the changing attitudes of the republican readership that Freneau had been attacking and resisting during the late 1780s and 1790s. Thus, Barlow confidently went about revising *The Vision of Columbus* into an American epic, *The Columbiad*, which he fully expected would have wide appeal among American readers. Even after he returned to America in 1804, he ignored signs that his epic would face a cold reception. As a result of this failure to grasp the changing currents of taste in his own country, his *Columbiad* was doomed to a failure more severe than that of *The Vision*. These two poems, or better, two versions of one poem, mark the beginning and end of the transition period in this epoch between the time that American poets could assume their audience's response to religious symbols and a time when only a minority of readers would respond to religious symbols with genuine feeling.

Barlow was aware that he was living through a time in which European writers and intellectuals were consciously rejecting the sacred history, the biblical types, and the religious language that had been an unquestioned part of American writing before 1776. For sophisticated readers in the 1790s the uses of such language without irony or a hint of embarrassment was certain to reveal the writer to be a fool. *The Columbiad* is a marvelous example of the effort of this American writer to teach the uninformed reader at the same time that he tried to please and impress his intellectual friends. Yet Barlow's artistic principle that moral and political instruction must take precedence over aesthetic beauty led him time and again to violate the artistic integrity of his own poem in order to argue a social doctrine. In the preface he attempted to justify his method by expanding the theoretical aside of his footnote in *The Vision* into a full-blown critical manifesto about the function of literary works in a republican society and the authority of the man of letters as a social leader. "There is one point of view in which I wish the reader to place the character of my work, before he pronounces on its merits: I mean its political tendency. There are two distinct objects to be kept in view in the conduct of a narrative poem: The *poetical* object and the *moral* object. The poetical is the fictitious design of the action; the moral is the real design of the poem" (pp. 377–78).

After explaining that Homer and Virgil were bad writers because their works supported a political system that fostered war and barbarism, Barlow argues that a modern epic should not be occupied with the operations of war and the pomp and circumstance of aristocrats. The heroic presentation of human pretensions and bloody destruction will only lead the young onto paths of destruction. The object of the modern epic should be quite the opposite: "to enculcate the love of rational liberty, and to discountenance the deleterious passion for violence and war." In a statement which some critics like to see as an excuse for bad writing, Barlow is quite explicit about the didactic purpose of his own epic: "My object is altogether of a moral and political nature. I wish to encourage and strengthen, in the rising generation, a sense of the importance of republican institutions; as being the great foundation of public and private happiness, the necessary aliment of future and permanent meliorations in the condition of human nature" (p. 389). This purpose, Barlow explains, "arises from the most pure and ardent desire of doing good to my country." Whatever sacrifice of personal gain or aesthetic indulgence may be necessary in fulfilling this goal, Barlow is convinced that the process of history has made his role as a political poet imperative: "This is the moment in America to give such a direction to poetry, painting, and the other fine arts, that true and useful ideas of glory may be implanted in the minds of men here, to take the place of the false and destructive ones that have degraded the species in other countries" (p. 389).

Because Barlow was trying to appeal to readers of varied educational backgrounds and literary tastes, he developed a form of narrative exposition quite different from the simple dialogue of *The Vision*. In the manner of Freneau and Dwight, he used a number of different voices who address different kinds of readers. Though the major voice of the poem is Hesper, the "guardian genius" of the Western continent, who replaces the Angel of *The Vision*, Barlow himself also enters as a teacher in the "Arguments" at the head of each book and in the extensive footnotes which inform readers on matters of classical history, mythology, and literary traditions. Some of these notes contain extensive essays, including the retitled "Dissertation on the Institutions of Manco Capac." In fact the most striking differences between *The Vision* and *The Columbiad* are the change in

attitude toward religion that emerges in *The Columbiad* and
the conversion to prose as a preferable medium for speaking
to popular readers on a level they might understand.

Critics have always felt Barlow's *Vision* to be a more
interesting poem than his *Columbiad*, but they have not been
able to explain why. They usually attribute the difference
to changes in Barlow's own personality over the years. The
younger and more passionate, though clumsier, Barlow is
preferred to the later, deliberate, self-conscious, and more
calculating poet.[15] But the real differences between these two
poems are in the language and symbols of the two versions.
In *The Vision* Barlow used the religious associations of the
imagery of light and darkness as symbolic of progress, cultural awakening, and political conversion. His masterful
adaptation of the old Puritan idiom added a symbolic
dimension to *The Vision*. The poem was the product of a
period in which Barlow was more concerned about expressing his own vision of America than in reaching or impressing
an audience. More comfortable with the place of America
in world history, more certain of its role in history and in
the successful progress to come, he composed a smooth and
balanced poem. The imagery functions to strengthen the
central theme of America's emergence into the light of divine
favor.

In *The Columbiad*, however, Barlow intentionally undercut the religious imagery. He was more conscious of himself
as the "American bud" addressing at once the cosmopolitan
world and a native audience in desperate need of instruction
—social, historical, and moral. The poem is torn by these
three contradictory purposes. The classical imagery and
literary allusions, which Barlow added probably to impress
learned readers, clash with the American place-names and
pedagogical apparatus designed to appeal to his own countrymen. For example, whereas the dissertation on Manco Capac
in the first poem is a daring and fitting intrusion of prose into

the poetic discourse, in *The Columbiad* the digressions are placed in extensive footnotes. Barlow had come to see *The Vision* as a provincial poem, and he was willing to sacrifice local appeal for what he hoped would be universal recognition and historical permanence. The result is that *The Columbiad* is less provincial but more pretentious.

Barlow's *Vision* was written out of a sense of participation in a massive and irresistible movement of progress toward a political millennium; *The Columbiad* conveys a sense of exhaustion—as though the poet is trying to push forward a movement that has lost its inherent power. The light and sun imagery of *The Vision* glow with spontaneous fervor, and the characters seem nearly blinded by what they see in the future. That light is diffused in *The Columbiad* as the poem stops and starts and the speaker tries to fan the sparks of ideas into a larger flame of international significance. For all its contradictions and confusions, *The Vision* is a poem celebrating and reflecting social change, economic and religious progress and fulfillment, and millennial hopes for the arts and letters as part of a carefully designed unification of the American landscape and historical evolution.

The Columbiad lacks that confidence and seems obsessed with asserting a collective national identity. While the mood of the earlier poem is open and optimistic, the tone of the second is apprehensive. At its very outset Barlow seems defensive of the patriotic theme and the awkward forcing of his material into the mold of the classical epic: "*The Columbiad* is a patriotic poem; the subject is national and historical. Thus far it must be interesting to my countrymen. But most of the events were so recent, so important and so well known, as to render them inflexible to the hand of fiction. The poem, therefore, could not with propriety be modelled after that regular epic from which the more splendid works of this kind have taken, and on which their success is supposed in a great measure to depend. The attempt would have been highly injudicious; it must have diminished and debased a series of actions which were sadly great in themselves and could not be disfigured without losing their interest" (p. 376). In other words, Barlow admits that the material is larger than his talent.

In *The Vision of Columbus*, Barlow had been trying to assure his readers with his own confidence about the future, but in *The Columbiad* he was trying to teach and preach to them with an awareness that the experiment might fail. In doing this, he destroyed the engaging simplicity of the patterns of light and dark imagery. Whereas in *The Vision*, America and the future are in light while Europe, Canada, Indians, and the past in shade and darker hues, in *The Columbiad* the imagery is mixed. Conscious of having been himself seduced by the religious language of his youth, Barlow was reluctant to impose these symbols upon his readers. Thus, he systematically tried to eliminate religious reverberations and to focus the attention of his readers upon the pure light of science and commerce and upon political liberalism. But without their metaphysical associations these metaphors lose much of their power.

The Vision is also more exciting because it reveals a poet in the midst of an age of transition, attempting to create a new dream in the language and conventions of the old. In *The Columbiad*, the dream has become concretized into a political ideology. The private visionary has become a party member and his voice—once the entrancing voice of an angel looking into the future—is that of a civil engineer and social planner, employing established rhetoric to argue how things should be done and practical problems solved.[16] Barlow was now a more systematic thinker and urgent reformer who believed that an evolution in religious ideas of the people was necessary if the society was to advance. Thus, in the revision of the poem he tried to make the religious ideas consistent with his own personal beliefs— something Freneau never dared to do. But he thereby drained the poem of its metaphorical power, losing the depth of mythic meaning the religious images and associations had provided. While some of the associations of light and darkness in the earlier version had sprung from Barlow's own unconscious acceptance of traditional connotations, in the later poem he was more aware of the religious sources of those terms, and his social and political beliefs led him to reduce their symbolic significances.

What Barlow did accomplish in *The Columbiad* was to give the poem the potential for reaching a wider audience. The additional notes, his authorial presence, the expanded prose arguments, the heightened characterizations, and the addition of a sentimental subplot were all designed to increase the appeal of the poem to his unlearned readers. At the same time, the additional classical allusions, elaborate geographical descriptions and allusions, details of scientific and naturalistic information, and the loftier language could appeal to the taste of more sophisticated readers of the European and American elite. Barlow tried to expand the religious and philosophical appeal of the poem as well but ran into difficulty. Although he did not remove all references to God, he did reduce their number considerably, and he especially eliminated references to Christ. He also left in some passages that stress divine intervention and images of America's founding derived from biblical types because, in spite of his personal skepticism, he still recognized the dimension of the national symbolism in this imagery. To balance the religious idiom, however, he went to great lengths to stress the political and social power of enlightened reason and the danger of religion as an irrational force that nearly always leads to war and large-scale human destruction.

However, Barlow's changes in *The Columbiad* are not so

clumsy and detrimental to the poem as they are sometimes
depicted. For example, the interweaving of the hymn to
Freedom into Book IV is quite smooth, appropriate to the
meaning and flow of that book, and serves several important
functions: it properly expands the idea, left undeveloped in
The Vision, that human freedom would be the key to the
opening of new political horizons on the American continent.
The passage also links the imagery of light and darkness
and day and night to themes of political ignorance and
enlightened freedom and thereby establishes the symbolic
dimension of this imagery for the political meaning of *The
Columbiad*. The blending of the religious imagery from
The Vision with the Prometheus motif of *The Columbiad*
operates neatly to reinforce the millennial theme of the later
poem. As William Channing was to do later, Barlow used
light imagery to depict human intelligence and moral perfection over the darkness of moral ignorance and human injustice. Barlow also anticipated Channing by using the
metaphor of organic human growth to symbolize the progress
of history toward perfection.[17]

The most intriguing addition to *The Columbiad* is a
powerful section on slavery in America, which illustrates
Barlow's courage to criticize his nation's most sensitive issue.
The attack is also an excellent example of Barlow's willingness to fracture the artistic unity of the poem for moral and
social preaching, and it represents Barlow at his rhetorical
best. As he announces in the Argument to Book VIII, he
enters the poem as his own character: "The Author addresses
his countrymen on that subject [slavery] and on the principles
of their government" (p. 680). And there is a significant shift
in tone and style when he opens his oration to the American
people:

> My friends, I love your fame; I joy to raise
> The high toned anthem of my country's praise;

but he soon asks, "Land that I love! is this the whole we owe?/ . . . Dwells there no blemish where such glories shine?" (p. 689). But in a clever tactical move, Barlow withholds his own abolitionist sermon until he has tried another well-established rhetoric of rebuke. In recognition that there are members of his audience who still respond to the thunder of the Puritan jeremiad, the "Author" invokes another speaker, the "Guardian Genius of Africa," who chastises the Americans in the imagery of fire and brimstone and the language of impending doom. With a visage like the wrathful Old Testament God, the Atlas, the "great brother guardian of old Afric's clime," approaches Barlow's pulpit:

> High o'er his coast he rears his frowning form,
> O'erlooks and calms his sky-borne fields of storm,
> Flings off the clouds that round his shoulders hung
> And breaks from clogs of ice his trembling tongue:
> While far thro space with rage and grief he glares,
> Heaves his hoar head and shakes the heaven he bears.
>
> [p. 690]

First, the Genius presents a litany of the crimes committed by the Americans against the African slaves. Repeating the phrase "Enslave my tribes" throughout the recitation, he depicts the suffering and brutality that the slaves endure. Then, after accusing the Americans of gross hypocrisy in proclaiming their doctrines of republicanism while engaging in the greedy and indulgent practice of slavery, he goes on, in the manner of the Puritan fast-day sermon, to predict that natural disasters will annihilate the slaveholding and supporting countries. Volcanoes, earthquakes, and violent storms will rack the land, and the oceans will rise up and pour across the lands and destroy the populations:

> Far heavier vengeance, in the march of time
> Attends them still; if still they dare debase
> And hold inthrall'd the millions of my race;

A vengeance that shall shake the world's deep frame,
That heaven abhors and hell might shrink to name.
Nature, long outraged, delves the crusted sphere
. . .

Her cauldron'd floods of fire their blast prepare;
Her wallowing womb of subterranean war
Waits but the fissure that my wave shall find,
To force the foldings of the rocky rind,
Crash your curst continent, and whirl on high
The vast avulsion vaulting thro the sky,
Fling far the bursting fragments, scattering wide
Rocks, mountains, nations o'er the swallowing tide.

[pp. 694–95]

All that will be left of Europe and America after this explosion of Nature's wrath will be one "dim lone island in
the watery waste" which

Stands the sad relic of a ruin'd world,
Attests the wrath our mother kept in store
And rues her judgments on the race she bore.

[p. 694]

Having allowed the "Genius of Africa" to berate Americans with the fiery Calvinist rhetoric that the poet hoped
might strike responsive chords in the pious, Barlow himself
enters the poem to present the enlightened, rationalist case
against slavery. First, he apologizes for the previous speaker
whose emotional outburst is excusable given his subjective
view of the issue and whose words may be useful if they
touch the hearts of those persuaded by appeals to passion. But
for those who are motivated only by logic and reason's voice,
the author has his own considered thoughts.

Fathers and friends, I know the boding fears
Of angry genii and of rending spheres
Assail not souls like yours; whom science bright
Thro shadowy nature leads with surer light.

[p. 695]

Barlow's own approach argues for an end to slavery on the grounds of self-interest and duty. Once men are well instructed, he says, they always act reasonably, and because men realize that the common good is the key to happiness, they seek to remove all social evils. Reason teaches that the master of the slave soon becomes a tyrant, and a society of tyrants will be corrupt and unworkable. So men must realize that the abolition of slavery is necessary to a successful society. In case this argument is not sufficient, the author also takes another tack. The inspiration of America was in founding a society on the sound principle of equality—a principle that clearly reflects nature's plan for the future of mankind. Slavery contradicts this American wisdom and thereby runs counter to the national purpose. Since the American system is the best in the world for bringing profit and glory to the people, a closer adherence to the true American principles will result in greater, not less, material gain.

Slavery remained for Barlow the worst example of the pattern of the strong's exploitation of the weak, which all the moralizing, common-sense reasoning, the rhetoric about the rule of law and justice could not hide. Barlow believed that the system of slavery resided behind the same veil that masked an array of other evils: land speculation, corrupt politics, the sustained ignorance of the many, the religious hypocrisy of social climbers and clergy, the flabby doctrines of benevolence, and the emptiness of all the language supporting these crimes against mankind, which the Revolution was to have eliminated. Slavery was not just a blemish on the pure cloth of democracy, it was part of the basic fabric and design of an entire tapestry of evil justified by naturalistic thought, which was the dirty undergarment of the republic. But in 1790 only a fool or a resurrected New England Calvinist would think or dare to suggest that behind the new Constitution there lurked a hidden license for continued human selfishness and corruption.

Through his juxtaposition of Calvinist and Enlightenment appeals and through the use of a range of rhetorical devices, Barlow supports his preachments against slavery with several different strictures. To do so, however, he had to intrude himself into the poem, wrench the narrative line severely, and create new characters who serve no function in the poem except this overtly didactic one. Evidently, Barlow felt so strongly about the issue that he was willing to risk the criticism the section was certain to receive.

Lest any reader think he was not aware of the risks he was taking here and throughout *The Columbiad*, Barlow used his footnotes to furnish his readers with some explanations. Tucked away in Note 49 is a justification of his work and of the mode of his writing. In condemning "heroic" writing because of its appeal to the senses by the depiction of war and strife, Barlow makes his case for a sympathetic reading of his works on his own terms. Of most writers of the past it must be said "that they have injured the cause of humanity almost in proportion to the fame they have acquired" (p. 847). Their fault has been in attempting to entertain readers by delighting them with bold actions instead of instructing them in the true and the good; thereby, they have "led astray the moral sense of man" (p. 849). Thus, Barlow says a book should be written which instructs both writers and their readers in the fundamental purpose of literature and in the merits of proper writing: "It should be a *Review of Poets and Historians*, as to the moral and political tendency of their works." With the aid of such a text "future historians and poets" would know how to write and how to judge the writing of the past, and "at the least it would prove a guide to readers by teaching them how to judge, and what to praise or blame in the accounts of human actions." Once readers knew what they should be looking for, "the public taste would be reformed by degrees" (pp. 429–32).

Again, in expressing his notion that a writer stands at a

certain point in the evolution of the history of his own nation and must bring his writing in line with the needs of his culture at that time, Barlow argues that Homer failed because he dealt with the wrong material: "If, instead of the *Iliad*, he had given us a work of equal splendor founded on an opposite principle, whose object would have been to celebrate the useful arts of agriculture and navigation . . . mankind, enriched with such a work at that early period, would have given an useful turn to their ambition thro all succeeding ages" (p. 848). Historians, too, have a moral duty to perform. While it may appear that the historian's task is simply to narrate facts, that chore "is part of the duty of the historian; but it is not his whole duty. . . . he would likewise develop the political and moral tendency of the transactions he details." Because historians teach the young of human nature and help the rising generation to form their own principles for the future, it is imperative that historians be moral men, who judge and evaluate what they report. Historians of the past have failed to make such evaluations: "History in general, to answer the purpose of sound instruction to the future guides of nations, must be rewritten." As an example of the errors of history, Barlow argues that those who have written of the "Roman Republic" have failed to mention one important fact, "Rome never had a Republic" (p. 849). After reviewing the past errors of nations, Barlow concludes in all modesty that the world would have been better run if the poets had been the leaders:

> I know I must be called an extravagant theorist if I insinuate that all these good things would have resulted from having history well written and poetry well conceived. No man will doubt however that such would have been the tendency; nor can we deny that the contrary has resulted, at least in some degree, from the manner in which such writings have been composed. And why should we write at all, if not to benefit mankind? The

public mind, as well as the individual mind, receives its propensities; it is equally the creature of habit. Nations are educated, like a single child. They only require a longer time and a greater number of teachers. [p. 850]

Finally though, *The Columbiad* is a tortured work. Barlow believed he had a new vision of an American society freed from the stifling values of the old order, but in fact, he had not advanced far enough to depict in poetry what he had envisioned in prose works such as *Advice to the Privileged Orders*. So encumbered by the classical form of the epic and the mixture of biblical and classical types and allusions of *The Vision*, Barlow tried to force his new world into archaic literary dress, and in the process he unwittingly infused the poem with the values and meanings of the old order he rejected. Unlike Timothy Dwight, who consciously embraced his American heritage and brought his epic into complete, though perhaps unfortunate, harmony with the classical and biblical traditions, Barlow struggled against these forms and yet succumbed to them. The result is a work that strives to present a radical reappraisal of the transmission of culture but achieves an opaque vision of a new world obscured by the forms and values of the old.[18]

Like Freneau, Barlow was a better poet in the 1780s, when he was still formulating his social philosophy and grappling with the question of his role as a poet in America. Once he had settled into his new ideas and became persuaded of his authority as an intellectual, poet, and statesman, he transformed his lively *Vision* into an aloof and static national product. The choicest fruit of his period of confidence was certainly "The Hasty-Pudding," the mock epic he composed in high spirits at an inn in Chambéry, France, in 1796. This breezy satire moves with the ease and grace of an accomplished writer not burdened by the need to stop to examine the political and moral implications of every line and image.

Self-assured of his place as the political and literary representative of his native land, Barlow mixed Columbus, the
gods, and the muses with Virginia "Hoe-cakes," the "Yankey,"
cornhusking, and pumpkins into his tasty New England dish.
But an American poet of the 1790s—and perhaps of any time
since—could only become so convinced of his place as a
national bard while living for several years outside the
country. When Barlow returned to America in 1807 and
published *The Columbiad*, readers at home and abroad
rejected or ignored it. He was surprised and disappointed.[19]

When Barlow returned to France to negotiate a commercial treaty with Napoleon in 1811, he had a more accurate
view of the place of the man of letters in America and of his
own diminished stature as one of those who, it was repeated
by English and American critics, wrote during the time that
America produced no literature of merit. After chasing
Napoleon across Europe, Barlow found himself seriously ill
and in the midst of the massive retreat from Moscow. His
moving letters to his wife Ruth give the details of the ordeal
he endured, traveling ten days in a stagecoach, fifteen hours
a day. As his companions tried to outrun the pursuing army
and get the dying Barlow to a place of safety, the poet-
statesman left his countrymen an astonishing work, quite
different from all he had previously written.[20]

Surveying the scene of destruction left in the wake of
Napoleon's army, Joel Barlow composed one of his most
poignant and most pessimistic works, which stands as a
reminder that he was not blind to the threat of an era of
continued world revolution and destruction in which he and
his country would play a major formative role. Of course,
it is not known whether he had long suppressed fears and
doubts about the future of America and other republics in
order to maintain an optimistic exterior for his own and his
country's purposes. But in "Advice to a Raven in Russia" the

lines ring once more with the truth of a vision, though now
the visionary sees not the best but the worst of the coming
ages. He fears that those sweeping global political reforms
he had supported may leave in their wake massive human
destruction. Turning away from the poetry of light and
returning to his Calvinist roots, Barlow re-creates the imagery
of darkness of the Puritan poetic heritage. In a tone
reminiscent of Michael Wigglesworth's *The Day of Doom*,
he creates a picture of chilling slaughter on a frozen
landscape, which symbolizes the waste and destruction he
fears will follow in the years after his own impending death.
The ravens who futilely try to pick out the eyes of the frozen
bodies of dead soldiers come from the same scriptural
passages that frightened the Puritan poet Edward Taylor
when he was a boy. Significantly, it is this shadowy biblical
type of received vision that Barlow made the central symbol
of "Advice."

> Fear nothing then, hatch fast your ravenous brood,
> Teach them to cry to Buonaparte for food;
> . . .
> Now can you tear one fiber from their breast.
> No! from their visual sockets as they lie,
> With beak and claws you cannot pluck an eye.
> The frozen orb, preserving still its form,
> Defies your talons as it braves the storm,
> But stands and stares to God, as if to know
> In what curst hands he leaves his world below.[21]

When Barlow's political faith failed, his poetic vision was
restored, and the religious idiom of his youth came to life
for a brief final moment.

"Advice to a Raven in Russia" is a poem that would have
pleased Increase Mather and Timothy Dwight. Yet it is also
a work that vividly expresses an apocalyptic vision that would
become a recurrent theme in American writing from Poe,

the later Twain, and the naturalists in the nineteenth century to John Barth, Thomas Pynchon, and Joyce Carol Oates in our own time. At last, with this poem of darkness Barlow earned his place as one of the fathers of American literature.

IV
PHILIP FRENEAU:
POETRY OF SOCIAL COMMITMENT

It had been a particularly onerous wait for the Critic, the Poet, and the Novelist. . . . Mailer, of course, had been preparing an extempore speech for the odd chance they might call on him; he would have liked to address fifty or one hundred thousand people: . . . but the call never came, which did little to improve his impatience.

NORMAN MAILER
The Armies of the Night, 1968

When Philip Freneau joined the Princeton class of 1771 to study for the ministry, he fulfilled the dream of his immigrant wine merchant father, Pierre Fresneau. As the oldest of five and the son of financially successful parents, Philip was well prepared to play the part of the intelligent youth who would give the family respectability and status by entering the elite of the ministry. In Monmouth County he prepared to enter college under the tutelage of Alexander Mitchell, a recent graduate of Nassau Hall at Princeton, an institution then headed by the New Light theologian, William Tennent. When Freneau entered Princeton as a sophomore in 1768, however, the joy of that occasion was marred by the death of his father in 1767, and the promised career was placed in jeopardy by financial losses that Pierre had incurred shortly before his death. Still, his Scottish mother's commitment to the family's dream and Philip's own thirst for learning resolved the question of whether he would attend college. Through three years of hardship and sacrifice, Freneau displayed what would be a life-long inclination to subordinate self to moral principles and social ideals that would characterize his choices in life and shape his most mature literary work.[1]

When Freneau left the quiet life of the village of Middletown Point, New Jersey, he entered a whirl of debate and conflict in which he was under constant pressure to make political choices and take stands on social and religious issues. As his friend James Madison immediately recognized, young Philip possessed the wit and verbal skill to become a dangerous protagonist in any conflict. At first, Freneau confined his literary inclinations to reading and to composing private poems. But Princeton was fast becoming a hotbed of political and religious radicalism, and Freneau was soon in the fray. When President Witherspoon preached of the moral and religious responsibility of Americans to resist the decadent authority of England, the Cliosophic Society of conservative undergraduates launched a series of rebuttals. Madison, Freneau, and their friends Hugh Henry Brackenridge and William Bradford, Jr., responded by reviving the defunct Plain Dealing Club and renaming it the American Whig Society. Freneau become the literary leader of this group, and his success in verse and prose satire caused him to question his plan for a life as a country clergyman.[2]

When he left college, however, Freneau was leaning toward a career in the ministry. He tried teaching, hated it, and returned to the advanced study of theology. The early 1770s, however, were not times that made it easy to cling to one's plan for the future. Philosophical and religious uncertainty kept intruding upon Freneau's theological study to the point that he finally vented his frustration in his theology notebook: "It was a vain notion that a Parson's occupation was the high road to wealth and independence in Life. . . . And so farewell to the study of Divinity—which is, in fact, the Study of Nothing! . . . and the profession of a priest is little better than that of a slothful Blockhead."[3] In spite of his vitriolic tone here, this explosion does not mark a major

change in Freneau's thought from Calvinism to Deism or
Romanticism or to the beginning of an enduring anti-
clericalism. In subsequent pages of the notebook, Freneau
returned to the serious consideration of texts for sermons and
other theological matters. The outburst signals his inner
turmoil and self-doubt rather than a turning point in his
life.[4] It reveals however, a pattern of conflict and resolution
in Freneau's life that appears in much of his most interesting
work.

Although Freneau did give up the study of theology and
his plan for a career in the ministry, he never abandoned his
commitment to employ his talents in service to his fellow-
men. Whether inspired by his father's dream, the determination and faith of his mother, or the teachings of Witherspoon,
which in spite of himself he was never able to forget, Freneau
seldom put his personal ambition ahead of his sense of social
and moral duty. He understood his calling to be to use his
knowledge and literary talent for the improvement of the
morals, social order, and literary taste of the American
people.[5]

Freneau's calling was always a burden to him. When faced
with the failure of others to appreciate or benefit from his
commitment, he became as ambivalent about his career as a
poet as he had been about the ministry in 1774. Repeatedly,
he threatened and tried to withdraw from public life and
escape to some pastoral retreat. In the poems in which critics
find a pre-Romantic spirit, he often created images of repose
and sanctuary where the personal poetic self might take
flight into new realms free of political and social burdens.
Indeed, Freneau was even known to leave the city or the
country in times of crisis as when he sailed to the West Indies
at the start of the Revolution. But he always returned, just
as he returned to the colonies in 1778 to earn the title "Poet
of the Revolution" with his patriotic verses and bitter satires.
Even the poetry he wrote extolling retreat from society always

suggested on a deeper level his conscious and ultimate acceptance of his social role.[6]

Still, throughout his life, Freneau complained. He protested the use of violent conflict rather than reason to solve
the problems between England and America; he was outraged by the treatment he received when held captive on a
British prison ship; he chastised his society after the war for
moral and social decay; he fumed at the Federalists who, he
thought, wanted to reestablish monarchy; and, most of all,
he protested his countrymen's indifference to literature. In
one critic's view, Freneau was a "good hater."[7] Yet it would
be a mistake to assume that in his writing he was out of
control and that what may appear today to be flaws are
simply the results of confusion, impatience, or anger. Perhaps Freneau's politics or opinions ruined his opportunities
for greatness in his own time, but he was always a conscious
craftsman who wrote each of his works to achieve a particular
set of effects. His poetic practice, the social, psychological,
and artistic complexities of his works were always the direct
result of intellectual positions and critical theories he embraced at the time he was writing.

Although Freneau seldom wavered far from his commitment to literature as a form of social influence, there are
recognizable stages in the development of his attitudes toward the function of literature and corresponding changes
in the form and style of his works. Most of his modern critics
have been inclined to trace his career as a gradual decline
from a daring Romantic vision and form in the early works
toward increasingly conventional ideas and pedestrian verse
in his later writing. The assertion that Freneau was "dead
as a poet after 1786" is too common in Freneau criticism not
to be taken seriously as describing a significant change in his
career and writing, and much of the poetry he wrote after
1790 is strikingly different in tone and style from the poems
of the 1770s.[8]

The argument that the change is a degeneration, however, rests upon adherence to aesthetic principles of judgment formulated in a post-Romantic age. Modern readers tend to favor the personal lyrics. If we judge Freneau's writing and poetic intentions on his own terms, a more objective explanation of the progress of his career is possible. Instead of the picture of a promising pre-Romantic poet who forfeited a chance to be the father of American poetry for political ambition, we may more justly view Freneau as a writer who devoted himself to becoming a moral preceptor and public poet. Freneau possessed an abiding faith in the power of the imagination to shape ideas and events, and, in spite of his constant yearning for escape, he believed it was his duty to use his power to serve and instruct his fellow citizens. Although not always successful or pleasing to modern readers, his shifts in literary method were the result of his constant search for the words and forms that would reach and influence his American readers.

When America first entered the war, Freneau was uncertain whether a change in the political situation would really make any difference in the lives of the colonists, and he feared that blood would be shed for a futile cause. Although his public poems like *The Rising Glory of America* expressed fervent hope, Freneau's knowledge of history inclined him to see the war as another senseless episode in the chronicle of man. This ambivalence is evident in "George the Third's Soliloquy" where a human and sympathetic King George emerges from the stock political rhetoric concerning his villainy.[9] Once Freneau became convinced of the validity of the war in 1778, however, he joined the militia and sailed the Atlantic as a ship captain. After being captured and suffering six weeks on a British prison ship, he became passionately committed to the American cause and produced vitriolic attacks on England. After the war he became an enthusiast of republican principles and devoted himself in the 1780s to the belief that Americans truly were socially, morally, and artistically superior to the British.

As a new social order emerged from the old in the late 1780s, Freneau recognized that the lines of power and influence in the republican society were to be redrawn. In Freneau's view, the constitutional squabbles and the dubious arguments of the Federalist papers made it evident that, because of their special, private interests, the leaders of government neither wanted nor could be trusted with the moral and spiritual leadership of the people. While the lawyers and politicians could write and enforce laws, they had to depend upon other elements of the social leadership to raise the intellectual level of the populace so that the people would elect wise and honest lawmakers. Since the clergy seemed to be losing their authority as moral leaders and spokesmen, there was a void of leadership which Freneau felt he had an obligation to fill. Yet he had to find a way of convincing the people to listen and read. During the 1780s Freneau tried to reach the ordinary literate citizen, but he was frustrated by the failure of the very readers who needed his works most to purchase his poetry or read his essays and journals.

During the 1780s and 1790s Freneau alternated between periods of fervent dedication to the causes of politics and literature and sudden departures from the city for months on his Jersey farm or long stretches at sea. In 1790 he married Eleanor Forman and tried to settle down into a quiet job as an assistant editor in New York. But politics called again. His friends Madison and Jefferson persuaded him to set up his own newspaper in Philadelphia to counter the powerful Hamiltonian paper of John Fenno. With fiery rhetoric Freneau's *National Gazette* upheld Jefferson's principles and attacked the policies of Washington. Jefferson later praised Freneau for having "saved our Constitution which was galloping fast into monarchy" while Washington grumbled of "that rascal Freneau."

Throughout these political involvements Freneau's primary interest remained the role of the writer and the place of literature in the new nation. He often threatened to abandon the calling of the writer, but he never lost sight of the fact that more was at stake than personal pride and his own literary success.[10] With the great emphasis upon commerce, economic expansion, invention, and entrepreneurship, which occurs in a new nation seeking an economic leap forward, the people were already beginning to grant the most successful members of the merchant and business classes the kind of moral authority accorded the giants of industry in the nineteenth century. In a society with no established tradition of literary and artistic patronage, merchants such as Philadelphia's Robert Morris were already taking control of the nation's cultural development and literary production.

Perhaps more than anything else, Freneau feared that such men would exercise a form of censorship that would force writers to help the rich and powerful to preserve their own status rather than to further the development of the mass of people. Thus he complained of these new elitists: "Of *Bank Directors* of the town,/The home-made *nobles* of our times,/Who hate the bard, and spurn his rhymes."[11] And identifying the Philadelphia magnate with the Roman courtier who was a prosperous sycophant of Tiberius during the time of Christ, he courageously attacked Morris directly in "Epistle to Sylvius":

> Sejanus, of mercantile skill,
> Without whose aid the world stands still,
> And by whose wonder-working play,
> The sun goes round—(his flatterers say)
> Sejanus has in house declared
> "These States, as yet, can boast no bard,
> And all the sing-song of our clime
> Is merely nonsense, fringed with rhyme."
> With such a bold, conceited air

> When such assume the critic's chair,
> Low in the dust is genius laid,
> The muses with the man of trade.[12]

Nowhere was Freneau more explicit about the effect of politics upon the literary situation than in his essay, "Royal Dangers in the Stage." There he argued that those who controlled the popular imagination would wield great political power, and theatrical entertainments approved by the wealthy and powerful for public consumption were merely tools for enforcing aristocratic values. The simplistic themes of such plays served only to distract the people from their political, economic, and social conditions: "It has ever been the policy of *ministers of state,* in all monarchical government, or *governments verging towards monarchy,* to create, and countenance *alluring amusements,* in order to prevent *the people* from thinking. . . . Fancy and imagination among mankind are everything. Aristocracy and Royalty by taking hold of these leading faculties in human nature, have rendered the theater subservient to *their own purposes.* In a Republic like America . . . the theater . . . should be a school of virtue and public good."[13]

Freneau was not an opponent of freedom of expression, but he feared that literary works that favored ideas and values contrary to accepted ones would be systematically eliminated while the works of political favorites would be endorsed. In his private war against this tendency in American culture, Freneau thereby established lines of division between those businessmen who used patronage to encourage certain kinds of docile or neutral writers, or artists like himself whose works challenged accepted values or criticized aspects of the society.

In spite of many poems in which he threatened to abandon writing, Freneau kept taking up his pen with new energy, trying new techniques, and exploring new themes and issues. The tension between a desire to escape and a social commit-

ment itself is a theme in much of Freneau's writing. In the
1790s he became a spokesman for the poor and oppressed
and aimed many of his works at the least sophisticated
readers, whom he felt needed literature to provide them with
moral guidance and social truths even if standards of literary
taste had to be lowered.[14] Believing himself to be living in
a transition period of history in which the taste of the people
would gradually be raised, Freneau was willing to sacrifice
both poetic beauty and critical acclaim for his social mission.[15]

In order to recognize the intensity of Freneau's moral and
literary commitment and its result in his works, it is necessary to begin a study of his writing by granting him a degree
of maturity and self-consciousness that he has not often been
given. To do so is to allow for the possibility that the voice
of the angry, ranting, and the later more simplistic poet is
not always that of Freneau himself. If we permit a distance
between the speaker of Freneau's poetry and the person of
Philip Freneau, we are in a better position to see his complex
response to his society.

In the prose essays of the 1780s and 1790s this distance
between Freneau the man and his speaker is easier to recognize because he often adopted the Addisonian method of
creating characters to serve as personae. In fact, in tracing
Freneau's shifting attitudes toward his audience and toward
the moral and social function of literature, it is helpful to
examine the evolution of his speakers in the early poems and
the prose essays. Even the poems written before 1788 are not
simply personal expressions—indeed, it is quite evident that
he was manipulating speakers in many of his best poems of
this period. Then, his experiments with personae in the prose
essays led him to devise more rounded characters as speakers
in the later poetry; some of these new characters spring
directly from the essays themselves.

With this interplay of techniques of poetry and prose in
mind as a context for examining his literary development,

we may begin with a brief examination of the tension between the private and public poet even in what have been
called the "Romantic" poems of the 1770s. Many of Freneau's early poems illustrate his conviction that the cultural
revolution coming upon the world would allow the poet
freedom to let his imagination lead society to new frontiers
of understanding, social organization, and artistic expression.
In "The Power of Fancy," which was written in 1770, he
gives his own fancy the freedom to explore:

> Wakeful, vagrant, restless thing,
> Ever wandering on the wing,
> Who thy wondrous source can find.
> Fancy, regent of the mind; . . .
> [I, 34]

First, Freneau equates the human imagination with the
creative power of the Divine mind, which generated the universe through an act of Fancy.

> Ah! what is all this mighty whole,
> These suns and stars that round us roll!
> What are they all, where'er they shine,
> But Fancies of the Power Divine!
> . . .
> Ideas of the Almighty mind! [I, 35]

Then, the speaker comes to a realization of the extent of
Fancy's power. Just as acts of the Divine mind have dramatic
consequences in the real universe, so too the imaginings of
the poet create the present and re-create the past. Therefore,
the traditional view of history as a record of actual events
is no longer adequate; history is a collective myth shaped by
earlier poets who produced the scriptures, the classics, and
the great works of the last centuries. The only records of men
like Caesar and events like the Trojan Wars are those left
by Virgil and Homer:

> Troy, thy vanish'd pomp resume,
> Or, weeping at thy Hector's tomb,
> Yet those faded scenes renew,
> Whose memory is to Homer due.
>
>   [I, 37]

The great poets of the past are gone, but universal Fancy passes down to the present generation. As a new epoch begins, it is for the imagination of the modern poet to create fresh images and new myths that will engender new possibilities for the expression of the human spirit and the progress of mankind:

> Yet must those eyes in darkness stay,
> That once were rivals to the day?—
> Like heaven's bright lamp beneath the main
> They are but set to rise again.
>   Fancy, thou the muses' pride,
> In thy painted realms reside
> Endless images of things,
> Fluttering each on golden wings,
> Ideal objects, such a store,
> The universe could hold no more: . . . [I, 39]

Even in such sanguine work, however, Freneau's Scottish Common Sense training led him to balance these assertions with a warning that Fancy must also be held in check by the poet's public duty. The speaker implies that without limits poetic Fancy may lead people to new forms of social order or may also be dangerous and destructive for Fancy may be a "fickle Goddess." The mind of the poet, which has the power to call up images and place them in a chosen context, may influence people toward a given course of action. Thus, rather than give Fancy total freedom, the speaker decides to restrain it to private flights at present because its domain is only one-half of human experience and thus it must be held in check by reason's power.

> Fancy, to thy power I owe
> Half my happiness below;
> By thee Elysian groves were made,
> Thine were the notes that Orpheus play'd;
> By thee was Pluto charm'd so well
> While rapture seiz'd the sons of hell—
> Come, O come—perceiv'd by none,
> You and I will walk alone. [I, 39]

While "The Power of Fancy" investigates the tension and interplay between imagination and reality within the mind of the poet, "The Beauties of Santa Cruz" explores the conscious conflict between the poet's desire for escape from the turmoil of politics and society and the moral imperative of the poetic vocation. Written in 1776, the poem at first appears to approve the speaker's romantic yearning for freedom. The speaker tries to persuade his reader, and himself, that it is foolish to endure the cold winters of the North and the burdens of city life when he may depart for a land of beauty and peace in the Caribbean. In support of his claim, he puts forth a description of this paradise that is supposed to enchant the reader; throughout the description, however, there are hints that Santa Cruz is not paradise. Allusion to human mortality and evil and images of shade and death, such as the "threat'ning rooters on every side" or the "enchanting plant" that may bewitch travelers, dot his descriptions and undercut his argument.

As the speaker himself begins to recognize the flaws in this all-too-real world, the poem moves toward a different conclusion. In this green southern world—always a symbol in Freneau of imaginative escape—there continues to be slavery, death, and the violence of natural destruction exemplified in the fury of hurricanes which wash away the cheap shelters and the lives of the poor and weak. The speaker comes to see that the evils of his exotic retreat equal those of the gray northern city and that there is no escaping the human situation. Accepting this reality, he also acknowledges his poetic duties and takes a new stand regarding such temporary retreats and self-delusions.

> On these blue hills, to pluck the opening flowers,
> Might yet awhile the unwelcome task delay,
> And these gay scenes prolong the fleeting hours
> To aid bright Fancy on some future day. [I, 266]

Memories of the pleasanter aspects of Santa Cruz will sustain the speaker and restore the power of his fancy when he returns to the city to labor once again. Echoes of Milton's "Lycidas" throughout the poem also alert the reader to the parallel situation of the poet who perished in his effort to fulfill his poetic calling and the need for retreat which the speaker claims. At the end of "Lycidas," the speaker is preparing to return to society to take up his poetic vocation and serve the world as Lycidas had hoped to do. While the sense of duty is less strong in Freneau's original version of "The Beauties of Santa Cruz" than in the revised version of 1786, the moral and aesthetic assumptions of the poem link it more to Milton than to the Romantics.[16]

The third poem often used to represent Freneau's period of romantic searching is his graveyard poem, "The House of Night." With many of his poems, Freneau changed the poem considerably between its first appearance in 1779 and its inclusion in the volume of 1786. As in most cases, Freneau made the later version more secular, less personal, and more conspicuously didactic. The addition of a prose explication of the poem's meaning on the first page indicates how apprehensive he had become about being misunderstood. Although some critics find the early version to be superior because of its seeming simplicity and spontaneity, the second version better illustrates Freneau's conscious attempt to reconcile the demands of the poetic imagination with the moral duty of the poet. By the mid-1780s Freneau had a better perception of the capabilities of his audience, and he was able to place his own philosophical inquiries regarding death in the context of the ideas current among his potential readers.

Unlike the 1779 "House of Night," which has an immature poet-speaker who confronts his fears of death and human corruption, the later version presents a mature social poet who has gained control over his own personal confusions and is ready to lead others out of their ignorance and confusion—whether political, philosophical, or spiritual. Examination of a few of the revisions exposes Freneau's estimate of the religious attitudes and intellectual sophistication of his audience. He added two opening stanzas that create a frame for the personal experience of the speaker. These stanzas distance the experience of the speaker from both Freneau and the reader. This semblance of detachment creates the illusion that the reader and Freneau are together observing the experience of a third person. In this way Freneau does not shock the reader by revealing a personal experience that might raise doubts about his religious faith and cause the reader to reject the subject of the poem out of hand. For this purpose also, he removed the earlier subtitle of the poem, "Six Hours Lodging with Death," and the Latin epigraphs, which might suggest a purely fanciful subject not worth the time of a serious republican reader.

Early in the poem he also added a religious dimension. In the fourth stanza of the original, he had claimed the value of poetry to be its power to introduce readers to deeper human truths that the rational mind might never explore. In 1786 he tried to strengthen this argument by adding a stanza on the religious value of the imagination, which may depict scenes of heaven and hell to inspire piety and discourage sin. This point had long served ministers as a justification of metaphoric language and vivid images in Calvinist sermons. Throughout the remainder of the revised version, Freneau continued to stress the religious value of poetry and fancy.

Instead of taking one stanza to point out the inadequacy of
the explanations of death by learned theologians, Freneau
expanded the point to two stanzas and is even specific about
the failure of theology.

At every point of revision Freneau had his Christian
readers in mind, readers who were not prepared to understand Freneau's nihilism, which he had exposed in the
earlier version and which he still held privately in 1785. At
the end of the first version he leaves the reader with what
Lewis Leary calls the "vision of a young man for whom death
was oblivion," whereas in the second he presents a picture of
eternal joy in paradise. The speaker proclaims Christ's victory over the fear of death that torments every heart lacking
the shield of Christian faith. While there is no evidence that
Freneau himself had experienced a renewal of Christian
faith, it is clear that as he matured and defined his role as a
poet, he held that the function of poetry was not to disturb
readers with personal doubts but to mediate beween the
truth as seen by the poet and the error or ignorance to be
corrected in society. Until the people were ready to cast off
the trappings of Christian theology and find for themselves
a new foundation for treating the fear of death and controlling the appetites of men, the old religious values and images
might still serve.

Freneau's purpose in "The House of Night" is closer to
what Eugene O'Neill identified as the purpose of modern
art: "to dig at the roots of the sickness of today—the death
of the Old God and the failure of science and materialism to
give any satisfying new one for the surviving primitive religious instinct to find a meaning for life in, and to comfort
its fears of death with." It was such a conception of his literary calling that guided Freneau during his period of reassessment between 1781 and 1790.[17]

Freneau expressed his position on the issue of the poet's
role in a democratic society most fully in his prose essays of

the 1780s where he developed a number of public personae who appear again in poems throughout the remainder of his career. It is useful to examine the narrative techniques he tested in these essays and his explicit statements about the function of poetry and the role of the writer, to appreciate the personal reassessment that underlies the changes in his poetry during this period and to understand the rationale for his new literary strategies and the revisions of his earlier poems.

In his first prose essays for the *United States Magazine* in 1779, Freneau spoke in his own voice. He called himself a "young American Philosopher and Bel Esprit, just returned from several small voyages." When he composed his essay series for the *Freeman's Journal* in 1781–82, however, Freneau decided to create a voice quite separate from his own. His "Pilgrim" is an authority figure of a very significant type who can be found not only in Freneau's work but in many literary works of other American authors of the period. Similar in some features to Franklin's Father Abraham in *The Way to Wealth* or Fielding's Man on the Hill in *Tom Jones*, the Pilgrim is a benevolent fifty-six-year-old hermit who lives at a distance from the town and whose best friend is a clergyman.[18] Although he maintains a philosophical and physical detachment from the engagements of the city, the Pilgrim has a thorough knowledge of current activities and is willing to share his keen perceptions with those who care to come to him or who read the missives he sends to the *Journal.* In this character Freneau found both a device for expressing his views in a congenial mode and a symbol for the tenuous relationship the poet must have with his society if he is to pursue truth and be able to give reasoned and detached advice to his fellows. The poet, like the Pilgrim, must finally stand outside the turmoil of events and can only speak to those who choose to listen.[19]

Throughout the nineteen Pilgrim essays Freneau developed

many features of the character he thought would appeal to republican readers. He established the wise man's authority as a spokesman for reason and morality by associating him with traditional authority. The Pilgrim is at work on a large book of natural theology titled "The Soul of the World," and he says this work has been commissioned by Divine Providence. Of course, Freneau creates much humor around this character as well, and he frequently peeks out from behind the mask to laugh with his more sophisticated readers. When the Pilgrim refuses to duel the ardent Tory Jonathan Simple who writes letters to the *Journal* attacking him, the hermit answers that he cannot risk being killed for fear that his Summa will not be completed: "Better would it be that ten, nay ten score of such persons as my correspondent should perish, than that one page of that bulky *folio* be lost to the generation to come" (p. 48). But such winks from Freneau do not deflate the authority of the wise man whose counsel it would profit his readers to heed.

With an unpretentious yet impressive mixture of classical and biblical learning, the Pilgrim gives advice on various aspects of society and morals. His style follows his own advice to those clergymen who wish to reach American listeners: he writes plainly. Warning against the display of too much learning in a country that values practical wisdom rather than showy knowledge, the Pilgrim explains that in America the Minister (and we may assume the poet) is always speaking to two or three levels of audience at once: "Adapt your discourse to plain understandings. . . . But remember it is possible to display elegance of language and true dignity of stile, and solid sentiment, in your sermons, which yet, without giving offence, shall be easily comprehended by the most vulgar, as well as by the middling class, and be received with real pleasure, and improvement by those of more elevated tastes" (p. 57). Interestingly, in this series the irate Tory, who serves as a foil to the judicious Pilgrim, writes his letters to the *Journal* in the kind of fiery rhetoric that Freneau himself often employed to attack his own political enemies.

Once Freneau established this disguise and some semblance of ironic detachment, he used the voice of the Pilgrim to set forward many of the most serious ideas that are recurrent themes in all his work. Through the mouth of this hallowed elder, Freneau preached directly upon the need for reflection, the certainty of death, and the dangers of materialism and ambition: "the perpetual amusements and avocation of a citizen's life are enemies to the future peace of the mind, as they prevent men from looking into themselves, by which neglect they commonly live and die strangers to that self knowledge which it would be to their constant study and ambition to acquire" (p. 43). He criticized those "perpetually engaged in the hurry of business" who fear the moments of repose, and also tried to explain the temporary retreat and detachment needed for the restoration of imaginative powers and philosophical clarity of thought: "Every rational man, let his business or station in life be what it may, should, in my way of thinking, at least once a year withdraw himself from the numerous connections and allurements that are apt to give us too great a fondness for life; he should then take time to reflect, as a rational being ought to do, and consider well the end of his being" (p. 43).

In spite of his own education Freneau was always suspicious of those who flaunted their knowledge. For that reason and perhaps to encourage readers to forget that the writer behind the mask was actually a learned poet and a college and divinity school graduate, Freneau has his Pilgrim attack pretentious university learning and praise intellectual simplicity. In "The Evils of Learning—the Advantages of Simple Living," the Pilgrim argues that the best educations are wasted on the sons of the wealthy who squander their advantages: "they are very great blockheads, whose education no one would suppose to have been superior to that of their coachmen were it not that they have a collegiate diploma ready in their pockets" (p. 58). And he observes that there are even economic dangers in such a system, for "a country overrun with scholars is observed never to be a thriving country." In contrast he proposes that, if left alone, the brightest and most talented will rise to the top by their own merits. "Plain, unlettered persons have commonly been the original authors of those areas and sciences" that are most valuable to society (p. 59). Perhaps Freneau felt that even his Pilgrim was too learned an authority figure, for his next persona represented the plain, unlettered persons of the republic.

The character of Robert Slender, who appears in 1786 in *The Miscellaneous Works of Philip Freneau*, is a stocking weaver by trade who invented his own loom and left for his executors a strongbox full of manuscripts signed with his name and the title "O.S.M.," for "one of the swinish multitude." Slender died lamenting the tragic fate authors endure in his society and warning the young against the folly of writing. While Freneau certainly borrowed the device of the deceased author from Addison's *Spectator* #50, he developed this character into a particularly useful American type who was to reappear in his essays and poems over the course of fifteen years.

Because Slender is supposed to possess a sort of natural republican genius, Freneau used him to explore sensitive subjects such as Christianity and authorship in America, which he may have felt were too close to his own interests to discuss in his own voice. In an essay "Advice to Authors by the late Mr. Robert Slender," Freneau used Slender to argue for an ideal to which he himself was constantly trying to adhere. In America, he says, writers are "at present considered as the dregs of the community," but authors should do all they can to establish a foundation for their authority among the common people of the country. If they cannot find support in the literate middle classes, writers will seek patrons among the rich, and as soon as they do they will make their writing begin to serve the special interests of literary patronage. Slender says: "By this ridiculous practice you degrade *dignity authorial*, the honour of authorship, which ought ever more to be uppermost in your thoughts. The silly unthinking author addresses great men in the stile of a servile dependent, whereas a real author, and a man of true genius, has upon all occasions a bold, disinterested and daring confidence in himself, and considers the common cant of adulation to the sons of fortune as the basest and most abominable of all prostitution" (pp. 92–93). Although Freneau feared that wealthy merchants would exercise increasing censorship over the arts, he never abandoned his conviction, based on the arguments of Witherspoon and the Common Sense philosophers, that the true genius and artist would overcome such resistance and find or create his own audience.

In the persona of Robert Slender, Freneau could also risk observations on the function of religion and the role of clergy in America. Slender seems to possess the kind of Christianity that the clergy claimed characterized too much of the religious thinking of the postwar period. In one essay, Slender explains that while reading a journal, he was about to skip over a letter to the editor that was addressed to the President because he assumed it would be over his head, but then he noticed it was written by a clergyman. He decided "it must be good, and it would be a sacrilege not to read it." Given his general suspicion of religion, it might seem contradictory that Slender would take an interest in the letter of a clergyman; however, he claims that he still admired the clergy because his father had been such a devout Christian. "My father, who loved religion, not for *the name of it* but for its *life* and *power*, paid always the greatest respect to the clergy. They labour for the good of our souls, he would say, and are therefore worthy of double honour" (p. 402). Thus, Slender decided to read the long, difficult letter because it must be "a sermon" that would be spiritually uplifting. What Slender is shocked to discover, of course, is that the clergyman has nothing to say about God, morality, or the individual soul but only writes about politics—even worse, his opinions are conservative and Federalist. Slender cannot understand why men of God would engage in political affairs or why they would work in complicity with the wealthy and the powerful.

In the later *Letters* (1799), Freneau used Slender to make one of his most direct attacks on American clergy's complicity in the crimes and immorality of the newly rich and powerful. Of the corrupt leaders of business and politics Slender says to his neighbor, "Do you suppose they can be *Christians*, and yet strive to cheat and defraud? . . . Do they think religion a cheat, or a bug-bear only to frighten children?" (p. 401). When the neighbor responds that such men attend church but care nothing about the meaning of Christianity, Slender replies that the clergy must therefore excommunicate them. The neighbor stoically answers,

> "Do you know, said my neighbor, any wicked men who are rich? Yes, says I, there is X. Y. and Z. they are very rich and every body knows they are great rascals. Well, says my neighbor, are they excommunicated? No—I protest, said I, now when I think of it, the rev. Mr. W. dined with X. on __, and with Y. on __, and six or seven clergymen dined with Z. a few days ago. God preserve us, I said, where shall we look for help; in the *great* depravity is permitted, some kinds of wickedness counted laudable, and every species winked at." [p. 401]

Because there are many such stinging attacks upon the politics of the clergy and their misuse of influence, Freneau's readers too quickly concluded that he was an enemy of religion and the clergy in general. This oversimplification of

Freneau's religious attitudes misses the point of his criticism entirely. Although Freneau never returned to his early Calvinist faith, he agonized privately all his life over philosophical and theological issues, and he did believe that religion was essential to the moral order of a republican society. As Nelson F. Adkins has observed, "Even as Freneau grew older and the ceremonies of the church, . . . [may] have lost their power, a careless disregard of the devotional proprieties seems honestly to have shocked the man's religious sense."[20] For all his seeming anti-clericalism, Freneau had only praise for the honest, unambitious clergymen whom he felt played an essential part in American life. In "The Orator in the Woods," a poem "occasioned by hearing a very elegant discourse preached in a mean Building by the Parson of an obscure Parish," Freneau had praised the good parson whose humble work is like a "flower beneath the shade" (III, 42). In his essays, he actually tried to warn the ministers that the common people were only being driven farther away from the church and from the moral benefits of the "life and power" of true religion by those highly visible ministers with political and social pretensions.

After the limited success of the first volume of poems published in 1786 and his *Miscellaneous Works* of 1788, Freneau grew more desperate to reach the widest possible audience. During the 1790s he edited, co-edited, and contributed to several journals. In his many essays in these publications he tried variations on the characters of Slender and the wise man, using a modification of "the Pilgrim" called the "Philosopher in the Forest" and the "Hermit," who sends pieces from a cave to the *City Gazette*. The character of Hezekiah Salem, who appears in essays of the late 1790s, combines characteristics of Slender and the hermit-pilgrim in the figure of a good but outcast clergyman who sends brief sermons for publication in *The Time Piece* (1797). With each of these voices and in the several personae he created for his poems, Freneau was attempting strategies for capturing readers, but popularity kept eluding him.

The character of Tomo Cheeki represents Freneau's attempt to combine the voice and insights of the wise man in the forest with those of the native American observer under the guise of a noble-savage philosopher. Again, Freneau used a somewhat conventional fictional frame to create the illusion that Cheeki was genuine. Tomo Cheeki, whose name is later echoed as "Tommo" in Melville's *Typee*, was a Creek who had come to Philadelphia thirty years before with a group of thirty Indian chiefs and several squaws to settle a treaty with the republican government. While his fellow Indians were interested only in amusement, it was evident to all that Tomo had a philosophical temperament. After the departure of the party, the landlord of the cabin in which Cheeki had stayed discovered a large bundle of papers the Indian had left behind. These were eventually sold and recently translated by a white man who had been held prisoner by the Creeks for twenty years. Freneau has now come into possession of several pieces of Cheeki's works which include letters, essays of observations on the whites, reminiscences of the "savage way of life," and a dream vision.

Of the many observations of Tomo Cheeki, the most striking for its revelation of Freneau's insight into the changing nature of his society is his essay on "The Slavery of Whites to Many Wants." Sounding much like Thoreau in *Walden*, Tomo observes that the white men have become obsessed with material things and no longer know the meaning of true human happiness: "These white men have enslaved almost the whole of creation of living things, in order that they, in their turn, might become the slaves of all. They have multiplied wants 'till it is no longer possible to gratify them. They have persuaded each other that the mere luxuries of life are the absolute necessaries; and endless labour, pain, and watchfulness are the consequences. . . . If he have any happiness at all, it is centered in some one object only" (pp. 342–43).

Interestingly, Cheeki discerns that the passion for material things and the organization of society that serves that materialism has also affected the relationship between the sexes, making it less possible for men and women to stand on equal footing. In the natural state of the human species, barriers of ownership, property rights, and financial status do not stand in the way of spontaneous expressions of mutual interests and love. But in the white man's society one of the great sources of human pleasure and happiness has been distorted and denied by the system of economic gain.

> He is constantly encompassed with jails, laws, government, society. He has been taught to be in pain for the future; and the tormentors of this world have taken care that he shall not enjoy the present. . . . Love itself has been degraded by the confusion arising from these invasions of the benign Law of Nature.—How comes it that love, as things go here, is directed only by sordid interest; and why is a link in that chain of amity which is thought to extend throughout the universe, broken, by one half of the human species (and that by the most amiable and virtuous) being forbidden to declare their passion on equal terms with the object of their love? [pp. 343–44]

In looking for the source of these problems, Cheeki turns to the leaders of the community. This blind pursuit of material objects and the resulting social ills have led, he argues, to a failure of leadership which, in turn, is caused by the self-aggrandizement of those in power: Thus, he urges: "Let the head men begin with shewing the simplest people that they may be satisfied with three or four enjoyments, and the people will soon follow in their path. It is the example of the great chiefs and big men that must govern the conduct of the laborious people to make them happy" (p. 344).

The character of Tomo Cheeki allowed Freneau to be more scathing in his attacks upon the evils of the society because there was no need for the pretense of aged benevolence that characterized the hermit-pilgrim figure. Similarly, he did not need to maintain the pose of naïveté and somewhat humorous simplicity of Slender. The voice of Tomo Cheeki, of stern and intelligent observation, comes closest to Freneau's own, but the mask of the insightful Indian was also a vehicle for expressing Freneau's private hope for a return to a pastoral golden age of human harmony. Although he touched upon this theme in several of his poems, the figure of Cheeki provided a way for Freneau to be explicit about his personal hope for the future and his fears that America might trade the dream for dollars.[21]

In "The Return of the Golden Age" the wise Cheeki recounts a conversation he once had with an optimistic philosopher. The Indian observes that the expectation of the coming of a new order is widely held among the white men: "I find it is a common opinion among the white men of this village of many wigwams, that a time will arrive, when a general change is to take place in the constitution of this world; when things will be brought back to their natural order, and merit and virtue will be avenged, that are not debased by the injury of fortune, the fickle being that seems to direct the destinies of men" (p. 345). After recounting the observations of the philosopher that support the expectation of a new age, including the notion that Nature herself had been out of joint but is "again visibly returned into the right way," Cheeki presents his own jeremiad on how far the present age is from the ideal:

> I see nothing but misery among these white men. Their
> race seems born to be unhappy. Cruel cares are from day
> to day preying upon them. Perpetual jealousies of all
> around them, and a suspicious eye cast upon futurity,
> damp all the pleasures, and embitter the most joyous

bowl. I see them enslaved and enslaving. . . . I see jails, gallowses and jibbets. I see these same white people trampling upon the dignity of their species by hanging up in the air men like themselves, who from the nature of their crimes ought to be confined as mad men. . . . Assuredly, their age of shepherds is yet very far off! [p. 346]

The more explicit Freneau became in his criticism of the ills of society, the thicker was the mask of his persona, the more fictional his prose essays became, and the more contrived are the frame devices. When he wanted to discuss political issues directly or to answer the criticism or charges of his enemies, he did not hesitate to speak in his own voice and to pour out his wrath in fiery rhetoric. But when he wanted to enlighten the people about their misguided materialism, their lack of reflection, their philosophical ignorance, or their religious and spiritual impoverishment, he turned to fictional speakers, and his essays become more like works of fiction.

Nearly all critics of Freneau's poetry have recognized that there are three marked phases in his poetic development: the philosophical pre-Romantic poems of the early 1770s seem quite distinct from the social satires, sea lyrics, and topical poems of the late 1770s and the 1780s, while his work after 1790 is often characterized as less symbolic, more prosaic, comical, and sometimes trivial. Lewis Leary's estimate of Freneau's "literary failure" is founded upon the view, held by others as well, that Freneau died as a poet if not after 1779, then certainly after 1790. The disease to which his death is usually attributed is a political ambition that caused him to waste his talent in the service of Jefferson as well as of himself. Once we recognize, however, his conscious and persistent efforts throughout the 1780s and 1790s to create effective voices of authority in his prose essays, the many changes that occur in his poetic techniques as well as the revisions in subsequent versions of early poems make more sense, even if they are no more pleasing to modern taste. While Freneau struggled in the prose essay to find appropriate speakers for addressing the moral and social evils of the republic, he also experimented in the poems with new ways of speaking on different levels at once, so as to appeal to a wide range of readers. Freneau's most interesting and ambiguous poems are those he produced during the 1780s as he tried to mediate between his private poetic impulses and the social and moral needs of his readers.[22]

It would probably be a good wager to say that there is no other American poet who wrote so many poems complaining about the problem of being a poet and declaring that he would never write again. Freneau often composed such poems when he was closing down a journal, embarking on one of his voyages of retreat, or simply contemplating escape. Critics are inclined to read these poems, such as "The Departure" or "To Sylvius on the Folly of Writing Poetry," as sincere expressions of Freneau's intention to abandon his poetic calling. Thus, the fact that he always returned to take up the pen again only seems to confirm the image of Freneau the temperamental Romantic whose inconsistency was one cause of his failure. But we might ask: If he really intended to write nothing more, why did he bother to write poems saying so? The answer is that even with these poems Freneau was experimenting, was actually adopting a familiar ritual of recommitment. Imitating the old Puritan form of church covenant renewal, he used these mini-jeremiads to define the ambivalent relationship he perceived between writers and readers in America, and he provided a formula for expressing discouragement while assuring the continuation of the poetic dialogue. Like the blasts of Puritan ministers on the ingratitude of their congregations with warnings of abandonment by both God and the clergy, Freneau's poems of poetic frustration and threatened departure were part of a continual rhetorical, one-sided debate with his imagined audience.[23]

For example, in one of his most famous poems of this type, "To an Author," Freneau complains that he lives in a land "where rigid Reason reigns alone,/Where lovely Fancy has no sway," where his efforts to court readers must be futile, for "An age employed in edging steel/Can no poetic raptures feel." Yet he does not end the poem with the intention to quit writing, but with a resolution to continue to attack folly and to turn to satire as the most effective form of verse. Similarly, in "Lines Written at Port-Royal, in the Island of Jamaica," Freneau expresses the need to escape from society for a time, but he does not profess to abandon his poetic calling. Instead, he vows that he will use the adventure as a source for future verse: "Why sail'd I here to swell my future page!" Just as his poem "To Misfortune" argues that hardship is necessary in acquiring strength of character, his poems on the poetic calling are resolved in a reassertion of duty. In these poems the particular conflict of the artist also becomes a symbol for the life struggle of every individual and, on another level, for the general condition of man.

In his earlier poems Freneau had let his imagination roam, and the visions he imparted were of death without salvation —obliteration in an empty universe where religion had failed to create myths of consolation. His fancy had also led him to a vision of a prosperous and populated American continent where the self-interest and greed of the people would lead to self-destruction. After his philosophical and artistic wanderings of the 1770s, he tried in the poetry of the 1780s to express some of the truths of life and death he believed he had discovered. At the same time, he knew his countrymen well enough to recognize that most of them did not want to face or even consider what he had to say. He understood the fundamental conflict in his society between the impulse toward daring in ideas, art, politics and the impulse toward restraint, security, withdrawal, peace, and comfort. It was his hope to keep the spirit of adventure alive. His faith in the ultimate goodness of human beings led him to the hope that with poets to lead the people to a better moral and aesthetic life and with leaders convinced that their own best interests lay in sharing wealth and power with the people, humanity and America might be saved. There were many times when such hope seemed a delusion, but, as with his decision in "The House of Night" to bury the fear of death through an act of the imagination, Freneau was convinced that only by retaining hope could mankind advance.

Freneau knew that few readers were prepared to grasp the truth that lay behind the rhetoric of the American Christian mission, of the fancy dress of politicians and merchants, of easy false art and fast money. He believed the most destructive element in his society was the spiritual emptiness that he saw in the heart of his fellow citizens, yet to have told people directly that they were shallow fools would only have incurred their wrath and hardened them against reflection and truth. Thus, in the 1780s Freneau crafted a series of remarkable poems in which he repeatedly created dramatic situations through which the reader might be led to wisdom and to consider alternatives for action and thought. Freneau no longer let his own personal doubts intrude upon his poems, and the more he revised them, the less he was present in them. They are heuristic lyrics, designed to convey ideas subtly only to those prepared to grasp their meaning. The detachment of Freneau himself from his characters and speakers is crucial to his strategy as a social poet. Such poems as "The Lost Adventurer," "Stanzas Written at the Foot of Monte Souffriere," and "The Hurricane," involve complex symbolic treatments of many of his most urgent themes such as the poet's role in society and the present condition of the/ American nation.

In "The Lost Sailor" (also titled "The Argonaut," or "The Lost Adventurer") the speaker describes a sailor he once met on a paradisical Caribbean isle. The sailor, named Ralph, had explained how he had come to leave his wife and home to become a sailor, why he had then left the sea to inhabit the isle, and why he was about to return to the perils and hardship of sailing. As the poem ends, the speaker recalls the day he watched Ralph's "black ship" fade from sight and implies that the journey may have been Ralph's last. "Though long I walked the margin of the main,/And long have looked and still must look in vain!"

The situation of Ralph, the lost sailor, before he first sailed the sea, may be compared to that of any individual who is fundamentally satisfied with things as they are. But as a young man might be encouraged by a teacher to become a poet, or a people inspired by their leaders to become a free people, Ralph was enticed by the voice of a captain and the colorful sails of a ship to seek the pleasure and rewards of bold adventure. So he leaped at the opportunity to leave his Amoranda at her spinning wheel and the "shallow stream" of his "one poor valley" in order to mingle "my labors with her [his ship's] hardy band" and "To guide the foaming prow/As far as winds can waft." But as all men mature and have second thoughts about their youthful choices, so did the sailor suffer a crisis of faith, and he jumped ship to live in pastoral retreat on the green sweet isle where the speaker found him. The sailor had lost faith in the ship and his crew and had chosen the life of the land again, but in a "monkey clime where limes and lemons grow."

The focus of the poem is upon the central moral choice of the sailor. Having learned the risks of the sea, he realizes that human life cannot be spent trying to escape from danger in the safe valley of his former home or of his southern retreat. Thus, the sailor decides to return to the sea, now strengthened by mature "Fortitude" and guided by wisdom born of experience and reflection. The courage of his choice to return to the "wintry worlds" where he must "face the cold glance of the northern bear" (presumably not his patient Amoranda), which symbolizes the trials of human survival, is underscored by the new awareness he possesses of a personal philosophy of life's ultimate meaning and purpose: "Tis folly all," he says, both unpredictable and perhaps pointless, and he will not expect others to mourn for him if he becomes one of those "who sink in storms, and mingles with the deep." Even though he fears the outcome of his voyage, he has come to accept that the impulse that led him to the sea in the first place is the guiding force of his life and must be followed. As the poem concludes, Ralph advises the speaker to remain in the "happy shades, be happy there" while he departs to his uncertain fate.

"The Lost Sailor" is clearly a symbolic poem, which speaks of more than the career of sailing. Ralph's lament that "the sister of the harp" will not complain if he is lost suggests a symbolic dimension of his activity that relates his experience to the arts and literature. When Ralph leaves the domestic safety of his valley, he also rejects the social and moral complacency symbolized by the "charming shade" of the "woody wild." In his quest he abandons his pastoral myths of the countryside as the world of "Damon's cottage" or "Palemon's fields," as well as his image of the sea as "Neptune['s]" garden. His search for a new personal philosophy suggests both a personal spiritual development and the political progress of a people. Freneau had used the image of the ship and crew as a northern society earlier in "The Beauties of Santa Cruz" as a symbol of the whole generation of the American Revolution. Echoes of Milton's "Lycidas" also evoke a world of revolutionary actions and dangers where personal choices

about art and one's social role have to be made under the
pressure of social and religious imperatives. Thus, Ralph
becomes a type of the new man joining with others on an
uncertain voyage into unexplored realms of promise and
peril.

On the surface of this poem, Freneau gives his readers a
somewhat comic tale of innocence and experience, but the
central paradigm of the sailor and the ship at sea call up
other meanings which involve himself as a poet and his
readers as crew members in a social experiment. While no
one of them "can truly tell what storms disturb the bosom
of that man/What ravenous fish in those dark climates dwell
that feast on men," the crew cannot turn back from the
course on which they have embarked, nor can they remain
forever in a state of political stasis. For a poet or a society
jumping ship for the safety of a sweet isle is an illusion,
which leads ultimately to death without the invigoration and
satisfaction of adventure. A return to the opening stanza
reminds the reader that until his decision to return to the
sea, Ralph was "a slave of fortune," but at the end of the
poem, though his fate is uncertain, he has set a course for a
destiny of discovery that has freed him "from the magic of
the enchanting shore." The irony of the speaker's worry that
Ralph may now be a "lost sailor" is that the sailor was truly
lost to himself until the self-discovery preceding his latest
voyage.

In the poems of the 1780s that treat religious or philosophical themes, Freneau usually spoke in two voices and
on two levels. There are many signs that by the early years
of the decade Freneau had abandoned Christian answers for
his own philosophical questions. The myths of a life after
death and of paradise seemed especially ridiculous to him,
and he was already leaning toward a concept of a transcen-
dental oversoul, or eternal spirit, of mankind in which the
life of each individual participates. But he also knew the

common people were not yet ready to give up the Christian myths of death and rebirth or the eschatology of a national-Christian mission. Often, therefore, the same poem that mocks Christian expectations for the future and other easy solutions to philosophical questions will, on a deeper level, seriously address matters of truth, eternity, immortality, or national significance. But, like the speaker of Robert Frost's "Mending Wall," Freneau did not want to tell his neighbor the truth as he saw it but wanted to let his neighbor discover the truth for himself.

"Stanzas Written at the Foot of Monte Souffriere" (II, 314) appears at first to be simply a description of a western isle in the manner of a travel narrative. The speaker explains in the first stanza that the islands of the West Indies had hardly been discovered and their beauties conveyed to the world before they were spoiled by tyranny. He laments the introduction of slavery, the loss of liberty, and the stark contrast that now exists between the natural beauty of the landscape and the painful frowns of suffering people. The only comfort the people have are the dreams of heaven and of a beautiful land without slavery and tyranny. The more they suffer, the more they withdraw mentally into fantasies of future joy. In case readers might overlook the social implications of this symbolism for America, Freneau makes them clear: Should greedy tyrants gain control in the United States, the citizens will be lost in dreams like the Caribbean slaves; but if America remains true to its ideals, it will lead the slaves of the world out of bondage. In the last two stanzas the speaker observes that if these Caribbean slaves knew about the freedom existing in America, they would take hope in the possibilities for the future of mankind in the real world rather than in the myths of "Elysian magic."

On one level, this poem appears to have a simple social meaning. It tells of misery and slavery in the islands in order to inspire Americans to continue to resist tyranny, for Americans are the hope of all oppressed people. The last stanza asserts that "freedom's sun" will ascend in America and enjoy a "long, unclouded circuit . . . Till little tyrants disappear;/ And a new race, not bought or sold,/Rise from the ashes of the old." However, because the poem focuses upon the function of the imagination among the island slaves, it also raises an important question about the social role of the artist.

In the opening stanza, the speaker says that "Art" was the means by which mankind learned about the glories of the islands. The artist has the power to re-create their beauty for those who have never experienced them, but in so doing the artist may also be partly responsible for luring future tyrants to those new worlds. At the end of the poem the speaker's exhortation of Americans recognizes other dimensions of the role of poetic artist—chronicler, messenger, and inspiring leader.

Yet, throughout the poem the speaker makes clear the potential harm that can result when artists, poets, or others inflame the imaginations of the people to their own detriment. In the Caribbean, priests have used religion to feed the slaves false illusions. While this spurious myth-making, superstition, and magic enables the oppressed to escape some of their pain in dreams of a peaceful afterlife, this misuse of the imagination is actually in opposition to the pursuit of truth by the real poet and artist. In America, too, false poet-prophets could encourage delusions in the people by creating images of past glories that mask the reality of present conditions and needs. For the speaker, the resolution of this conflict must finally depend upon the sincerity of the political and social purpose of art. Therefore, the motive of the poet and artist is all-important in determining the kind of poetry he will write and the effect his work will have for social good or ill.

By the mid-1780s Freneau had come to believe that all art is political. If a writer deludes his readers, he betrays the mission of the true artist. Where social ills are present and the need for reform urgent, the task of the artist is to expose those problems. The luxury of artistic escape and self-indulgent excursions into imagined beauties are only possible in a society that has fulfilled the goal of genuine social freedom. The honest writer must be engaged in battle against those who seek to exploit the people and must constantly strive to remove the ignorance that makes the people vulnerable to exploitation.

As a sea captain, Freneau frequently borrowed his metaphors from the sea and saw many parallels between the role of the sea captain and that of the poet. In both capacities he embraced the challenge of leading others from one safe harbor to another. He saw no opposition between land and sea, for the object of every sailor must ultimately be to return to land. Instead, Freneau liked to depict the conflict between man and the sea, which threatens to swamp man at every moment either because he ignores its natural power or because he lapses into dreamy or suicidal reverie, like Ishmael on the mast or O'Neill's Edmund on the crow's nest. In pursuit of truth and art, the poet always runs the risk of forgetting his personal mission and social obligations to the other members of the crew. For all of his belief in political freedom and liberation from organized religion, Freneau recognized that personal and cultural self-destruction could result from venturing too far from the course of social and religious order.

Some of these themes are central to the meaning of "The Hurricane" (II, 250–51), which recounts Freneau's experience of a hurricane at sea in July 1784, in which he nearly lost his ship. In many ways, the poem is similar to Stephen Crane's famous short story of the next century, "The Open Boat." There are contrasts between the "happy man safe onshore," the animals safe in their caves and hollow trees, and the "wretched we" in "our feeble barque" who must endure the "tempests roar." The sun descends to leave the vessel wandering on the "dark abyss" for an entire night with no shore or star to guide the crew to safety, "no voice of friendship for comfort in this dreadful hour." But as in many of Freneau's poems of the 1780s, there is more here than a simple adventure. As the ship "gropes her trackless way," the speaker sees "mountains burst on either side" and concludes in the closing lines: "Thus, skill and science both must fall;/And ruin is the lot of all."

This sudden introduction of the surreal elements of the bursting mountains suggests other possible meanings for the ship, the sea, and the near tragic situation of the crew, and the language of the earlier stanzas provides additional hints of symbolic meaning. The speaker mentions the "Pilot" and "Columbus" in the fourth stanza, which add a religious and a political dimension: "What Pilot shall explore that realm,/What new Columbus take the helm." The use of "pilots," with a lower-case "p," in the last stanza reinforces the implication that Christ is the Pilot of stanza four. The mention of Columbus points to the launching of the American ship of state. Thus, the speaker's barque becomes a symbol of the perilous state of man sailing the "dark abyss" of life without Christianity and of an American society adrift without the reliable guidance of a Columbus. These political dimensions are reinforced by the image of the weak "pilots," who have futilely tried to guide the ship, which is now lost in her "trackless way" and at the mercy of the elements: "The barque, accustomed to obey,/No more the trembling pilots guide."

In this context, the final statement that science and skill have failed to save the ship so "ruin is the lot of all" has important social and philosophical implications: good leadership and knowledge are needed to hold the ship on her course against the tempests of the human condition. The bursting mountains, perhaps of political factions and parties, threaten to destroy the ship from either side. In this context too, the "happy man who is safe on shore," who sits by his fire and is "unmoved" when "he hears the tempests roar," takes on a new meaning as well, for socially he is the complacent individual who dreams of joining the animals in their caves and shares their unconscious faith that in their hollows they are protected from the storm. But the man safe in his home is only deluding himself if he thinks that "death and darkness [which] both surround" only threaten the ship at sea for, the "tempests which rage with lawless power" have social and political analogues on land. Thus, what seems at first an occasional poem with a somewhat overstated ending about the ruin of all, is upon closer examination a social and philosophical work through which Freneau is again trying to awaken the sleepers.

As social conditions in America seemed to worsen, Freneau became more tempted to write works of explicit social criticism. Poems of the 1780s, such as "The Projectors" and "Picture of the Times," indicate the direction toward more explicit satire that his writing would take in the 1790s. In these transitional works, however, he was still inclined to probe deep issues more directly. "Picture of the Times" appears to be a straightforward criticism of the rampant greed and ambition that threaten to ruin the republic. In the first six stanzas the poem develops as might be expected. The first stanza laments the continuation of war and seeks a cause for such events in the world: "Can scenes like these delight the human breast?" Passion prolongs the scenes of war while "slighted Reason says, they must be wrong." In seeking to understand the present condition of man, the speaker looks back upon a golden age ruled by the "patriarch sage" when there was no ambition and, therefore, none of the evils of slavery, murder, greed, and war. In contrast, in the present age, of which "George the tyrant" is typical, men are tormented by a "demon, hostile to human kind" which has "planted fierce disorders in the mind." Although the common pursuit of all should be happiness, the demon has deluded men into thinking that war will lead to peace and prosperity, and thereby to true happiness. Freneau sees, however, that such hopes are often false and are created by the few who expect to gain from the war, which only brings suffering and loss to the many.

In the last two stanzas the speaker carries forward the pattern of contrasts by addressing personifications of the brute "Ambition" and the desired "Happiness." At this point, however, the poem opens more philosophical questions: How do people perceive reality? What is the function of imagination in life? What are the causes of widespread moral decay? The poem argues that these ideas are closely related to the current social conditions in America. Because ambition has led people to mistake happiness for "extent of power," they have been left in a liminal state between reality where reason should reign and a fantasy world of ever-retreating objects of desire. Like Fitzgerald's Jay Gatsby pursuing his orgiastic dream of Daisy symbolized by a distant green dock light, Americans are yearning for vaguely defined goals of freedom, success, and achievement, which were created by the imaginations of men to motivate them to fight and rebel but now threaten to drive them to "fierce disorders in the mind." Pursuing what they think is happiness, Americans, "in a circle, chase thy shadow round"; but true happiness—the peace for which the poet longs—"which yet possessing, we no more possess" eludes them. He concludes that the cause is a failure of moral vision which may lead to self-destructive tragedy.

> Thus far remov'd and painted on the eye
> Smooth verdant fields seem blended with the sky,

But where they both in fancied contact join
In vain we trace the visionary line;
Still as we chase, the empty circle flies,
Emerge new mountains or new oceans rise.

[II, 165]

Of course, Freneau was aware that he too was using the power of fancy to create an image of Americans. In this instance he chose to depict them as a nation of people blinding themselves to reality by subordinating their reason to delusions of their imaginations. When controlled by the demon of "Ambition," the fancy may become like Circe, who paints pictures on the eye to lure people to their death as they seek what they think is happiness. As a serious moral poet with the insight to perceive truth and the skill to depict it, Freneau had the task of dispelling these destructive dreams with his equally powerful images of genuine happiness.

Freneau's early poetry was psychologically immediate but socially isolated, to borrow Clifford Geertz's two very useful and pertinent terms.[24] It had to be for a young man working out his own perceptions of life close to the surface of his poetry. After he had reconciled most of his theological and philosophical doubts, he tried to write the kind of poetry that would enlighten his readers intellectually and heighten their level of aesthetic appreciation. But few of Freneau's readers were willing or able to give his works the close scrutiny they required. He soon learned that artistic complexity was at odds with what he felt to be social necessity, and he chose to sacrifice art and the artist in himself to the service of his republic.

On March 15, 1790, Freneau published in the *Daily Advertiser* a short poem celebrating the 1789 publication of the first collection of poems of the English satirist and humorist Dr. John Walcott, whose pen name was "Peter Pindar." As Frederick Lewis Pattee has noted, Walcott's "influence upon the poetry of Freneau was considerable."[25] A few lines from Freneau's "Epistle" explain Pindar's appeal for the frustrated American poet:

> Peter, methinks you are the happiest wight
> That ever dealt in ink, or sharpen'd quill.
> . . .
> How happy you, whom fortune has decreed
> Each character to hit—where all will read.
>
> [III, 28]

The poem concludes that there is a need for an American Pindar, and though Freneau offers his American material to Walcott, he clearly has his own literary future in mind:

> But, Peter quit your dukes and little lords,
> Young princes full of blood and scant of brains—
> Our rebel coast some similes affords,
> And many a subject for your pen contains
> Preserved as fuel for your comic rhymes,
> (Like Egypt's gods) to give to future times.
>
> [III, 28]

From this point on in his career, Freneau began to write his satires in a style much closer to the plain and direct verse of Walcott. But history proved him wrong. He neither attained the kind of popularity that Walcott enjoyed nor did he witness much social or moral improvement resulting from his work. He also nearly forfeited his critical reputation down to the present day.

After a decade of feverish publication and public involvement, Freneau withdrew again in 1801, when Jefferson was elected President. He retired to his farm and returned occasionally to the sea. During his last thirty years, he worked on his poems, wrote essays attacking the greed and selfishness of corrupt politicians, and sold pieces of his lands to produce a small income. He discovered that he had given his best years of literary productivity to his country, for it had been in the few stolen moments of the hectic 1780s that he had found the inspiration for his best poems.

Perhaps the poem that best expresses Freneau's situation as a self-sacrificing American poet is the curious "Hermit of Saba." Although probably written earlier, the poem was published in 1788, when Freneau was contemplating a new literary bent, before his exposure to the poems of Pindar. The speaker is another hermit-pilgrim—a wise and generous-minded man who has escaped the world of "avarice" and "ambition" and lives in harmony with "Nature planted" enjoying "heaven-born contemplation!" One day three mariners are shipwrecked on the rocks of his island. As though he has some premonition of his fate, the word he utters when he first spots them on the rocks is "Perdition!" Still, he shares his food with them and offers his cave for shelter. Whether a country printer, an orator in the woods, a good country parson, an observant Indian, or a pilgrim-philosopher, the figure of the hermit in Freneau is usually a symbol for the poet. The hermit of Saba is especially interesting.

In response to the mariners' questions about his life, the hermit tries to explain that he can "find the bliss more pure" alone in nature than those who live in "civilized domains." He attempts to explain the "riches" of simple living. Of course, the sailors are incapable of understanding his truths, and with the aim of stealing his riches, which they assume to be treasures of gold, they kill him and throw his body off a cliff to the rocks from which he had saved them. As the poem closes, one of the mariners returns from the hermit's cave where he has learned the truth of the hermit's situation.

> Deep have I fathomed in his cave, but find
> No glimpse of gold—we surely did mistake him:
> His treasures were not of that glittering kind.
>
> [II, 368]

And repeating the word the hermit had uttered earlier, the sailor expresses his new understanding of himself and his fellows, which the hermit's death has taught him:

> While here we stay thy shadow will torment us,
> . . .
> Crying—Perdition on these fiends from Europe,
> Whose bloody malice, or whose thirst for gold,
> Fresh from the slaughter-house of innocence
> Unpeoples isles, and lays the world in ruin!
>
> [II, 368]

Significantly, however, the hermit, perhaps like the poet in a new republic, had to give his life in order to convey this truth.

As critics have lamented, Freneau might have become America's first Romantic poet and truly earned the title "father of American literature" if he had followed the literary impulses of his youth. To do so, however, he would have had to have been a very different person in temperament, in training, and in his social and religious assumptions. From his earliest experiences in his proud but struggling family through his impressionable years under the guidance of Tennent and Witherspoon to his exposure to war, slavery, and the injustices of postwar America, Freneau was constantly made aware that he had to choose between escape into the self or engagement with the world. Though he may have preferred the peace of isolation on his farm in Monmouth, New Jersey, and might have written more poems that would please modern readers, Freneau's commitment to minister to the needs of his own generation was too strong.

Philosophically, Freneau saw the life of an individual to be like the duration of the flower, as described in his famous poem, "The Wild Honey Suckle." While this poem can be read as a romantic celebration of the beauty of nature, which blossoms apart from the crush of human hands and feet, a deeper understanding of Freneau's sense of the moral duty of the poet casts new light upon this work. Another way of reading it is to see that the speaker recognizes the blossoming and death of the isolated flower "in this silent, dull retreat" to be a cruel waste of nature's beauty. It would have been better had the flower been exposed to people who might enjoy it, even at the risk of its being damaged, than for it to reside in the "guardian shade" "smit with those charms that must decay." For death is always certain, and "unpitying frost, and Autumn's power/Shall leave no vestige of this flower." Thus, what is gained for the world by a flower, or a poet or a person, that possesses remarkable beauty that is not shared by others? The answer in the poem, and in Freneau's poetic philosophy, is nothing.

> From morning suns and evening dews
> At first thy little being came:
> If nothing once, you nothing lose,
> For when you die you are the same;
> > The space between, is but an hour,
> > The frail duration of a flower.
> > > [II, 307]

V

HUGH HENRY BRACKENRIDGE: THE REGENERATIVE POWER OF AMERICAN HUMOR

Failing to fetch me at first keep encouraged,
Missing me one place search another,
I stop somewhere waiting for you.
WALT WHITMAN
"Song of Myself," 1855

In his various careers as preacher, poet, magazine editor, lawyer, judge, and novelist, Hugh Henry Brackenridge adjusted quickly and completely to the world of postwar America, forging a unique identity for himself as an eccentric writer-teacher-judge. More than any other member of his generation, Brackenridge established a public role for the democratic writer that enabled him to have an important impact upon his times and that has been a model for others such as Whitman, Twain, Hemingway, and Mailer.[1]

A master of public self-presentation, Brackenridge created the stereotype of the frontier judge by wearing smallclothes in the courtroom and sputtering wise and reasoned judgments interlaced with jokes and social criticism. His success and notoriety indicate how well in touch he was with the direction of American society. When he wanted to preach to the citizens on some folly such as dueling, he did not approach the pulpit as he had learned to do at Princeton; he cooked up a humorous piece of fiction for the local paper. When he wanted to write a lasting work of literature that might educate thousands, he did not reach for his Homer and his Bible and compose an epic as his fellow university graduates were doing. He turned his ear to the language of the

people and produced a serialized fiction in the tradition of
Franklin and Fielding. To show that he did not give a feather
for the carping critics, he included a mock preface in which
he claimed to write only for the purpose of refining the
English language and style—thereby engaging in a literary
spoof that anticipated such comic masters as Twain, James,
Mencken, and Nabokov.[2]

A true original in every way, Brackenridge began to surprise people when he was fifteen years old and applied to be
a schoolteacher in Gunpowder Falls, Maryland. The son of
Scottish emigrants who spent his boyhood behind a plough
in the rough barrens of York County, Pennsylvania, Brackenridge would not have had an opportunity to acquire knowledge of the Latin, Greek, and the classics, but in his interview "the trustees were not less surprised at the application
than by the qualification of the applicant." Perhaps even
more shocked were his first students when the young teacher
demonstrated his method for quieting an unruly bully: he
took "a brand from the fire, knocked the rebel down, and
spread terror around him." Brackenridge learned early how
to awaken an audience and give his ideas of social order
added force.[3]

The twenty-year-old Scotsman also captured the attention
of his classmates at Princeton when after a special admissions
decision he entered the class of 1768. As his quick and lasting
friends James Madison and Philip Freneau soon recognized,
this farmer's son possessed impressive classical learning,
oratorical skills, and a ready wit. His passion for knowledge
and for moral and public improvement would lead him to
a varied career in public service and letters. Before he was
through, he would be elected to Congress, appointed to the
bench of the Pennsylvania Supreme Court, and established
as a prominent American novelist. Perhaps most remarkable
of all, his novel was even popular during his lifetime.

An avid Whig at Princeton and later a Jeffersonian Democrat, Brackenridge joined Freneau, Madison, and others in forming the American Whig Society. These activities led Freneau and Brackenridge to collaborate on *Father Bombo's Pilgrimage to Mecca*, a satire on American manners that may be the first work of prose fiction written in America.[4] They also combined their talents in composing a patriotic poem of epic design, *The Rising Glory of America*, which Brackenridge read at the 1771 commencement. After graduation Brackenridge completed his training for the ministry and taught and served as headmaster of a Maryland academy until the Revolutionary War when he signed on as an army chaplain and preached fiery patriotic sermons to the soldiers. Hoping for a wider sphere of influence after the war, he moved to Philadelphia in 1778 to start *The United States Magazine*. The ideals, dreams, and glowing enthusiasm that Brackenridge expressed in his statement of purpose for the magazine may have been dampened by later disappointments, but he never really lost faith in the beliefs he set forth:

> We regard it as our great happiness in these United States, that the path to office and preferment, lies open to every individual. The mechanic of the city, or the husbandman who ploughs his farm by the river's bank, has it in his power to become, one day, the first magistrate of his respective commonwealth, or to fill a seat in the Continental Congress. This happy circumstance lays an obligation upon every individual to exert a double industry to qualify himself for the great trust which may, one day, be reposed in him. It becomes him to obtain some knowledge of the history and principles of government, or at least to understand the policy and commerce of his own country. Now it may not be the lot of every individual to be able to obtain this knowledge from the first source, that is from the best writers, or the conversation of men of reading and experience. In the one case it would require a larger library than most of us are able to procure, and in the other a greater opportunity

of travelling than is consistent with our daily occupations.

The want of these advantages must therefore be supplied by some publication that will in itself contain a library, and be the literary coffee-house of public conversation. A work of this nature is *The United States Magazine*.[5]

Unfortunately, the journal survived only from January to December 1779, when lagging subscriptions convinced Brackenridge to change his profession and location. Discouraged by the cultural provincialism he saw in Philadelphia, he decided to go west, where he might still have an impact upon his countrymen. In the early 1780s he took a law degree and moved to the tiny village of Pittsburgh, where he later reflected that his aim in "offering myself to the place" was "to advance the country and thereby myself."[6]

Soon he became a distinguished citizen of Pittsburgh, founder of the first western newspaper, the *Pittsburgh Gazette*. In 1786 he was elected to the state assembly, where he fought for the adoption of the federal Constitution and obtained endowments for the establishment of the Pittsburgh Academy, which became the University of Pittsburgh. Outspoken and uncompromising, he lost a bid for election to the Constitutional Convention in 1787 because he followed his conscience and opposed popular sentiment in supporting federal controls; he also nearly lost his life when he attempted to mediate the Whiskey Rebellion.[7]

During his years as a judge (1799–1814), Brackenridge continued his untiring efforts to instruct the people. In addition to a steady flow of satires, narratives, and sermons, he devoted himself to his masterwork, *Modern Chivalry*, a long comic narrative modeled on *Don Quixote* and *Tom Jones*. Written, he said, as an entertaining lecture on morals and society for "Tom, Dick, and Harry in the woods,"[8] the novel exposes the folly of a people whose ignorance and greed cause them to elect corrupt and hypocritical leaders. Through this work, published in several volumes between 1792 and 1815, Brackenridge finally achieved his goal of reaching a large portion of the people with his moral precepts. His novel was called "a textbook for all classes of society," and it was reported that his name "became a household word for half a century."[9]

Although he gave up formal practice of the ministry after leaving the army, Brackenridge remained a thoroughgoing preacher throughout his career. A practical yet sensitive and artistic man, he had learned from personal experience that it was possible for a person of humble birth to rise through study and learning to a place of respect and influence in America. Thus, he was convinced that America could become a nation of learned and moral people as long as everyone was afforded the chance to achieve his potential without being duped and exploited by those who sought to profit from the ignorance and weaknesses of others. For this reason, all of his works are sermons upon the doctrine of republican genius.

Better than any of his contemporaries, Brackenridge mastered the technique of telling people what they ought to do without seeming to care whether or not they listened. The sense of detachment of the narrator of *Modern Chivalry* is the key to the success of that work. What makes his instruction engaging is that his tone is neither strident nor condescending. Brackenridge succeeded in creating this mask of the nonchalant and ultimately detached comic observer because he expected neither fame nor wealth from his writing. Since he was not economically dependent upon his audience, his writings have an integrity that gives them a tone of true moral conviction and authority. Although he was not overtly religious, in all of Brackenridge's work there is a faith that there is something larger than the individual, the local community or even the nation itself.[10]

To say that Brackenridge himself really felt detached from

the political and social conflicts of his society, however, is
to mistake the persona for the man. In moving to the frontier,
he was not seeking a "neutral territory" or acting the isolate;
quite the opposite, he was so deeply involved in the affairs of
the day that his fervor sometimes crept into his writing and
threatened to shatter the fragile veneer of his stoicism and
the artistic unity of his work. Early in his writing career he
developed a rhetorical posture of philosophical detachment
that he used to present controversial issues with the seeming
objectivity of a magistrate. In many instances this posture
was necessary to protect him from charges of libel and sedition and from the public rejection that would have rendered
his writing ineffective.

Sometimes Brackenridge was inclined to employ a comic
aloofness in real life, as when he faced armed rebels in the
famous episode of the Pennsylvania insurrection. As federal
troops advanced toward Philadelphia and insurgents pressed
inside the gates to meet them, Brackenridge was the only
mediator who understood the positions of both sides. His
subtle, understated humor and seeming detachment saved
the day and perhaps hundreds of lives. An insurgent yelled
a question above the mob: Would a battle result in a great
loss of life? Brackenridge snapped: "Not at all; not above a
thousand killed and five hundred mortally wounded." With
that he began entertaining the rebels with stories and told
them of the whiskey and women awaiting them if they put
down their guns and postponed the revolution. He later
recalled, "It cost me four barrels of whiskey, that day, and
I would rather spend that than a single quart of blood."[11]
Brackenridge's comic rhetoric masked his deep commitment
to republican ideas and proved a useful tool for teaching his
fellows the value of reason and the rule of law.

Hugh Henry Brackenridge was a brilliant writer with
acute social insight. At a time when other learned men were
perplexed, he perceived his nation with remarkable clarity:

he saw that the changing social conditions after the Revolution and the new mixture of habits, heritages, and languages furnished a breeding ground for money-grabbing land-buyers and ignorant yet conniving politicians. He recognized the danger of the growing indifference toward religion and morality and took upon himself the task of trying to counteract the greed, lust, and violence in the city and on the frontier. Like the other writers and intellectuals he was frustrated by conditions in which literature and art were ignored, but he had the genius to see that in America the most fitting and most effective response of all was laughter. One hundred and thirty years later, in her work *American Humor*, Constance Rourke explained what Hugh Henry Brackenridge had already known about his country: that the cement which kept this fragmenting society from coming apart was a comic spirit born of the same diversity and competing interests in which Madison had placed his faith in *The Federalist* #10.[12]

After writing sermons, "rising glory" poems, and essays and trying to find patrons and contributors for a serious literary journal, Brackenridge recognized the taste of the American readers and the proper form for reaching them. He finally turned his talent for bombast, masquerade, and satire to the creation of a rambling, comic narrative which, in its confusions, interruptions, and absurdities, symbolized the America Brackenridge knew. Brackenridge was the first of America's great comic novelists.

But before he embarked on his ambitious *Modern Chivalry*, Brackenridge explored the possibilities of fiction in his short romantic tale of personal searching, "The Cave of Vanhest."[13] This tale, perhaps America's first genuine short story, is a fascinating work that reveals Brackenridge's psychological state in 1779 and shows him experimenting with the techniques of fiction that he was to employ in his novel. The main character is a young man like Brackenridge who has experienced war and learned of politics and seems rather provincial, ambitious, and a bit smug. On a journey across New Jersey, he and his companion become lost and are given refuge by a wise man who lives with his family in retreat from society in a cave. Brackenridge's use of a first-person narrative allows the reader to watch the process of deflation the young man undergoes as he tests his assumptions about life and society in conversation with the learned hermit. The narrative strategy that allows for the exposure of the naïveté of youth is similar to that used later by Hawthorne in "My Kinsman, Major Molineux."

Although apparently left uncompleted, the tale does reach a proper conclusion and is quite interesting in its characterization, narrative method, and theme. When the narrator enters the world of the cave, he seems to enter a different realm of time and space, giving the tale a dreamlike quality suggestive of the narrator's inner search for a proper calling in life. The abrupt ending does not seem inappropriate as a proper conclusion, even though it leaves the narrator with a new perception of the absurdity of his past and present life but no idea of his future direction. The mystery and ambiguity is as effective as that at the end of Poe's "Cask of Amontillado" or Hawthorne's "Young Goodman Brown." It is possible that the story of the fantastic hermit and his beautiful daughters is all a dream.[14]

Within its basic contrast between the quiet seclusion of the cave and the chaotic clamor of the outside world, where the American Revolution is still raging, the story sets up a series of comparisons between the ideal and the actual. In the forest, the narrator and his companion find humanity, affection, and stability, best illustrated when the servant, Barnardus, injures his foot, and the members of the family all care for him. These people live in harmony with nature; they enjoy a variety and abundance of foods and have no need to compete with others. Even their speech is colored by the imagery of their natural surroundings and suggests the blending of nature and man.

But outside the cave the engines of war are destroying nature and people. As the narrator reports, cannonballs tear and burrow the fields and destroy the crops with the same devastation as when they rip off the heads of good men. Competition creates greed and ambition and causes young men to waste their talents and become lost in the pursuit of unsatisfying goals. The political paranoia of this world is also revealed through the narrator's suspicion about the Tory leanings of the hermit. At first he thinks the hermit to be a loyalist sympathizer evading capture. Then, when he tells the hermit of the Battle of Monmouth and sees his eyes glisten, the young man concludes he must be a Whig. Actually, the hermit is simply saddened to hear of man's continued inhumanity.

At the request of the lady of the cave, the narrator recounts the story of his life. Although he begins with pride and self-confidence, the constant questioning and reflection of the hermit causes him to begin to see his past blindness and errors. Of course, this technique allows the reader to recognize the narrator's weaknesses before he sees them himself. He explains that his father was "a worthy good man, who wishing to see me step along the quiet vale of life, as he had done, had entertained the thought of matching me with a farmer's daughter of the neighborhood in which he lived" (p. 91). But the youth "had heard of the Miss Muses, who were great beauties," and he courted three of these ladies in succession—Miss Theology, Miss Urany (Milton's poetic muse), and, presently, Miss Law. He confesses, however, that he has been unsuccessful and dissatisfied in his experience with each, and he begins to see that the motives which drove him—desires for fame and wealth—led him astray from the start.

As the fragment ends, the young man is coming to a realization that his life has been one of self-centered ambition, which has led him away from genuine human experience. As he looks at the beautiful daughters of the hermit in this setting of pastoral abundance, he contemplates a different future for himself: "But I begin to apprehend that the beauty of some persons not so far distant as the head of the gulf of California is in a confederacy to draw me away from her [Miss Law], and whereas I first set out with a warmth of affection for the young ladies of the hill [Brackenridge's foot- note cites Parnassus], I shall this day fall a victim to the young ladies of the cave" (p. 92).

It is not surprising that shortly after he published this narrative, Brackenridge made his radical choice to abandon his career in religion, literature, and law in Philadelphia for new life in a frontier village.[15] With scornful words for the narrow preoccupations of money and property of the city residents, he decided that he might have a better chance to enlighten and guide the less pretentious citizens in the West.

> There is one sort of people to whom the news of the suspension of this work will not be disagreeable; I mean those persons who are disaffected to the cause of America. These have been sorely pricked and buffeted with the sharp points of whiggism, . . . and will be ready to believe, that in the suspension of the work is accom- plished that prophesy of the Apocalypse, *And Satan shall be bound a thousand years.*
>
> There is yet another class of men that will be sensible of some happiness, now that the mouth of this publica- tion is in a fair way to be, at length, closed; I mean the people who inhabit the region of stupidity, and cannot bear to have the tranquillity of their repose disturbed by the villainous jargon of a book. Reading is to them the worst of all torments, and I remember very well that at the commencement of the work, it was their language, *Art thou come to torment us before the time.* We will now say to them, *Sleep on; and take your rest.*[16]

Brackenridge was persuaded that in the eastern cities the established, moneyed interests were already resistant to the development of a true democracy that would encourage literature aimed to educate the common people. He feared as well that the common people were already too dulled and complacent to recognize their own interests. The enemies of the arts would be the politics of the rich and the ignorance of the poor.

Yet Brackenridge had faith that cooperative spirit, paternal care, and freedom of mind, symbolized by the family in "The Cave of Vanhest," could still be possible in the western forests. Certainly, he found personal fulfillment there, in his marriage to a young woman who had attracted him by the way she could leap a corral fence and in his success as a community leader and popular writer.[17] Whenever he returned to the East on business, he was even more convinced that he had made the right decision. Although the subject of "The Cave of Vanhest" is a very personal one, the effective narrative technique and dramatic irony transform private experience into a metaphor for the identity crisis many of the members of Brackenridge's generation were experiencing. The tale presents a portrait of a young American man of letters in the making.

Although literary histories have always acknowledged the importance of Brackenridge's *Modern Chivalry* as one of the first successful works of American fiction, the novel has never received much critical acclaim, nor has it many readers today. There are a number of reasons for its fate. Literary critics have, from Brackenridge's time to our own, tended to admire fiction more imitative of the nineteenth-century social novel, in the manner of Jane Austen and George Eliot. The long neglect of Herman Melville, the disregard of James's American humor, the deafness to Emily Dickinson's social meanings, and the early disdain for Faulkner are a few examples of the mistreatment writers receive when they seem too

eccentric, iconoclastic, clever, or crude for tastes formed by
British standards. Brackenridge's rambling plot, rough-hewn
characters, use of dialect, and seeming lack of attention to
structure and style caused the cliques of writers and critics
in late-eighteenth-century New York and Boston to react with
embarrassed silence, and only in recent years has his work
begun to be reexamined.[18]

As in all picaresque novels, the basic plot of *Modern Chivalry* is quite simple. Captain Farrago has decided to travel
around the country to learn about the habits and ideas of
the citizens, accompanied by his servant, Teague O'Regan, an
Irish immigrant referred to as a "bogtrotter." Social satire
springs from the interactions of the pair with local characters, while more complex social assumptions and attitudes
are revealed through the repeated attempts of Teague to
leave the Captain for the opportunities offered by the new
society and through Farrago's effort to hold him back. Inter-
spersed among the comic episodes are Farrago's observations
and reflections, the narrator's commentaries, and the "author's" digressions. Though these interruptions, too, are
sometimes just amusing intrusions, they usually underscore
or explicate the serious themes. Starting with this fundamental structure, Brackenridge expanded the novel over the
course of fifteen years of writing, from the first two volumes
published in 1793 to the seven volumes, which together
exceed eight-hundred pages in Claude M. Newlin's one-
volume edition. In this modern edition the first four volumes
constitute Part I and the last three are grouped together as
Part II.[19]

Even among those who have now recognized the value of
Modern Chivalry as an early example of American humor,
local-color fiction, and high-level and successful popular
literature, there are still problems which have led to misreadings and a lack of full appreciation of Brackenridge's
achievement. First, critics find it difficult to decide whether

to read the seven volumes as one book, as seven, or as something in between. Those who focus attention on the first volume alone tend to be more admiring than those who try to encompass the entire corpus. Others treat the first four volumes grouped as Part I as a single narrative.[20] This confusion continues to lead to widely varying evaluations of Brackenridge's narrative skill. In Volumes III and IV he began to alter his approach significantly, and in the three Volumes of Part II he practically reversed the narrative methods of the first volumes. Thus the fairest approach, one which is commonly used in the evaluation of modern novel sequences, is to treat each volume as a separate novel in a series in which Brackenridge's general aims and narrative strategies were continually evolving. It is especially revealing to examine these changes. Once each of the separate books is assessed, the overall achievement of the sequence can be established upon firmer ground.

Another obstacle to reading this work is the strong tendency to associate Brackenridge's characters, particularly Captain Farrago, with Brackenridge himself. Readers and critics have simply assumed the characters to be voices for the author's commentary. As a result, readers are baffled at the seeming contradictions and inconsistencies, which they conclude to be failures in point of view and narrative control. But Brackenridge is never Farrago. Those who assume that Farrago speaks for his creator will underrate the artistry and miss the rich ironies and meanings of this early masterpiece.

Perhaps even more misleading is Brackenridge's use of the character of the narrator-author. Although closer in viewpoint to Brackenridge than Farrago, the narrator does not always speak for Brackenridge either. Especially in the earlier books, Brackenridge often used the narrator ironically by having him address the audience about some issue with apparent innocence, when it is clear that Brackenridge himself held opposite opinions. For example, the reader should not take seriously the narrator's dissertation on the origin of races in Volume II; it is quite unlikely that Brackenridge believed Adam was white and Eve black, for all evidence about Brackenridge's religious ideas lead to the conclusion that he recognized the story of Adam and Eve to be a religious myth. The entire section is a joke on the speculations of the American Philosophical Society, which Brackenridge considered specious. Brackenridge repeatedly steps in and out of the narrative, sometimes speaking through the voice of the narrator and sometimes using the narrator ironically, and the reader must be sensitive to these subtle differences. In the later books, however, he dropped the mask more frequently and spoke more directly through the voice of the narrator. Still, even in the early books, the narrator-author must be treated seriously as a major character in the novel.

Basically then, there are two ways to read this work: with the main character Captain Farrago as the hero or with the narrator-author as the hero. To confuse these two related but distinct readings is to fail to understand either. Only in the first two volumes did Brackenridge adhere to his original intention and narrative method of presenting the story of Farrago and Teague in which the narrator-author is, as he describes himself, a Greek chorus for the drama. As Brackenridge added volumes, the role of the narrator-author looms larger, and the narrative starring Farrago appears fragmented, constantly changing, and evolving in theme as Farrago moves from book to book. When the seven books are taken together, however, the story of the narrator-artist-hero emerges as the most important, with the theme of the struggle of the writer in American society—a minor motif in each separate book—as the central issue of the larger composite narrative. In the context of the decades of struggle for the first generation of American writers, this theme takes on a greater importance, and the novel as a whole may be seen as a masterwork, which expresses both in form and in meaning the condition of literature in the early republic.

The overall structure of *Modern Chivalry* is based upon a balance of competing perspectives that are constantly being reconciled into dissatisfying compromises that are necessary for social intercourse and cohesion but are the source of both guilt and frustration to those who do the compromising. Man, as Brackenridge presents him, constantly fails to achieve his ideals but moves society forward, if ever so slightly, with each effort. In the original two volumes, the opposing forces are clearly symbolized in the characters of Farrago and Teague. The Captain represents a member of the declining aristocracy in America, which is desperately clinging to the tradition, culture, and economic advantages of the landed gentry of the pre-Revolutionary War society. A bookish, fifty-three-year-old member of the intellectual elite, Farrago is a learned man, and for this reason readers are quick to identify him as Brackenridge's spokesman. However, quite unlike Brackenridge, Farrago no longer practices a profession. Though he has retained the title "Captain" presumably from his rank in the Revolution, he has no desire to contribute to society or to the education and advancement of men like his servant. Indeed, Farrago's most obvious trait is directly contrary to Brackenridge's principles: a desperate desire to cling to the privileges of the past by retaining his servant and keeping him ignorant of his republican rights for as long as possible. He uses every means to that end, including lying, fraud, and conspiracy, and rationalizes his deceptions with a social theory, so well expressed by Alexander Pope, that each should stay in his own place to make all right with the world.

Of course, Teague is not a spokesman for Brackenridge either. Illiterate, foolish, and undisciplined, Teague stumbles through life while pulled by his appetites and often benefits from Farrago's self-motivated paternalism. Although the Captain resorts to lies and instills blind fear into Teague to keep him in his place, it is clear that Teague is often better off because of Farrago's efforts. There are many sharpers in this fluid society who would soon ruin the ignorant Teague were it not for Farrago's paternalism. This point is established most clearly in a later book when Teague does accept a position as an excise collector, and is tarred and feathered for his efforts. Within this continued conflict between Teague's opportunities to succeed and Farrago's self-interested efforts to prevent him from doing so, the narrative provides ample opportunity for Brackenridge to satirize various sectors of the new republic—the American Philosophical Society, the Society of the Cincinnati, doctors, preachers, Indian negotiators, the government and its administrative methods, and the people and leaders of the democracy who exploit the system or are exploited by it.

What frequently misleads readers of the first volume is that while the ridicule of Teague is usually quite pointed, the satirizing of Farrago's self-interested deceptions and spurious reasoning is rather intricate and often not immediately apparent. In addition, Farrago's pronouncements frequently combine a mixture of wisdom and rationalization. For example, the Captain expresses shock when he meets one of the Indian treaty-makers who swindle the government out of tax money by writing phony treaties with non-existent Indian tribes. Outraged over this public swindle the Captain cries: "Is it possible that such deception can be practiced in a new country? It astonishes me." The treaty-maker calmly informs him that "these things are now reduced to a system; and it is well-known to those who engage in the traffic, that we think nothing of it" (p. 57). After expressing such moral indignation at this practice, Farrago immediately engages in a deception of his own by painting a false picture of what Teague may expect if he interviews for a job as a treaty-maker. Instead of telling the truth about treaty frauds, the Captain concocts a fantastic tale to terrify Teague into continued submission. Unless the reader stops to question the motive for Farrago's lie and the social assumptions that underlie his condescension, his tricking of Teague seems a simple comic device.

Similarly, detection of Farrago's fallacious logic in some of his arguments also requires careful attention to his verbal manipulations. In another episode, Farrago gives a young man in love the sage advice that "imagination governs the world," and love is based entirely upon the imagined value of the other to the lover; thus, he encourages the young man to laugh away this delusion. Sounding much like Brackenridge's narrator at other places in the narrative, the Captain advises self-mockery and humor to free the mind from such incapacitating imaginings: "Ridicule is a better cure for love than passion. It is better to make the patient laugh than think" (p. 67). Because of the similarity of tone and reasoning, readers identify Farrago's words as those of the author. However, Brackenridge immediately undercuts Farrago's advice by having him engage in a long naturalistic treatise on sexual selection among humans in which he argues that people never mate with those below their station because the law of nature demands that people marry their social equals: "Should the eagle come from the firmament, and make his advances to the pheasant, he will find himself unsuccessful; . . . or should the rein deer, which is a most beautiful creature, woo a frog, the croaking animal would recede into the marsh, and solace itself with a paramour of its own chusing" (p. 68). Yet this foolishness is contradicted by other episodes that demonstrate that people constantly marry outside their social class, as did Brackenridge.

Because Brackenridge feared the growth of a new American aristocracy, he was always eager to expose the pretensions of the Society of the Cincinnati, so he has his narrator ridicule their choice of the eagle as their "hieroglyphic." He explains that the predisposition of Americans to use biblical or classical types for all kinds of trademarks causes an officer of the Society special problems. When his countrymen see the symbol of the eagle on his coat, they tend to interpret it either literally or religiously. An innkeeper mistakes the eagle as a goose, takes it as a directive, and prepares the colonel a goose dinner—a meal he despises. More troublesome is a clergyman who looks upon the eagle as a graven image; he accuses the colonel of being an idolater and member of a cult that worships the "Gog and Magog spoke of in the Apocalypse" (p. 71). While the narrator presents such events in a serious tone, Brackenridge's guffaws are to be heard clearly in the background as he invites his more sophisticated readers to enjoy this confusion over the literal and symbolic meanings of icons.

In the first volume, then, Brackenridge begins with a rather intricate narrative method in which the observations of the narrator are to be taken as "something like the sentiments delivered in the chorus in the ancient plays; a kind of moral on what was said; or like the moral as it is to a fable" (p. 68). But as with many good writers, moral and meaning are not necessarily the same. To make that subtle distinction clear, Brackenridge went to some length to establish a pattern of comic winks to the sophisticated reader from the author's position, which he kept separate from those of both the narrator and Farrago.

To reinforce this comic distance from his text, Brackenridge opens with an introduction in which he disclaims any intentional meaning in the book. He says the work is purely an exercise in style, designed to provide "something to read without the trouble of thinking" (p. 5). Of course, this declaration is frequently countered even directly in the course of the narrative, as when the narrator observes, "Now it may be said, that this is fiction; but fiction, or no fiction, the nature of the thing will make it a reality" (p. 22). Yet he continues to declare his authorial detachment, as at one point when the narrator-author supposedly catches himself moralizing on a point and stops: "I have been affecting to speak sense, whereas my business is to speak nonsense" (p. 36).

The narrator also declares that if there is one thing his book is not, it is not a satire. He claims that he had been guilty of engaging in that activity in his youth but had learned that there was neither money nor power to be gained by it. He says he could not have become the important person he is in society today had he continued in that satirical mode. "I never knew any good come of wit and humour yet. They are talents which keep the owner poor" (p. 43). Thus, though friends keep urging him to use the opportunity of this book to satirize the follies of society, he says "the truth was, I could see nothing to be ironical about," and thus uses his digressions only to present "philanthropic and benevolent ideas" (p. 44). Brackenridge follows this declaration of intention with a wonderfully ironic piece on the virtue of dueling, a vice he repeatedly attacked in his sermons and editorials.

Brackenridge's narrative method, therefore, is that of the philosopher employing parables. While he declares that he merely has a tale to tell, which will neither offend nor teach, he slyly hints to alert readers that he will subtly intrude morals into the minds of the less sophisticated readers. Then through irony, seeming contradiction, and debunkings of his characters—the seeming heroes as well as the fools—like Shakespeare whose lines spoke differently to the groundlings than to the nobles, Brackenridge entertains and instructs different levels of readers with different facets of his craft.

The central theme of the first volume of *Modern Chivalry* is that the pretensions and self-interest of Farrago are directly related to his fear of the democratic impulses that provide new opportunities for O'Regan. Were Farrago less threatened by the loss of his servant and were he to depend more upon reason in advising and instructing Teague, he might have tempered the dangers of social upheaval. Farrago's refusal to be honest with Teague and help him to improve himself only leaves the servant vulnerable to confidence men. Such impulses to repress the poor and the ignorant only create more anger and unrest among the common people and lead to social anarchy. Without the generous, intelligent guidance of the members of the privileged class, Brackenridge thought, the common people freed by democracy would misuse their new powers because their only models would be the selfish elite who had exploited and despised them. This clash between greed and ignorance creates a self-destructive, vicious cycle that Brackenridge feared would end the American experiment.

Still, the conflict between Farrago and Teague is always balanced by the wit, learning, and patience of the narrator, whose seeming aloofness provides a mediating influence. Brackenridge's own laughter, verbal trickery, and his ironic detachment from his narrator-author soften the social satire. Because the real author behind all the masks is obviously humane and reasonable, the reader is led to trust the narrative as a sane representative of the strengths and weaknesses of the new republic. This image of the learned, democratic author is strongly reinforced in the closing chapter of Volume I when Brackenridge reiterates his point that the book is meant for the improvement of style and turns humor on himself as well as his English competitors: "The English language is undoubtedly written better in America than in England, especially since the time of that literary dunce, Samuel Johnson, who was totally destitute of taste for the *vrai naturelle* or simplicity of nature" (p. 78). For some readers this statement may seem a simple horselaugh on the British, but the self-mocking double-edged humor shows Brackenridge's awareness of the danger of American provincialism as well.

In Volume II Brackenridge sustained his technique of two-leveled humor, but, perhaps to avoid misinterpretation, he began to stress the distance between Farrago and the narrator and between the narrator and himself. The twisted logic of some of Farrago's arguments and the tongue-in-cheek philosophizing of the narrator alter the reader's relationship to the work as a whole and make it more difficult to assume that there is a serious author present at all. Brackenridge becomes like the pedagogical caterpillar in *Alice in Wonderland* who envelops himself inside circles of smoke and leaves his listener wondering if he will suddenly sweep the verbal cloud away and reveal his meaning, or will simply disappear into a smoke screen of absurdity.

For example, in the second chapter the narrator proposes that his remarks on the American tendency to elevate unqualified people to office is not intended as a "burlesque on the present generation" but is merely an observation on mankind in general, for throughout history the natural state of man has been to "magnify what was small and elevate the low." He then illustrates this point with outrageous examples: the Egyptians worshipped muskrats as deities and the Romans and Greeks often "worshipped small matters," for as some poets had observed "Cannons shoot the higher pitches, The lower you put down their breeches." This inclination to raise up the insignificant is, he says, in keeping with man's creative impulse, for it requires greater art to use a magnifying glass to make things appear larger than they are. As final defense of social elevation, the narrator cites Caligula who is remembered for "making his horse a senator" (p. 86). The satire here is more heavy-handed and the tone more Juvenalian than in any passage in the first volume.

The treatment of the character flaws of Farrago is also more explicit here than in Volume I. For the first time Farrago's duping and suppression of Teague arouse his guilt. Using a sentimental incident in a way that was to become

more familiar in the novels of Charles Brockden Brown and
later Dickens and Twain, Brackenridge involves Farrago in
the suicide of an unfortunate young woman (pp. 107–13).
Stumbling into a house of prostitution during one of his
searches for Teague, the Captain has a conversation with the
madam, who complains that since the war, American girls
have all been going into virtuous professions, making it
difficult for her to keep up supply to meet the demands of
her business. A young beauty just from the country then
becomes the subject of their conversation, and the Captain
expresses a desire to meet and help her. When the girl comes
in, she tells Farrago her tale of her mother's death, her own
seduction, and the conditions that led her to her present
state. The Captain responds with a compassionate speech to
encourage her and concludes with the remark that she must
keep hope even though it may be difficult, "if not impossible,"
to recover her lost reputation. After his dinner, a night's
rest, and a late breakfast, the Captain sets out to find aid for
the distressed young woman, but his delayed efforts are in
vain. After thinking about his statement on her lost reputation, the girl had hanged herself. In his ineptitude and subsequent nonchalance in seeking aid, the Captain shares responsibility for her death.

This episode is so unusual in the novel that its impact
upon Farrago is of some significance. So moved by this event
is Farrago that he resolves to treat Teague with new sensitivity to his needs and desires and to help him to establish
himself in the world. His guilt over the poor of the society
who are denied opportunities and fall into despair drives
Farrago to seek out Teague and offer to guide his career.
Significantly, it is in the context of this new sense of social
responsibility that Brackenridge introduces the problem of
slavery and the American Constitution.

Continuing the pattern of balancing serious and comic
elements, the first episode regarding black people in America

is an absurd scene in which a black man is sent in place of his master to give a speech to the American Philosophical Society. He explains his own theory of the origin of races. The speech is a burlesque both of the Society and of biblical and historical interpretations of human origins. The man's argument is that Eve was a black woman and Adam a white man, but his speech places this point in the context of a more extended debate between theologians about the nature of God and the existence of heaven and hell. The narrator observes that this racial theory is no more provable than the doctrine of heaven or hell or God's benevolence and concludes that the main reason for paying heed to such doctrines is to prevent them from becoming extreme and thus harmful to society. The narrator implies that it is a necessary folly for people to develop and argue such theories because it is through myths that people develop a sense of personal or communal identity. He says the only danger with the latest religious views in America is that if everyone believes the liberal preachers who say there is no hell, then the pendulum will swing and the prevailing theory will be that there is no heaven—a view that discourages the fostering of virtue.

At this point in the book, the question of slavery seems to be put aside. However, as the narrative returns to the development of Farrago's new spirit of generosity, the issue of slavery and the Captain's social conscience become the subject of the volume's closing chapters. When the guilt Farrago feels regarding Teague is diluted by his frustration at trying to help the ignorant bogtrotter to prepare himself for social progress, Farrago quickly forgets his noble ideals. O'Regan has a chance for another career as an actor, and Farrago's self-interest prevails again. Forgetting his resolutions, he accuses Teague of ingratitude and concocts lies about the dangers of the stage.

The appearance of a Quaker reopens the issue of slavery. Not surprisingly, Farrago is ready to argue against the Quaker and in favor of the Constitution's support of slavery. The debate that ensues is both intricate and thematically important. While the narrator seems to suggest that Farrago goes away from the argument having confirmed his convictions about the rightness of slavery, it is apparent that each of his arguments has been shown by the Quaker to be based upon false analogy and logic. A casual reader, or one who takes the narrator as the last word, may miss the thematic implications of the Quaker's quiet victory over Farrago. While understated, the major point of this episode and the slave's speech to the Philosophical Society is that people and societies use fallacious theories to justify what they want to do because people act not from reason and philosophical principles but out of economic interest.

Though the slavery debate is left to the reader's close analysis, the narrator is very clear about the legal dimension of the slavery issue: the contradiction in the state constitution of Pennsylvania which declared all men equal and yet condoned slavery. Sounding perhaps like Judge Brackenridge, the narrator says he opposes the idea of gradualism in freeing slaves on the grounds that if slaves are men and should be free, then holding them one day longer is like allowing a thief to keep stolen property because it would be inconvenient for him to return it immediately. In presenting this attack on slavery, however, the narrator again pretends to argue exactly the opposite case. "As opposed to the enfranchisement of negroes, generally," he says with tongue in cheek that he has "been under apprehensions" that some young lawyers might point out the contradiction between the ideals of freedom and the condition of slavery. After he makes his convincing case for the abolition of slavery and the immediate freeing of the slaves, the narrator pretends to join the pro-slavery men who hope to suppress the compelling logic of freedom: "I shall say no more on this head, lest I should furnish hints to pettifoggers, who may make ill use of their information" (p. 140). Without a clear understanding of Brackenridge's ironic distance from his narrator, there is the possibility of misreading this section as evidence for Brackenridge's own sympathy with slavery.

Perhaps because of such misinterpretation Brackenridge abandoned the mask of the narrator-author in the next volume and put himself more directly into the narrative. In evaluating and interpreting Volume III, it is important to understand how significantly he altered his narrative method. The narrator's voice is distinctly different in tone and style, especially when he deals with political and social matters. Brackenridge also refashioned the character of Farrago, making the self-interest in his nature explicit, in order to reduce possible confusion between the Captain and himself. Thus, much of the subtlety and irony of the first two volumes is lost, and the more penetrating reader is denied some of the pleasure of interpretation in order that the more literal-minded reader not be left confused or led astray.

Instead of playing the sly stage manager who manipulates events from behind the scenes, Brackenridge places himself in the spotlight at the opening of this book. With a commentary on the critical response to his first volume, he includes a mock review wherein the supposed reviewer misreads the work, to which Brackenridge adds his own witty response. Then, he explains that he had originally planned his work as a long narrative poem, written in the verse form of Samuel Butler's *Hudibras* and to be titled "The Modern Chevalier." Next, he tells an elaborate tale of his discovery of an unknown poet named McConus whose poem on the Society of the Cincinnati he publishes here for the first time. The humor in this introduction and the poem is strained to the point that its effect is nearly ruined.

Included in this volume also is the famous scene in which Teague receives lessons from a French dancing master. The comedy here reaches a new low, as when the Frenchman advises Teague: "you must not break wind from your mouth or any other part" (p. 213). Though the scene is funny, the nature of its humor indicates that Brackenridge was losing faith in the ability of his readers to respond to finer comedy. The fact that he also mentions the popular English poet of the common people, Peter Pindar, may be a signal of his own awareness of the lowering of his literary sights.[21] Finally, Brackenridge compares his task as a narrator to the role of the biblical prophets: he points out that he will interrupt this book more frequently with moral instruction because, having learned that "the human mind, from defect of attention or incapacity, cannot be reached all at once, in the manner of the prophet, imitating his zeal and knowledge of the heart, I give 'line upon line'; precept upon precept; here a little, there a little" (p. 224).

At the same time that Brackenridge gives the narrator a personality more like his own and makes him a greater participant in the narrative, he separates himself more completely from Farrago and paints him as an even more selfish and sinister character. Because Teague is illiterate and must trust his master to read his mail to him, Farrago now exploits this weakness and lies about the contents. In addition, the Captain conspires with others against the servant, whereas in the first volume he merely lied to Teague to keep him from advancing.

The most revealing episode of this kind also has very interesting social implications. What brings out the worst in Farrago is the threat that Teague presents to the sexual-social order of the community—what Farrago calls "Teagueomania." Teague has begun to attract ladies above his social station and is even on the verge of marrying into a higher class. In Farrago's view, such a marriage would violate the only taboo left in the republican society, and he says he would rather see Teague become President than marry a social superior. The Captain plots with the father of the smitten girl to discredit Teague to the girl and her mother. He then deceives Teague about the reasons for the girl's sudden rejection of him. While Farrago stoops to such stratagems to protect the social order, he rationalizes his knavery as indulgent benevolence: "By these artifices, certainly innocent as the object was good; for it can be no injury to deceive a man to his own advantage" (p. 246).

At the end of this volume, Brackenridge reduces the separation between himself and the narrator even further with a comic appendix in which he refuses to apologize for printing errors since the ignorant will not notice and the intelligent will not care: "Looking over the preceding sheets, and observing several errors of the press, I had thoughts of giving a table of them. But I recollect that in other books, a table of this kind has appeared to me as unnecessary.—Because the intelligent reader could in general himself see what were errors, and as to the unintelligent, it made no great odds, whether he did or not" (p. 250). His awareness that his audience was divided into two distinct groups of readers underlies both the technique and the meaning of the novel. Finally, he calls out in his own voice for critical reaction to his book.

> I have only farther to say at present, that I wish I could get this work to make a little more noise. Will nobody attack it and prove that it is insipid, libellous, treasonable, immoral, or irreligious? If they will not do this, let them do something else, praise it, call it excellent, say it contains wit, erudition, genius, and the Lord knows what! Will no body speak? What? Ho! are ye all asleep in the hold there down at Philadelphia? Will none of you abuse, praise, reprobate, or command this performance? It is ill usage; that is all I can say; and I will take my revenge in a short time unless the matter mends, by dropping my pen altogether, as I now do for the present. [p. 250]

With the third volume, Brackenridge established a new relationship between himself and his readers. It is possible to read the first two volumes as halves of a single work with narrative, structural unity, and a central theme. But with Volume III *Modern Chivalry* becomes a different kind of work: a fictional sequence flexible enough to include other forms, such as poems, sermons, essays, and political discourses. The story, such as it is, becomes a frame device for the witty observations and social commentary of the author. This organization is nearly the reverse of that in the first two books where the narrative was central and the commentary incidental. In keeping with this architectural change, the fictional elements and episodes now include baser material and humor, as though Brackenridge were pitching his work to the lowest level of possible readers. He becomes like a nightclub comedian facing a restless and resisting audience: he keeps talking and trying different approaches, hoping to engage people by getting them to laugh at themselves.

This new tone and strategy are immediately apparent in the opening of Volume IV where Brackenridge adds another low character and again alters Farrago's situation. As a result of a meeting with the President, Teague has finally risen to a new station, that of excise officer. So Farrago hires a new servant, a strict Scotch Presbyterian named Duncan Ferguson. But O'Regan meets violent resistance in his first attempt to collect taxes and so returns to the Captain for help. Farrago now takes on the role of overseer of Duncan and Teague rather than that of protagonist in a conflict with the bogtrotter and his constitutents. He loses some of his selfish meanness and becomes more of a paternal authority figure in the community. It is in this volume that Farrago's philosophical observations begin to sound a bit more like those of Brackenridge. Because these qualities are grafted onto the original character, readers sometimes confuse Farrago's ideas with those of Brackenridge; however, the two never do become one. The Farrago of Volume IV and the later works is a man more like the lawyer in Melville's "Bartleby the Scrivener": patient, condescending, and fairly benevolent, a man motivated entirely by self-interest who desires to maintain the status quo with the least amount of friction among those in his charge. The new Farrago is not necessarily a better man, but he is a more effective manipulator of those beneath his station. With this new demeanor and style he rises to the rank of governor.

In Volume IV the comic episodes become even more absurd. Teague's interview with the President and his appointment to office are ludicrous. Then, when he tries to collect taxes and is tarred and feathered for his efforts, he is captured and put on display by the Philosophical Society who mistake him for a rare specimen, half man and half bird. In all of these scenes the satire upon the follies of the republican society is more bitter than in the first three volumes. Writing in the context of the French Revolution and just after his experience in the Whiskey Rebellion, Brackenridge seems to have been obsessed with the dangers of demagoguery and the possibility of the American Revolution evolving into social anarchy. While the predominant voice in this book is the narrator-author whose speculations overshadow the contrived plot, Brackenridge tries to distract attention from this drift toward increased didacticism by asserting his detachment: "It may be observed, that as I advance in my book, I make fewer chapters by way of commentary and occupy myself chiefly with the narrative" (p. 278). Because the narrative itself is more rollicking and outrageous, a naïve reader might actually take this statement seriously, but the experienced reader will soon discover that Volume IV is actually closer to a sermon.

The new dimension in Volume IV is a deeper philosophical skepticism about the nature of history, progress, modern culture. There is one especially moving scene from which

emerges the central symbol of the book. While Duncan and
Teague are debating the merits of various denominations of
modern Christianity and the virtues of Saint Andrew versus
Saint Patrick, they happen upon an ancient cave once used
by the Indians as a burial ground. After observing that the
skeletons of this race of giants, many of whom were eight
feet in height, have been preserved better than Egyptian
mummies, they enter a section of the cave known as the
"petrified grove." They find trees with wasp nests in them
and buffaloes "hard as adamant." They are awestruck to
discover a petrified Indian: "an Indian man reduced to
stone, with a bundle of peltry on his back" (p. 277). This
image of the enduring burdens of life serves at least three
important functions in the work. First, it balances the criticism of the Indians that Brackenridge had included in the
earlier books. While Brackenridge was suspicious of Indian
treaties and promises, he recognized the tragedy the whites
had wrought on Indian civilizations. The petrified Indian is
also a reminder of the permanent hardship of the human
condition and the repetition of history; for all their optimism
and faith in progress, Americans too might one day be
stultified by the burden of their peltry. Finally, in a book in
which the competition among ethnic, social, and religious
groups for opportunities is so central a theme, the image of
the Indian is a reminder of the equality awaiting all in the
grave. Another dimension and a modern twist are later
added to this symbol when the trio happen upon the per-
formance of a play, "The Oppressed Politician." Here, a
republican leader is forced to carry a burden on his back—
one of his noisy constituents.

In Volume IV there is also a shift in narrative emphasis
away from the fictional plot with its theme of the guilt of
the aristocrat and the duties of the common man in the
republic toward the deeper conflict between the narrator-
author and his audience. The plight of the author-artist is

now laid bare as the subtheme of the entire work. Brackenridge makes this meaning explicit in a pronouncement by
the narrator-author about the role of art in American culture. After nearly three hundred pages of understatement,
this passage is startling in its directness. Its irony signals a
new relationship between the author and reader that will
continue throughout subsequent volumes. In the midst of
describing the peace and harmony that must have prevailed
among the Indians during the centuries they ruled the American continent, the narrator speculates on the high place of
the imagination and the arts in Indian culture compared to
the insignificance of the life of the mind in contemporary
America:

> Happy savage, that could thus amuse himself, and
> exercise his first preeminence over animals we call
> Beasts. They can hunt, and devour living things for
> food; but where do you find a wolf, or a fishing hawk,
> that has any idea of these abstract pleasures that feed
> the imagination? Why is it that I am proud and value
> myself amongst my own species? It is because I think
> I possess, in some degree, the distinguishing characteris-
> tic of a man, a taste for the fine arts; a taste and
> characteristic too little valued in America, where a sys-
> tem of finance, has introduced the love of unequal
> wealth; destroyed the spirit of common industry; and
> planted that of lottery in the human heart; making the
> mass of the people gamblers; and under the idea of
> speculation, shrouded engrossing and monopoly every
> where. [pp. 280–81]

Brackenridge throws into new perspective all of the subtler
statements in the previous volumes about the role of the
leaders of business, government, the banks, and the churches
in relation to that of the artist. In fact, in many ways the
entirety of Volume IV acts as a gloss upon the understated
conflicts and tensions in the first three books.

Indeed, Brackenridge expanded the role of the narrator-author so much in Volume IV and subsequent volumes that his authoritative voice overwhelms the whole work and risks distorting a reader's perceptions of the early volumes. He even provides critical commentary on his own method, observing that Volume IV was designed like a homily, with parts carefully divided to hold the attention of the readers; there is even a final section which is similar in purpose to those parts of the Puritan sermon labeled "application" and "uses": "It is time now to make some reflections, were it not only for the sake of form; just as the clergyman who divides his text into several heads, and then adds, 'we shall conclude with an improvement of the whole; or with a few practical observations, or reflections' " (p. 306). Rather than seeing these later books as an extension of the novel, it might be more useful to view them as an extended commentary on the conflicts and themes presented more artistically in the original design.

The three volumes of Part II of *Modern Chivalry* cannot be read in the same way or evaluated with the same criteria as the books of Part I. By 1804, when he completed Volume V, Brackenridge had abandoned his original plan of putting the narrative forward and relying upon brief intrusions to teach his moral and social lessons and to hint at the importance of authorship in America. Like the other writers of his generation, he came increasingly to realize that the only possibility the writer had of altering attitudes and beliefs of readers was to confront established ideas with direct, overt statements. Thus, he adopted a new strategy for the second part of his series, and any critical assessment of the entire work that does not take this into account will find Part II a narrative catastrophe, for the story is very much secondary to the preaching. These final volumes are worthy of study, however, because of the many remarkable statements about important social, political, and religious issues and about the role of the literary artist in the republic.

In these books the narrator becomes the hero—an author-prophet-social leader who appears only incidentally concerned, almost annoyed with, the continuing comedy of Farrago and Teague. This artist-protagonist is engaged in a more compelling conflict with his audience and is constantly battling the American society whose follies are depicted in the narrative. But these volumes are more than just segments of a journal in which Brackenridge recorded his anger over the mudslinging of the "mully-grub" press or his thoughts on democracy. He was too much of a self-conscious artist to lapse into mere preaching. Close examination reveals that he maintained a thematic unity and narrative consistency, giving these volumes autonomy from the earlier books. At the same time, Part II may be understood as part of the larger novel sequence of *Modern Chivalry* because it exposes the frustration, anger, and sense of mission of the novelist whose conscious intentions were masked in the earlier books. Then, the overarching theme of the whole of *Modern Chivalry* becomes evident: the struggle of the man of letters in the new republic.

In Volume V, the two central themes are established early. The spokesman for one of these themes is the Captain who has become the respected governor of his state. Constantly consulted on all manner of issues, Farrago is now a ready defender of democracy. Sounding more like the learned narrator-author of the earlier volumes, the Captain voices his new stoicism in his favorite statement: "Human nature is the same everywhere" (p. 375). He responds philosophically to an attack on the two-party system: "Political divisions will always exist, said the Captain. It [division] is inseparable from the nature of a community. And it is not in the nature of things that the power can be long on one side. *The dura-*

tion depends upon the judgment of using it. The people will
revolt from themselves when they find they have done wrong,
and that side which was now the weakest will become the
strongest" (p. 358). This is not the Farrago of 1792.

Early in Volume V, Brackenridge also establishes the
importance of the main theme of republican authorship.
First, to alert the reader to presence of deeper meanings in
his work, he presents a key metaphor for the roles of the
serious author and the critic: "The spider is found sometimes
in the cellar; and his weaving is an emblem of the composition of an author; while the wasp [who inhabits the attic]
resembles the critic" (p. 355). Then, Farrago elaborates upon
the difference between the author's function during the
Revolution as inflamer of passion and the writer's new role
as teacher and moral leader:

> For though at the commencement of a revolution, active
> and uninformed spirits, are useful, or perhaps absolutely
> necessary, like the subterranean fire throwing up con-
> tinents; yet as in this case, the fostering dews, and the
> breath of the atmosphere, are necessary to give soil and
> impregnate with vegetation; so after the stirrings of
> men's minds, with a political convulsion, deliberate
> reason, and prudent temperament are necessary, to
> preserve what is gained, and turn it to advantage.
> [p. 348]

To illustrate the disregard the writer experiences in America, however, this pronouncement is followed by an extraordinary scene in which Farrago enters a madhouse. He meets
three intellectuals there who have been declared insane by
the citizens of the republic: a philosopher who believes in
moral choices and responsibility; a "Lay Preacher" who tries
to teach industry as a duty of independence; and a poet
(obviously Brackenridge) who has been declared a bedlamite

because he is writing a poem in Hudibrastic verse about Farrago—he is allowed to keep ranting but has been confined to a small garret where he can do no harm. This idea of the artist and intellectual who does not add his voice to the ideological consensus and is thus declared insane was to become a recurrent theme in American literature through such works as Melville's "Bartleby the Scrivener" and Joseph Heller's *Catch-22*. Brackenridge's narrator claims that he will include some of this poet's verse, while Farrago goes away from the madhouse wondering if the men he has met are really mad: "At the same time doubting with himself, whether those he saw confined were more devoid of reason than the bulk of men running at large in the world" (p. 387).

The two themes are kept in balance throughout Volume V. Farrago preaches on the need for virtuous citizens in a democracy, and the narrator expounds on the importance of letters to the democratic society. When Teague again considers public office, Farrago advises him to seek an appointment, not for personal gain but for the service he can render others: "You a republican, and yet destitute of republican virtue, the basis of which I take to be *humility and self-denial*" (p. 392). In this vein Farrago explains that self-interest springs from the aping of the British system of education and social order, which was founded upon notions of hierarchy and aristocracy. Since the American educational system still retains certain features of the old values, it is destroying democratic virtues at a critical point of their development in the young: "I take it to be a great error of education in our schools, and colleges, that ambition is encouraged by the distribution of honours, in consideration of progress in letters; that one shall be declared the first scholar in languages, another in mathematics. It is sufficient that the fact be so without announcing it" (p. 391). He says that this formal acknowledgment of superiority "takes away the friendship of

others, and corrupts the moral feelings of the successful com-
petitor himself. Ambition springs up, that accursed root
which poisons the world" (p. 391).

Then, in the context of the Captain's attack upon the love
of honors and the ambition for wealth and power that infect
the educational system, the narrator expresses for the first
time his formulation of the growing antagonism between
the self-indulgent moneyed classes and the artist. Because the
calling of the artist necessarily involves the poverty and self-
denial that make him a true republican, he is a special threat
to wealthy hypocrites: "There is a natural alliance between
liberty and letters. Men of letters, are seldom men of wealth,
and these naturally ally themselves with the *democratic
interest* in a commonwealth. These form a balance with the
bulk of the people, against power, springing from family
interest, and large estates." Just as the ministers so often
argued that the people's best protection against exploitation
is a strong learned clergy, so too does the narrator plead for
the social value of men of letters.

> It is not good policy in republicans to declare war
> against letters; or even to frown upon them, for in
> literary men is their best support. They are as necessary
> to them as light to the steps. They are a safe auxiliary;
> for all they want is, to have the praise of giving
> information. . . .
>
> There is ground, for the regret, that literary institu-
> tions are not favoured; that it has become a popular
> thing to call out against learning, as not necessary to
> make republicans. The knowledge of our rights, and
> capacity to prosecute, and defend them, does not spring
> from the ground; but from education and study. [p. 401]

In the remaining section of this volume Brackenridge
presents a remarkable analysis of the function of literature,
especially fiction, and the role of the writer in the new
republic. He is now quite explicit about the parallels be-

tween the role of the author and that of the preacher—even
prophet—and of the competition between the man of affairs
and the writer for the hearts and minds of the people. The
section begins with an actual sermon in which Brackenridge
borrows heavily from the rhetoric of the Puritan jeremiad
in asserting the identity of the "true democrat" (like the
"true believer") versus the hypocritical democrat, who does
not possess true faith in the people. One can tell true republicans by their virtues of self-sacrifice and their good deeds
toward their fellows: "The democrat is the true chevalier,
who, though he wears not crosses, or the emblazoned arms of
heraldry, yet is ready to do right, and justice to every one.
All others are imposters, and do not belong to the order of
democracy" (p. 404). From this, he turns to an elaboration
upon the virtues of fiction and romance as touchstones for
discovering truths about human nature and society.

> I would ask, which is the most entertaining work,
> [Smollett's] History of England; or his Humphrey
> Clinker? For, as to the utility, so far as that depends
> upon truth, they are both alike. History has been well
> said to be *the Romance of the human mind; and
> Romance the history of the heart. . . .*
>
> The Eastern nations in their tales [by which he means
> their histories], pretend to nothing but fiction. Nor is
> the story with them the less amusing because it is not
> *true.* Nor is the moral of it less impressive, because the
> actors never had existence. This, I have thought it
> sufficient to say, by way of introduction in this place.
> [p. 406]

Having asserted this social function of literature, Brackenridge contrasts literature to modern organized religions. As
early as the first volume, Farrago had propounded the demise
of the clergy's influence: "You think it a great honour to
preach now a days. It was an honour once; but the thing is
now become so common, that it is of little consequence to

reach or not" (p. 39). In Volume V, Brackenridge probes the deeper causes of the failure of the churches. In his view, the clergy have become misguided in their recent concern with social and political matters and have thereby lost their proper mission and their spiritual power: "But our modern churches, have not the zeal of the primitive: or that zeal is directed to a different object, *the building up the faith at home*; and that in civil affairs, more than spiritual, doctrines. It is not the time now to go about 'in sheepskins, and goatskins,' to convert the heathen, to the gospel; but the citizens to vote for this or that candidate" (p. 408). Because the clergymen have come to occupy themselves with politics, the writers have had to fill the spiritual void. To the novelist has fallen the duty of warning the people against their errors and their backsliding from their ideals; it is now the writer's task to arouse the hearts of people to renew their faith in the truth of expressed beliefs.

The narrator explains this new role for the artist to be the key to the kind of satire that the reader may expect to find in his book. He says those who look for simple sarcasm directed at individuals and social organizations do not understand the more penetrating social criticism of the work:

> We have been often asked for a key to this work. Every man of sense has the key in his own pocket. His own feelings; his own experience is the key. It is astonishing, with what avidity, we look for the application of satire which is general, and never had a prototype. But the fact is, that, in this work, the picture is taken from human nature, generally, and has no individual in view. [p. 411]

Such rebukes of society found in this book, he says, are closer to those of the great Jewish prophets who were the philosopher-authors of their people. What has happened in the republic is that fraud and misplaced values have made it difficult for the people to tell the difference between the sage and the demagogue. With the example of Napoleon never far from his mind, the narrator explains that it is in the interest of the demagogue for the people to squander their freedom, misuse their power, and grow ignorant, confused, and corrupted. Therefore, the demagogue is always praising the people in everything they do and encouraging them in their folly. The demagogue's hope is that when social collapse occurs, he will be able to grab power by offering himself to the people as an authority figure to lead them from their perilous state.

The task of the man of letters—the prophet-sage of the republic—is to warn the people and chastise them when they drift from their ideals. In so doing, he stands in direct opposition to the demagogue as well as to the aristocrats who are scornful of the people and wish to see them prove irresponsible and fail. Unfortunately, in their blindness the people mistake the writers as their enemies and reject their criticism and truths. If the republican experiment is to succeed, however, the people must heed such criticism and acknowledge the prophetic role of the artistic genius.

> How do you distinguish the demagogue from the patriot? The demagogue flatters the clown, and finds fault with the sage. The patriot, and the sage, unless you mean the vain philosopher, mean the same thing. The Jewish prophets were all of them sages. They were seers, or *men that saw far into things.* You will find they were no slouches at blaming the people. "My people Israel, is destroyed for lack of knowledge." "*I am wounded* in the house of my friends." *This may be said of liberty, when republicans give it a stab.* The lamentations of Jeremiah are but the weepings of a patriot over the errors of the people. Yet the people are always right, say the demagogues. I doubt that. *Tom fool,* may laugh at the expression, "save the people from themselves."

Nevertheless, there is something in it. It is a Scripture phrase, "go not with a multitude to do evil;" which would seem to imply that the multitude will sometimes do wrong.

Do the multitude invent arts? Or some individuals among them? It is sometimes a matter of accident. Sometimes a matter of genius. But it is but one out of a thousand that happens to hit upon it; or that has the invention to contrive. [p. 415]

In this striking analysis of the clash between the emergent republican ideology and traditional moral, religious, and artistic values, Brackenridge laid bare the ritual of blame, purgation, and reform that had been the strength of the Americans in previous generations. This emotional process had played an essential function in the shift of power from the king to the people, but it was now being short-circuited by those who flattered the people and exploited their ignorance and innocence. Without the restraining hand of a chastising clergy, there would only be a downward spiral of error and accommodation that would lead to despotic rule. The reforming impulse founded in guilt would no longer exist. In the face of this disaster, only the artist-prophet could assume the role previously held by the Jewish prophets and the American clergy, warn the people of their errors, and recall them to their original professed beliefs. The press might have played this role, but the self-interest of the editors and journalists has led them to be caught up in partisanship and in their own exploitation of the people. Thus, the artists must become the "preservers of the balance," the trimmers of the vessel of state. Yet these "trimmers are unfavourably spoken of" (p. 416).

Continuing his analysis of the rejection of the imaginative writer in American society, Brackenridge next includes an interrogation of a man suspected of being a scholar. If proven to be a scholar, he will be condemned to jail or an asylum, exposed as either a fraud or a madman. In one part of the interview appears this exchange, which also focuses upon the relationship of narrative fiction and history to reality and truth:

> You are a man of books—
> A little so.
> What books have you read?
> History, Divinity, Belles-lettres.
> What is the characteristic of history?
> Fiction.
> Of novels?
> Truth. [p. 431]

As though to test this assertion, Brackenridge has his characters stumble upon the presentation of a play "The Oppressed Politician." Here they, and the reader, are asked to judge whether the images of fiction in the play do not present a truer picture of political leadership than the public images actual politicians try to project.

In the scene presented, a congressional representative is forced to carry a number of his people upon his back. Of course, he stumbles and falls, makes no progress, and many of those clinging to him fall by the wayside. This tableau is then interpreted by one character as representing the problem of democracy, which burdens one man with the problems of many. Another spectator views the scene as a statement about the folly of politicians who take on such a ridiculous job. But a wise man asserts that this interpretation has a partisan slant, for it is favorable to the Federalists, who wish to discredit the republican politicians and their constituents. Then, the narrator-author presents a more complex reading: the point, he says, is that some people think that the best way to lead is to carry all the burdens of others on their shoulders, but they only hold that view because pride blinds them to the ability of the people to help themselves. Such leaders harm democracy because they either pretend or believe the people to be fools and thereby assure that the people will fail to participate in their own governance. Such leaders want to believe that the nation will not be able to go on without them when they die, but often, he says, the best leaders are those who seem to lead least.

To this point, the narrator draws an analogy between the political figure and the author and argues that it is the writer, like the playwright who created this instructive figure, who really carries the weight of society upon his shoulders, for he strives to teach others how to use their own talents. A humorous spoof on the function of criticism and the multiplicity of interpretation, this tableau links the roles of political leader and author in a single image, and in its echo of the figure of the petrified Indian and his universal burden of Volume IV; it also places the entire discussion in a philosophical context.

Perhaps still fearing that the meaning of such episodes might be too subtle, Brackenridge resorts to direct statement in the closing pages of this volume. He explains that some of his meaning might not be evident to the present generation of readers, but he does not expect to be understood all at once or even in his own time: "We mean it for the coming generation, as well as the present; and intending solid observations, *we interlard pleasantry to make the boys read*" (p. 443). He says that what disturbs him most about the audience of his own generation and about those who pretend to leadership as well is not "the want of learning that I consider as a defect; but the *contempt of it*" (p. 447). A candidate for public office will "affect not to be able to write, . . . will take care to have it known that he is no scholar; that he has had no dealings with the devil in this way; that he has kept himself all his life, thank God, free from the black art of letters" (p. 446). Again he asserts that careful interpretation of the works of serious writers is the only defense the people have against the tyranny of despotism. The writer is the warning beacon of the republic, whose imaginative projections in literature present the only unadulterated truths about the nature of society.

> [D]espotism is not of a day; it is of gradual increase. Will not the people give him credit that can point out to men, where a germ of it exists.
>
> In what is hinted at, in several pages of the preceding chapter, of hostility to laws and a disposition to overthrow establishments, . . . I have in view, not the proceedings of a public body, but the prejudices of the people. . . . It is therefore into this pool that I cast my salt. It is to correct these waters that I write this book. [p. 449]

Affecting exhaustion and frustration, Brackenridge declares at the end of this volume that his imaginative powers are weakening and that he has merely tried to keep the narrative flowing "to let people know that I am alive" (p. 463). This apparent confession is often taken seriously as an apologia for the breakdown of unity and the drifting of the narrative from its original design. However, it is by no means certain that Brackenridge can be taken any more seriously in these disclaimers than in the earlier assertions that his intentions were only to improve style and not to affect ideas. Like his old friend Freneau, Brackenridge understood that the literary taste of Americans had changed drastically since the time he had begun his novel and that he could not at once reach a popular audience and meet high critical standards. Yet his love of America and his fear for its future led him to sacrifice artistic fame to try to attain social and moral ends.

Indeed, in the two volumes that follow there does not appear to be any lessening of energy and intellectual liveliness in the writing and ideas. The narrative technique established in this first volume of Part II is continued, with the narrator sounding more and more like the author as he seems to grow even more desperate to maintain democracy by conveying his advice to readers of all intellectual levels. Creating new characters to express his insights, he introduces a wise, blind lawyer who joins Farrago's group. Like Tiresias, the blind man perceives truths that the others fail to see. There are also sensible republicans in the crowds along the way who sometimes emerge in debates to contribute intelligent insights. Instead of the oppositional logic that provided the balance to the arguments in Part I, Brackenridge now seems to endorse a sort of pluralism of opinion in which reason and justice emerge from a multiplicity of opinions, once again in a manner similar to that described in Madison's *The Federalist* #10.

As the vigorous defender of the virtues necessary to a democratic people, the narrator continues to extol the merits of self-sacrifice and self-denial and to attack those who stand between the people and their own best interests. He declares that his book is intended as a social primer for the common man, and in a line anticipating Whitman's famous statement, he says, "This whole book from beginning to end has a purpose, which, if any one has not found it, let him read again" (p. 479).

In Volume VI, Brackenridge adds a new twist to the conflict between the demagogue and the men of learning. While the narrator again stresses the urgent need for courageous, learned men to do battle with this satanic enemy of the people, he also warns against false men of letters. Reflecting Brackenridge's lifetime wariness of pseudo-intellectualism, he says the danger is that spurious intellectuals may use obfuscation and pretentious knowledge for show and self-advancement rather than for the practical social benefits in which learning achieves its true purpose. The tendency of the people to value what they do not understand makes them vulnerable to being duped by such pretenders who infiltrate the churches, universities, and literary circles. He warns against the natural tendency to admire the dark and mysterious, even when the source is simply vagueness or ignorance.

> But is there not a sublimity in the obscure. . . . In the natural world there is something in darkness, which impresses the mind with awe! A lowering cloud brings an impression of dignity, of grandeur. In the moral world, is there not more in mystery, than in what is self-evident? Why, otherwise do we value preachers in the pulpit, in proportion to their dwelling on what is unintelligible? . . . [People say] give me the divine. . . . It is of no moment whether I understand his words or not; or rather, I would not wish to understand him, for if I did, I would take it for granted that it was not so deep as it ought to be. [p. 584]

As a last needle to the critics who scorned his populist fiction, Brackenridge again asserts that he has designed his book to appeal to all levels of intelligence and learning. In response to an intelligent and literate tailor who is untrained in the classics and complains that the author has included too many Latin phrases, Brackenridge says that he put them in to keep the intellectuals from getting bored but that he also made certain these phrases were not essential to the meaning so ordinary readers would lose none of the ideas. "This book is written for individuals of all attainments, and of all grades of intellects" (pp. 584–85). In fact, in an effort to avoid offending readers with some of his most radical ideas, he has consciously deleted "some of the more forward of them[.] I have actually knocked [them] on the head having reason to believe that they might do more harm than good at the present time. I thought a pity of several of them, for they struggled hard to live. But, dearies, said I, you must go. It is better you should die than your father. So they went, poor

things, to house themselves with the infantile images that
are heard only by their plaints in the entrance of the house of
night" (p. 576).

In these volumes of Part II, then, Brackenridge created a
different kind of narrative in which the narrator-author
emerges as the hero engaged in a tireless conflict with the
various enemies of the people, who threaten to divert the
power and wealth to their own ends. Because the democratic
artist does not seek wealth or power, he is in the position to
speak truth about the social conditions. To achieve this, the
author must use every rhetorical weapon at his disposal and
shrewdly compose his works in a style and manner that will
make them appeal to a republican audience more interested
in entertainment than in wisdom. In Part II Brackenridge
makes the unifying theme of *Modern Chivalry* boldly explicit. With the aid of this gloss, the reader may return to the
first four volumes with a heightened awareness of the cen-
trality of the question of the writer's role in America, which
Brackenridge had earlier subordinated to the political and
social satire.

The narrator closes the final volume by confidently claim-
ing success—America would be a worse place to live in today,
he says, were it not for these seven volumes. His book has
served the body politic like a preventive medicine. Opinions
sweep the society like influenza, and many absurd opinions
might have been accepted by the popular mind "unless this
burlesque prevents it." But "owing to this book" there is at
present in America "a very different state of things" than
might have been (p. 805).

Brackenridge accepted the role of the artist as that of a
man apart—like a judge—who oversees the affairs of his
fellows and works to expose error and resolve conflicts. He
may have been the first writer to recognize that the urging
of the common people toward moral reform was itself a
politically threatening act to the few in power. A people

dulled and lulled into moral apathy and social cynicism is more pliable than a socially and morally awakened populace. Some leaders were already counting upon the wasteful self-indulgence and moral uncertainty of the people as a foundation for social stability. With a skeptical but steady belief in moral progress, Brackenridge hoped that as the people became educated they would naturally take a greater role in assuring that their leaders adhered to the principles of the Declaration of Independence and the Constitution, to which he devoted his life.

VI

CHARLES BROCKDEN BROWN:
THE BURDEN OF THE PAST

DANTE'S LUCK LAY IN HIS GULLIBLE
& HEAVENLY WORLD   WE MY BOY DRAW FROM 2
SORTS OF READER: ONE ON HIS KNEES TO ART
THE OTHER FACEDOWN OVER A COMIC BOOK.
OUR STYLISH HIJINKS WONT AMUSE THE LATTER
& THE FORMER WILL DISCOUNT OUR URGENT MATTER

JAMES MERRILL
Mirabell: Books of Number, a Poem, 1979

Charles Brockden Brown grew up in the cultural center of Philadelphia during the 1770s and 1780s where he was witness to the tumult and confusion of the war and heard the declarations of America's promises and ideals. As he began to recognize his literary talent, he might have dreamed of becoming the anticipated American literary genius. Certainly his career constituted a remarkable effort to become a writer of popular and critical success, and his ability to make his living from his writing gave him the distinction of being the first professional man of letters in America.[1] Yet, as in the cases of Poe and Melville, with whom he shares many affinities, Brown's career ended in obscurity and personal failure. The story of his blossoming and fading literary career constitutes the final chapter in the tale of the frustrated efforts of the first generation of American writers to achieve the elusive goal of winning popular acclaim and critical praise in the new republic.[2]

The son of Elijah and Mary Armitt Brown, Brown was born in Philadelphia on January 17, 1771, the year in which Freneau and Brackenridge composed *The Rising Glory of*

America. Brown's father made a suitable income as a conveyancer, and both parents were active members of the Society of Friends. Embracing pacifist principles, which Brown himself held most of his life, the family remained loyal to the American cause but was not involved in the fighting during the Revolution. As a child Brown showed signs of unusual intelligence and interests. Frail and physically inactive, he gave his time to the study of geography and architecture, and his enormous curiosity led him to read widely in the arts and sciences. At the Friends Public School, which he entered at the age of eleven, Charles was fortunate to be instructed by one of Philadelphia's finest teachers, Robert Proud. Proud had been an opponent of the Revolutionary War and was a professed Tory; and it is likely that a spirit of challenge to prevailing opinions pervaded his teaching. Brown's tendency to question the commonly held beliefs of his society may have been nurtured under Proud's guidance.

When Brown left the school in 1787, he was apprenticed to Alexander Wilcocks to prepare for a career in law, although the drudgery of his legal duties left him quite dissatisfied. In his spare time Brown planned epic poems on the discovery of America and the conquests of Mexico and Peru, and he composed imitations of the Psalms, the Book of Job, and the Ossian poems. Of his work in the law office he wrote, "The task assigned . . . was perpetually encumbered with the rubbish of the law. . . . It was one tedious round of scrawling and jargon. . . . When my task is finished for the day, it leaves me listless and melancholy."[3]

At the invitation of a friend, Brown joined a literary society, the Belles Lettres Club, and pondered leaving the legal profession. Inclined toward a pessimistic temperament, Brown enjoyed the club members' discussions of the validity of suicide, the imperfections of government, and the repression of the human spirit and of freedom. These meetings encouraged his growing philosophical skepticism and his study of the idealistic and radical doctrines that he was to explore in his essays and novels. To please his parents and brothers, he continued the study of law until 1792, but devoted much of his energy to literary endeavors. In 1789, a series of his essays appeared in the Philadelphia *Columbian Magazine* under the title "The Rhapsodist."[4]

In these essays Brown adopted the semi-narrative essay form with which Freneau, Brackenridge, and Dwight had experimented. His persona is a hermit-explorer who has spent many months alone in the Ohio wilderness, meditating on human nature. The essays show Brown's inclination to separate himself from the political squabbling and rhetoric of urban America in the 1780s in order to reflect upon the complexities of the human situation and the many options that Americans might explore to create a just and liberal system of government.

But Brown himself could not remain detached or aloof. The general insincerity of political orations, the apparent hypocrisy of the moral teaching from the pulpit, and the contrast between the promises of the Revolution and the actuality of government policies prompted Brown to consider new schemes of social order. He became increasingly dissatisfied with the legal profession and the scorn for real justice it seemed to symbolize. He wrote to a friend during this period: "[I] was perpetually encumbered with the rubbish of law, and waded with laborious steps through its endless tautologies, its impertinent circuities, its lying assertions and hateful artifices."[5] In this bitter frame of mind, Brown studied Rousseau and the German sentimentalists, and began to question the systems of thought inherited from Puritanism, Quakerism, and Enlightenment rationalism.

In 1790 Brown formed a new friendship that was to have a significant impact upon his intellectual development. The arrival in Philadelphia of Elihu Hubbard Smith, a medical student with literary talent and radical philosophical views, was an important stimulus for Brown. When Brown visited Smith in New York in 1793, he met Smith's colleagues in the Friendly Club, a circle of New York intellectuals including William Dunlap, the writer and artist who became Brown's first biographer. The members of this group helped Brown to define important philosophical issues and nourished his confidence in his literary abilities. Brown said of himself at the time: "I am conscious of a double mental existence . . . my imaginative being [and] my social one."[6] His friends warned him that he must keep these two beings clearly separated, so that he might arrive at social and philosophical truths through rational thinking, and then use those insights to inform and deepen his imaginative work.

At this time Brown was also influenced by William Godwin's *An Enquiry Concerning Political Justice* (1793) and Mary Wollstonecraft's *Historical and Moral View of the Origin and Progress of the French Revolution* (1794) and *Vindication of the Rights of Women* (1792). He was stirred to compose a Utopian romance on women's rights, *Alcuin: A Dialogue*, which appeared in 1798 and was immediately reprinted in the Philadelphia *Weekly Magazine* as "The Rights of Women." A second volume, which may have been suppressed for it was not printed until 1815, shows him to have been disappointed by what he felt was the failure of the framers of the Constitution to remain true to the principles of the Declaration of Independence.[7]

Most of all, Brown questioned the confidence of his age in the rational faculties of man. From a recognition of his own emotional complexity and from his serious study of human psychology (a professional interest of Smith's), Brown came to believe that it is absurd to think that people are always guided by reason and that sense experience is completely valid. The workings of passions and illusions upon the mind from within, and the operations of unfamiliar elements of the external world, can deceive humans, leading them to build elaborate logical systems and make seemingly rational decisions based upon mistaken assumptions. In addition, for all their scientific knowledge, thinkers had yet to explain the forces that people refer to as fate or chance or God. Brown also recognized that the unconscious remained a mysterious and misunderstood aspect of experience that challenged the notion of reasonable action. He also believed that religion and the arts were necessary vehicles for expressing these deeper drives. In a paper delivered at a meeting of the Belles Lettres Club and later reprinted in *The Rhapsodist* and in Dunlap's *Life* of Brown, he talked of the close relationship between the sources and purposes of religion and literature: "The enthusiasm of poetry is no less strong and violent than that of religion; they flow in separate channels, but are derived from the self same fountain."[8]

In regard to social and political systems, therefore, Brown had serious doubts that human drives and passions could be controlled and guided by moral principles, or even by legal restraints. His work within the American legal system had shown him how legal procedures and terminology could be manipulated to serve those with power and money. He became convinced that the yearning of the crafty self-seekers for hierarchy and privilege and the ignorance and gullibility of the poor would impede genuine social revolution. The rhetoric of equality allowed unscrupulous confidence men superb opportunities to exploit the weak. In America, where rank and title and the trappings of social division had been abolished, a cunning individual could use imposture and duplicity to deceive both the rich and the poor. On the larger scale, Brown saw a situation in which the rhetoric of opportunity and freedom existed simultaneously with subtle social restraints designed to maintain the status quo. He was deeply troubled by this pattern; and he believed that, from this grand deception, tensions and repeated upheavals within and between nations would result. Despite these pessimistic convictions, Brown never relinquished his belief in the duty of all intelligent men of good will to encourage their fellow men to live up to their articulated ideals and to strive toward social improvement. In a prose piece in the *Monthly Magazine and American Review* in 1799, he clearly expressed this social purpose.

> A man, whose activity is neither aided by political authority nor by the press, may yet exercise considerable influence on the condition of his neighbors, by the exercise of intellectual powers. His courage may be useful to the timid or the feeble, and his knowledge to the ignorant, as well as his property to those who want. His benevolence and justice may not only protect his kindred and his wife, but rescue the victims of prejudice and passion from the yoke of those domestic tyrants, and shield the powerless from the oppression of power, the poor from the injustice of the rich, and the simple from the stratagems of the cunning.[9]

Thus, Brown decided on a course of authorship as the best means to awaken the people to the dangers and, even more important, to affect the sense and sensibilities of their leaders. In 1797 he wrote an announcement for the book that would have been his first novel, *Sky-Walk; or the Man Unknown to Himself*, in which he postulated a key element of his literary doctrine. Unfortunately, for reasons that are still unclear, this novel was not published and was subsequently lost, but Brown's advertisement expressed this important perspective:

> The popular tales have their merit, but there is one thing in which they are deficient. They are generally adapted to one class of readers only . . . [they] are spurned at by those who are satisfied with nothing but strains of lofty eloquence, the exhibition of powerful motives, and a sort of audaciousness of character. The

world is governed not by the simpleton but by the man
of soaring passions and intellectual energy. By the display of such only can we hope to enchain the attention
and ravish the souls of those who study and reflect.[10]

Although Brown aimed high for the sophisticated reader, he
also believed that "to gain their homage it is not needful
to forgo the approbation of those whose circumstances have
hindered them from making the same progress." And like
Freneau and Brackenridge, Brown knew that his approach to
moral reform had to be subtle and indirect: "so long as men
are led by their affections, I destroy in myself the power of
doing good, if I declare open hostilities with their follies
and weaknesses, and thus forfeit that esteem by which alone I
can hope to influence their judgments to choose the good
and refuse the evil."[11]

Each of Brown's major literary works represents another
stage in his continual effort to modify and alter his fictional
designs in order to win a popular audience while pleasing
his demanding intellectual peers. Despite the speed with
which he sometimes wrote his novels and the flaws in composition that resulted, he never strayed from his purpose of
addressing his works to these two audiences simultaneously.
It was partly this effort that led to the powerful ambiguity
and intriguing complexity of his narrative point of view that
can still hold the attention of learned readers.

Although Brown's major works are often admired for their
psychological depth and Gothic sensationalism, at heart they
are explorations of the impact of the social and economic
order on the lives of individuals. His most interesting and
oddly sympathetic characters are those whose poverty turns
them into villains or into deluded seekers of wealth or
comfort. At the most fundamental level, the philosophical
attitudes, the political notions, and even the psychological
compulsions of Brown's major characters are rooted in the
imbalance of wealth in Western civilization. Brown's own

feeling of financial failure, of possessing a talent that was not rewarded in his society, surely reinforced his view of economic injustice in the new republic. But whatever the ultimate source of his convictions, his intellectual position in his four major novels emphasizes the dangers of a political system that protects the interests of the wealthy while proclaiming the equality of opportunity for all. Such false promises create social tensions that can lead some to use their wits to defraud the unsuspecting and others to despair, violence, and insanity. Brown recognized that in a society built on such an unstable foundation, there would be mad and tragic figures such as his characters Ormond, Carwin, and Huntly roaming the land to make social upheaval or irrational violence an ever-present danger. The works in which he best gave expression to these overriding concerns were his two most compelling novels: *Wieland* and *Arthur Mervyn*.[12]

Brown's first published novel, *Wieland; or, The Transformation: An American Tale*, appeared in September 1798. Recognized as the first important novel written by an American, it is certainly Brown's most famous and readable work of fiction. Adapting the formulas of the Gothic horror tale and the sentimental seduction novel, Brown constructed a fast-paced, suspenseful narrative containing supernatural elements, insanity, and mass murder. Perhaps to add to the appeal of the novel for those readers who had made Susanna Rowson's *Charlotte: A Tale of Truth* and other sentimental novels so popular in America, he chose to cast the narrative in the epistolary form and to use a woman narrator, Clara Wieland. The fairly simple plot and the enormity of Theodore Wieland's crimes should have also attracted a large reading audience.

On the surface, Brown's first novel would not seem to have taxed the intellect of the average eighteenth-century reader of fiction. After protesting to the truth and objectivity of her narrative in the introduction, which contains titillating

promises of "incredible" experience, Clara Wieland recounts
the background of her family.[13] The elder Wieland, father
of Clara and Theodore, came to America after undergoing
a religious conversion in England to "disseminate the truths
of the gospel among the unbelieving nations" of American
Indians. For fourteen years, however, worldly affairs dis-
tracted him. Through his industry he prospered, married,
and acquired wealth and leisure. Finally, he remembered his
spiritual calling, but derision, sickness, and the "license of
savage passion" of the Indians defeated his efforts. He therefore built a temple on the land near his farm on the
Schuylkill River, where daily he engaged in private worship.

When Clara was six years old, her father became convinced
that a command had been laid upon him that he had failed
to obey, an omission for which he must pay a penalty. When
he went to his temple for midnight worship, a mysterious
flash of light and explosion reduced his clothes to ashes and
fatally injured him. Shortly afterward, Clara's mother died,
and the orphaned children were left to ponder the cause of
this catastrophe—whether their father's death was "a fresh
proof that the Divine Ruler interferes in human affairs" or,
as a learned uncle suggests, that it was the result of natural
spontaneous combustion, as had been documented in similar
cases (p. 19). The unresolved question lingers over the young
people and contributes to more disastrous events.

Financially secure and nurtured in the enlightened thought
of the last half of the eighteenth century, Clara and Theodore
grow up in a cheerful atmosphere and hold rational religious
attitudes that focus upon "the grandeur of external nature."
With a bust of Cicero and a harpsichord they transform their
father's temple into a setting for lively conversation and
mirth. Theodore marries their childhood friend Catherine
Pleyel, and Catherine's brother Henry arrives from Europe
to add to the delightful company. Although they feel no
antagonism for each other, the discussions between Henry and

Theodore define quite opposing philosophical and religious convictions. A "champion of intellectual liberty" (p. 25), Pleyel places his complete faith in the testimony of the senses and the guidance of reason. Wieland admits to a fundamental belief in religious truth and the operation of the supernatural in human affairs.

Suddenly, the confidence of these characters in the security of their wealth and intellectual position is undermind by a new phenomenon. One night, when returning to the temple to retrieve a letter, Wieland hears what he thinks is his wife's voice, warning him of impending danger. He later learns that she was too far away for him to have heard her voice. The mystery begins to play upon Wieland's mind. Soon afterward, as Henry is trying to persuade Theodore to accompany him to Europe, where he intends to court a recently widowed baroness, they both hear a voice like Catherine's announce that the baroness is dead. When her death is confirmed a few days later, Wieland is persuaded that the voice is supernatural, and Pleyel is forced to admit that his rationalist theories cannot account for the event.

A stranger named Carwin soon appears on the scene in the trappings of a common vagabond. Despite his ostensible social inferiority, he becomes a member of the little group, charming them with his wit and lively conversation. Clara is then frightened by voices in her closet that seem to be those of two men planning her murder, and Wieland and Pleyel are summoned to her rescue by another voice. Carwin dismisses all of this as pranks. When Clara begins to fall in love with Pleyel, he rejects her because he has overheard a conversation between her and Carwin that revealed her to be promiscuous. Clara returns home to question Carwin about these charges, but finds a note from him warning her of a horrible sight. With that she discovers the body of the murdered Catherine Wieland and meets her deranged, "transformed" brother. Pleading with heaven that he not be required to offer another sacrifice, Theodore advances to murder Clara, who is saved only by the arrival of neighbors. They later inform her that Wieland has also murdered his children.

As she wonders about possible connections between these events and the fate of her father, Clara learns that her brother believes himself commanded to perform deeds by the voice of God and that he is still under divine obligation to kill Henry and herself. At this point Carwin confesses to Clara that he had been using powers of ventriloquism to play tricks on the two couples and that his infatuation with her caused him to turn Henry against her. As Carwin is swearing that he did not create the voice that Wieland hears, the madman, who has escaped from prison, arrives to murder Clara. Carwin uses his skill to invent another divine voice that tells Wieland he has deceived himself. Wieland suddenly realizes the horror of his acts and commits suicide. Carwin's confession exonerates Clara, and three years later she and Henry are married. She attains enough peace of mind to recount the ghastly details in the narrative. Carwin, who is the victim of a mysterious plot started abroad, flees to the countryside to become a farmer.

For most of Brown's readers, the lessons to be drawn from this narrative are fairly obvious. Clearly, the tale points to the dangers of religious enthusiasm and superstition. With Puritan spirit still strong in the land and the signs of another religious revival already evident, the rationalist Brown was warning his readers against unbridled indulgence of religious emotions, which can have dire consequences, even for future generations. The burden of the sins, or saintly delusions, of the fathers is a theme that was to recur in American letters. *Wieland* also offers warnings against selfish jealousy, such as Carwin's, and rash judgments, such as Henry's. Some might view the catastrophic results of Carwin's intrusion as proof of the folly of admitting vulgar types, no matter how seemingly refined, into the circles of the educated and wealthy. Read in any of these ways, *Wieland* would seem to have a satisfactory conclusion with meanings that might bring Brown's readers practical or moral benefits.

For Brown's perceptive readers, however, the novel poses many complex philosophical and social problems that none of the above interpretations resolves. It is a book of questions —indeed, at one point Clara presents a series of rhetorical questions that runs to three pages. The main question is: How can man know that he knows anything to be true? The answer seems to be that he cannot. This dilemma leads to the moral question of how, then, can a man perform moral actions when he must act on deficient knowledge?

As Brown's friends Smith and Dunlap would have recognized, *Wieland* presented a direct challenge to the accepted optimistic psychology of the age. To readers who trusted in the power of human reason and the principles of divine benevolence, Brown presented a chaotic world of irrational experience and inexplicable events. The experiences of each of the four main characters in the novel constituted a denial of the Enlightenment epistemology.

Although Theodore Wieland has been educated in Enlightenment ideas and appears to be a normal individual, the unexplained death of his father secretly haunts him, and his brooding fears place him on the precarious verge of insanity. His emotional state allows the tricks of Carwin to set his mind on a course of tragic self-delusion. But unlike his father, Wieland is not a victim of religious fanaticism. It is his overconfidence in the validity of his sensory experience that destroys him, leading him to believe that the voices he hears are genuine and must have a supernatural source. Nor does he doubt his senses when he hears the voice of Carwin or when he hears the voice of his own unconscious. If he had been capable of admitting that there may be natural phenomena that men have not yet understood, or that his own

senses might sometimes deceive him, he might have questioned the source of his divine guidance. But his intellectual
position precludes such doubts and makes him vulnerable to
the tendency toward irrational behavior that he inherited
from his father. The combination of Puritan pietism and
Enlightenment optimism seals his fate.

In Henry Pleyel, Brown presents a case study of the folly
of formulating conclusions strictly upon sensory evidence,
without testing them against previous knowledge. Because
he has such faith in the validity of his impressions, Henry
simply adds up the facts as he receives them from his senses,
and concludes that Clara and Carwin are lovers. His former
awareness of Clara's virtue does not give him pause when
his eyes and ears provide evidence, however circumstantial,
of a new truth.

The most intriguing intellectual problems of the novel
involve the characters of Clara and Carwin. As narrator,
Clara has it in her power to affect the reader's perception of
events and motives. At one point she even warns that she
has necessarily transformed her experiences in the account
she has written: "My narrative may be invaded by inaccuracy
and confusion; . . . What but ambiguities, abruptnesses, and
dark transitions, can be expected from the historian who is,
at the same time, the sufferer of these disasters?" (p. 147). In
addition, she says these events have driven her to a mental
breakdown while the therapy of writing has saved her from
the "wild and fantastical incongruities" threatening to destroy
her mind. Indeed, a close reading of her narrative reveals
that Clara is not always fully conscious of her own motives
and impulses. Use of this narrative point of view allows the
reader to engage in a rigorous analysis of the thought process
by which Clara interprets her own sense impressions and
draws her conclusions. Brown thereby raises philosophical
and artistic questions about the validity of historical evidence,
as opposed to the deeper truths of imaginative literature.

Unlike Pleyel and Wieland, Clara is not satisfied with either rationalist or religious answers to the epistemological questions that her experience raises: "Which of my senses was the prey of a fatal illusion?" she wonders. Quite early in her account, she states her belief that the senses cannot be trusted and that human actions based on sensory impressions may be in error. "The will is the tool of the understanding, which must fashion its conclusion on the notices of sense. If the senses be depraved, it is impossible to calculate the evils that may flow from the consequent deduction of the understanding" (p. 35).

Aware of the possible defect of the senses, Clara is not ready to jump to conclusions, as her brother and her lover do. Faced by mysterious events, she tends to remain passive and rely upon her courage. Because Clara suspends judgments, she is able to be more intuitive than those around her. While she has no conscious reason to distrust Carwin, her first contact with him rouses an inexplicable impression that he is somehow the cause of the voices and delusions. Similarly, despite her love for her brother and her trust in him, her dreams warn her that there is reason to fear him. She cannot consciously act upon these forebodings, however, because intuition provides no factual evidence, and her education has taught her to trust only in sensory evidence. Therefore, Clara is unable to follow the more self-assured courses of Wieland and Pleyel and is left to ponder her premonitions.

Significantly, Clara's fears are turned inward and transformed into a form of self-torture and longing for martyrdom, tendencies that gradually appear as the novel progresses. Although she finds Carwin physically unattractive and fears him, she is drawn to him and sensually aroused by the sound of his voice. She admits at one point that the mysterious incidents deeply troubling her companions produce in her "a sentiment not unallied to pleasure." Clara seems to want to reach out and embrace the catastrophe she feels looming in her future. When she hears a potential ravisher lurking in her closet, she even struggles to open the door, in order to confront him and her fate (p. 87). Brown was greatly interested in the latest theories of abnormal psychology, and his portraits of Clara and Theodore contain evidence of his awareness of Oedipal and incestuous impulses. Clearly, he wanted to convince his educated readers of the truth of Clara's observation that "ideas exist in our minds that can be accounted for by no established laws."

For Brown, the most interesting character in his first novel was surely Carwin. In the "advertisement" for *Wieland*, he promised his readers a sequel that would tell the full story of Carwin; and he did compose several chapters of the "Memoirs of Carwin, the Biloquist" in 1798 before he put it aside. He later published the pieces as installments in *The Literary Magazine and American Register* in 1803–4, but the work remained unfinished. Although there is enough information about Carwin in *Wieland* itself to enable the reader to formulate an interpretation of his character and his place in the overall meaning of the book, the Carwin fragment is useful, for in it Brown filled out his background.[14]

Besides being the catalyst who sparks the dementia of Theodore and the villain who causes Clara distress and torment, Carwin provides the key to the social and philosophical meaning of *Wieland*. He is an outsider who lacks the educational and financial advantages of the Wieland group. But because he is audacious, clever, and skillful, he is able to move freely into the upper level of society and to threaten the group's security. His rootlessness and his poverty have bred a form of irresponsibility that causes him to indulge his curiosity by probing into the lives of the Wielands for mere thrills. The immorality of his behavior is emphasized when he engages in an illicit affair with Clara's servant Judith at the same time that he claims to love Clara. While he constantly tells himself that he means no harm and that he uses his power only to benevolent ends, it becomes evident that he little cares what the consequences of his actions may be. He is gradually exposed as a satanic intruder, a "double-tongued deceiver" in the Wieland garden, who creates havoc among the unwary. By introducing phenomena that can beguile the senses, this perverse impostor undermines the eighteenth-century confidence in Lockean epistemology and the fundamental goodness of human nature.

In the Carwin fragment Brown gives this portrayal even greater social implications. There Carwin is a penniless but shrewd son of an American farmer who headed to Philadelphia to make his fortune, an end that, for him, justified any means. A political radical named Ludloe, who is a ranking member of a utopian organization called the Illuminati, discovers Carwin to be a fitting candidate for the secret society and takes him to Europe to prepare him for his political role. Ludloe believes that he and his brotherhood act from purely benevolent and rational motives. But for all of the idealism of Ludloe's statements about the present social and economic injustices of the world, it is clear that he is motivated by selfish desires. The rules of the secret society, which dictate instant death for infractions, alert the reader to the dangers of misguided benevolence.

In "Memoirs of Carwin" Brown explores a theme that is central in *Wieland*: the persistent conflict between established society and individuals who are frustrated by existing political systems. If the Wielands are to be protected against men like Carwin, they must either strengthen their defenses against the ruthless and unprincipled or construct new ways to foster social equality. Brown was deeply affected by the radical thinkers of his time, but in his fiction he struck a balance: his reformers are justified in their complaints about their societies, but they often become selfishly motivated villains; at the same time the insulation and naïveté of his affluent characters shield them from real knowledge of the world, making them easy prey for sharpers. At first glance a novel of Gothic horror and sentimental romance, *Wieland* is also a serious intellectual document in which Brown questions some of the fundamental assumptions of his time.

Although the initial sales of *Wieland* were modest, Brown was encouraged by the warm critical acclaim he received and continued the extraordinary burst of productivity that led him to publish his four major novels in less than a year. After false starts in the "Memoirs of Carwin" and the "Memoirs of Stephen Calvert," Brown completed *Ormond; or, The Secret Witness* early in 1799. During this same period he was also contributing short stories and reviews to the *Monthly Magazine and American Review*. Best known of his stories is "Thessalonica: A Roman Story" (1799), which illustrates the social lesson that "no diligence or moderation can fully restrain the passions of the multitude."[15]

The *First Part* of *Arthur Mervyn or Memoirs of the Year 1793* was published by Hugh Maxwell in Philadelphia early in 1799. *Arthur Mervyn, Second Part* appeared in the summer of 1800. The two parts were published together in London in 1803 as *Arthur Mervyn. A Tale. In Three Volumes*. When considered as a single novel of two parts, *Arthur Mervyn* lacks the narrative unity, the force and clarity of style, and the logical character development of *Wieland*, yet it is in many ways a more intriguing and challenging book because in it Brown drew his narrative powers to their limits.[16] The plot of *Arthur Mervyn* is extremely intricate, but it is essential to understand the tangled events that shape the main characters and reveal their motives.

When the story opens, Mervyn is sick and leaning against a wall of a house in Philadelphia, expecting to die. He is saved by Dr. Stevens, who takes him into his home where he eventually recovers. Stevens is a benevolent man, inclined to think the better of people, and Mervyn pleases him by declaring that he yearns to be a simple yeoman with some time for study. Reluctant at first to talk about his life, Mervyn launches into his narrative when one of Dr. Stevens's friends, Wortley, accuses him of being an associate of a swindler named Welbeck.

As in Brown's earlier works, the difference between the surface meaning of the narrator's tale and the deeper meaning of the novel hinges upon the reader's perception of how the speaker may be slanting his life story. Throughout the book Mervyn protests his innocence, his total sincerity, and the absolute benevolence and selflessness of his intentions. Thus, on first examination the story appears to present the struggle of a virtuous country boy against the corruption of the city. This is what Mervyn would have Stevens believe and what Stevens wishes to believe, since it is not in his nature to be distrustful.

The son of a Pennsylvania farmer, Mervyn left home to make his fortune after his brothers and sisters died successively as each neared the age of nineteen, after his mother also followed them to the grave, and after a servant girl then enticed his father into marriage, destroying Mervyn's hopes of inheriting the farm. Soon after his arrival in Philadelphia, he was hired by Welbeck, who took him into his magnificent house. In the fine clothes that Welbeck provided him, Mervyn resembled a youth named Clavering whom he had known briefly and who had recently disappeared from Philadelphia. Mysteriously, Welbeck made Mervyn promise to reveal nothing of his real history. When Mervyn learned that Clavering was the son of the man who owned the house in which Welbeck lived, he began to worry that he might be involved in a plot. He protests vehemently to Stevens that he was preparing to extricate himself from Welbeck, but Welbeck's benevolent nature drew him in further. By accident he learned that Welbeck was to be the victim of a

local intrigue, and he delayed his departure in order to warn
him. Just then, he discovered his employer in his study, with
the body of a man he had just shot.

At this point Welbeck told Mervyn his own tale of passion,
dissimulation, and deceit. Like Carwin and Ormond, Welbeck was left with nothing by his father, and his humiliation
and strong "love of independence" made him willing to use
any means to attain financial security. He declared to Mervyn,
"My virtuous theories and comprehensive erudition would
not have saved me from the basest of crimes" (p. 86). Be-
friended by an American named Watson who brought him
from England, Welbeck proceeded to ruin the man's married
sister and drove her to an anguished death. With a burning
need to win the "esteem of mankind," he tried forgery and
counterfeiting before falling onto a rare chance to steal a
fortune from a young man who had died of yellow fever and
had entrusted Welbeck with the sum of $20,000, to be
delivered to his sister, Clemenza Lodi. Welbeck of course
kept the money and then seduced Clemenza, who remained
virtually his prisoner. Welbeck confessed that he was planning a new scheme in which Mervyn was to play an unsuspecting part; but he was stopped by the arrival of Watson,
the American. In a pistol duel Welbeck then killed Watson.

Despite his shock at the "scene of guilt and ignominy
disclosed where my rash and inexperienced youth had suspected nothing but loftiness and magnanimity" (p. 107),
Mervyn helped Welbeck bury Watson in the basement and
aided his escape to New Jersey. In the middle of the Delaware
River, however, Welbeck jumped out of the boat; and
Mervyn assumed he had died. After returning to Welbeck's
house to resume his rustic dress, he departed for the country.
He tells Stevens that he had had enough of the false appearances and corruption of the city and now sought the honest
rural life. He hopes that this narrative has satisfied the

insinuations of the doctor's friend, but other questions cause him to continue his tale.

Back in the country, Mervyn found employment in the home of the Hadwins, a simple Quaker family, and courted their daughter Eliza. He also intended to study and translate a manuscript that he knew to have been the property of the dead brother of Clemenza Lodi and which he had taken from Welbeck's house; one day he discovered in its pages $20,000 in banknotes. He concluded that the money was the same entrusted to Welbeck and decided to take it to Clemenza. But on an errand to disease-racked Philadelphia he contracted yellow fever and went to rest at Welbeck's house, where he discovered Welbeck himself madly searching for the missing manuscript. An argument ensued in which Welbeck deceived Mervyn into believing that the money was counterfeit; and before Welbeck could stop him, Mervyn set fire to the notes. The enraged Welbeck fled again, and Mervyn wandered the streets until he came to the place where Stevens found him. With declarations that there is "nothing which I more detest than equivocation and mystery," Mervyn ends the first part of his tale.

The first part of the novel could stand as a unified narrative, even without its sequel. It is a tale of virtue versus villainy, with the egocentric Welbeck serving as a foil to the well-meaning Mervyn. Unredeemed by any utopian social purpose, Welbeck appears in the first part as the total scoundrel who confesses to an "incurable depravity" that has made him "the slave of sensual impulses" and ambition (p. 87).

It may be that Brown originally intended this work to illustrate the lesson of virtue rewarded, but during the year that elapsed between the appearance of the first and second parts, he decided to expose the other side of Mervyn's character. The second part casts a shadow of doubt over all of Mervyn's professed motives. He appears to be a calculating opportunist who masks his real motives and self-interest by fashioning his rhetoric to strike the most responsive chords in his listeners. At the same time, Brown shows Welbeck to be a pathetic victim of passions generated by his early impoverishment and humiliation. In the second part, Welbeck is a broken and penitent man whose final punishment is Mervyn moralizing over him as he breathes his last in debtor's prison. Brown even balances the theme of the city versus the country by showing the darker side of rural life. Most interesting of all the shifts in the second part, however, is Mervyn's rise to wealth and leisure through a series of actions that he says are the results of chance but that the attentive reader may see as the result of his shrewd calculations and smooth dealings.

As the second part opens, Dr. Stevens informs Mervyn he has learned that Welbeck placed Clemenza Lodi in a house of prostitution (owned by a woman named Mrs. Villars) after she became pregnant by him. Anxious to aid Clemenza, and still concerned over the Hadwin family and Eliza, Mervyn departs for the country. In the meantime, Wortley investigates Mervyn's involvement in the affairs of Welbeck. Arthur's old neighbor, Mrs. Althorpe, charges that before he left his father's farm he committed a string of evil deeds, including the theft of his father's horse and money. When Mervyn returns, Stevens confronts him with new accusations, and Arthur relates the events that occurred after his departure for the Hadwin house. The plague, which spread to the country, took the lives of the Hadwin father and his daughter Susan, leaving Eliza the apparent owner of the farm until her callous uncle Philip Hadwin claimed the property. Arthur then rescued Clemenza Lodi from the house of ill repute, where he also met Achsa Fielding, a wealthy widow six years his senior, whom he eventually marries.

From Percy Shelley and William Dunlap to the most recent

critics, even Brown's sympathetic readers are bothered by his decision to have Arthur marry Achsa Fielding.[17] After establishing Eliza Hadwin as the young, attractive, forthright American country girl, Brown surprises everyone, including Dr. Stevens and even Mervyn himself, by having his hero chase a woman whom the usually moderate Dr. Stevens describes as "unsightly as a *night-hag*, tawney as a moor, . . . [having] less luxuriance than a charred log, fewer elasticities than a sheet pebble" (p. 432). Indeed, the shift so complicates the ending of the book that it forces the reader to reassess all of Arthur's previous narrative. If, as it seems, Arthur has chosen the financial security Achsa's wealth offers over the life of social purpose, moral purity, and vigorous labors he has claimed to desire, then his earlier idealistic expressions are called into question. And that is exactly the function of Arthur's choice: to send the reader back, with a new skepticism, to the beginning of his testimony for a retrospective look at the new American hero, his rhetoric, his methods, and his destiny. If this book leaves the thoughtful reader somewhat perplexed and provokes a vigorous moral debate about Mervyn's character, then Brown may have come closer in this novel than in any other to achieving the highest standard for good fiction set in his time.

As the title indicates, *Arthur Mervyn or Memoirs of the Year 1793* explores a single character and a historical social setting. The interaction between Mervyn and his society has moral consequences that demand the reader's intellectual engagement. Yet, while appealing to the reader to arrive at moral judgments, the intricate plots, internal contradictions, and multiple narrators seem to deny the presence of a controlling moral vision. As a result, readers tend to concentrate entirely upon the conscious actions of Mervyn and to choose sides over the issue of his guilt or innocence. Most interpretations of this novel therefore miss part of the richness and meaning of Brown's most ambitious work. To see

Mervyn as an innocent rewarded, and thereby to ignore the elements of the confidence man in his character, is to miss the novel's ironies and comic dimension. At the same time, to view Arthur as a total villain is to flirt with anachronistic misreadings that present the novel as a cynical and nihilistic forerunner of Melville's *Pierre* or *The Confidence Man*.[18] But Brown again struck a careful balance between the inclinations of the individual and the powerful effects of society upon him.

When Mervyn is examined in the context of his world, the full complexity of his character becomes apparent. Neither picaresque saint nor complete confidence man, Mervyn, a near anagram of Everyman, is a symbol of the amoral, unschooled but intelligent individual struggling to survive in the social turmoil of the post-Revolutionary age. Using every skill he can acquire and exploiting every advantage nature has given him, including the strengths and weaknesses of others, Mervyn struggles to create a place for himself in his society. Throughout this process of accommodation, Mervyn's motives, ends, and means are constantly changing, and a careful assessment of his adjustment to those around him provides the only sound foundation on which to judge his character. In the end, this kind of analysis reveals that the moral resolution of the novel does not depend entirely upon a verdict of Arthur's guilt or innocence. A deeper understanding of the novel's full meaning requires a recognition of the tragic limitations of his character and the complex nature of his response to the social order, or rather disorder, in which he exists.

On first reading it is difficult to look behind the mass of complicated events to determine how Arthur might be distorting the facts to suit his purposes. But Brown does provide the attentive reader hints along the way, such as the quick glimpse behind Mervyn's mask when he boasts about his skillful manipulation of "rhetorick" (p. 305) in the argument with Philip Hadwin over the legitimacy of Hadwin's claim to Eliza's estate. Mervyn explains to Stevens how he calculated each word and gesture to leave Hadwin with the impression that he was *"a queer sort of chap"* (p. 309), and he proudly declares: "the stuff that I was made of was damnably tough and devilishly pliant" (p. 308). Given his bias in Mervyn's favor, it is not surprising that Stevens fails to draw the logical conclusion that Mervyn may be deceiving him as well, but an alert reader cannot fail to catch that implication in this scene. In fact, Stevens even has extraordinary faith in the countenance of Mervyn rather than in his words, which is itself cause for the reader's suspicion. At one point Stevens admits that if *he* were the reader he would not believe Mervyn's story: "Had I heard it from another or read it in a book, I might perhaps have found it possible to suspect the truth . . . but the face of Mervyn is the index of an honest mind" (pp. 229–30). Yet for some reason, which he never explains, Stevens has chosen to make his faith in Mervyn's honesty the only thing between himself and total cynicism: "If Mervyn has deceived me, there is an end to my confidence in human nature" (pp. 248–49). But Brown's reader, who need not be swayed by what Wortley calls Mervyn's "smooth features and fluent accents" (p. 249), has the advantage of being able to reexamine his story in light of his later actions.

Certainly one reason to question Mervyn's honesty is that he is always entering people's homes without bothering to knock and is repeatedly caught in the act of taking someone's property. Of course, each time he has some excuse—he was lost, his mission was urgent, or, as he says at one point, "my mind was deeply occupied in meditation; and, with my usual carelessness of forms, I entered the house [without notice] and made my way to the parlour" (p. 354). The situation is repeated so often that it is prevented from becoming a running joke only by the moral questions raised by the nearly disastrous consequences that often result. When he first arrived in the city, Mervyn was duped by a young wag who left him inside a dark bedroom occupied by members of a merchant family named Thetford. There Arthur overheard conversation that revealed a business plot against Welbeck. This information about the local commercial intrigues later enables him to thread his way through the complicated interconnections among the friends of Dr. Stevens and the enemies of Welbeck.

This situation serves as a paradigm for Mervyn's relationship to all people in his society. He repeatedly intrudes into people's lives and somehow gains knowledge or makes contacts that enable him to survive. Indeed, he even meets Achsa after forcing his way into Mrs. Villars's house, an act that he almost pays for with his life when Villars tries to shoot him. Also, Welbeck has good reason to accuse Mervyn of being a thief, for Arthur stole the Lodi manuscript containing $20,000 and broke into Welbeck's house; and, on another occasion, unknown to Welbeck, Mervyn sneaked into his bedroom and read his private letters. Admitting that he has no regard for legalities or for the rights of private property, Mervyn tries to justify his intrusions with a spurious theory of ends justifying means (p. 322). Although the twisted logic of his rationalization is not challenged by any character in the book, Mervyn's dubious argument about "good intentions" (p. 329) is likely to cause the reader to think of the road to hell rather than to sustain confidence in Mervyn's honesty and reliability.

In view of Mervyn's final situation of comfort and security and in view of his readiness to use any means to attain his goals, there is also good reason to study the exact nature of Mervyn's relationship to Welbeck. Is Mervyn simply using Welbeck as he later plans to depend on Achsa? Mervyn admits that he had ample reason to flee Welbeck from quite early in the relationship. Welbeck required Arthur to hide his true identity from Mrs. Wentworth, Welbeck's wealthy landlady. Also, Mervyn watched Welbeck put on a false front when he attended a local social gathering. And because Arthur really believed Welbeck to be Clemenza's father, he interprets signs of their sexual intimacy as evidence of "the blackest and most stupendous of all crimes" (p. 76). But Mervyn stays and even allows Welbeck to believe that his anxiety over Welbeck's activities is the result of homesickness—a deception that contradicts his claim that "my lips [are] untainted by prevarication or falsehood" (p. 135). When he finally does intend to abandon Welbeck, Mervyn still tries to save him from Thetford's plot. As a result, he becomes involved in the shooting of Watson, aids Welbeck in the victim's basement burial, and assists the killer in his escape. The only explanation Mervyn can give for this loyalty, which makes him a partner in crime, is that he acted out of a sense of duty and gratitude to his employer. It is no wonder that Wortley calls Mervyn's story "a tissue of ingenious and plausible lies" (p. 226).

Either Mervyn is a complete fool, of which he gives little evidence, or he has other reasons for his attachment to Welbeck that he conceals from Stevens. Mervyn's own admission that his first thought was of marrying Clemenza and inheriting Welbeck's wealth lends strong support to Wortley's suspicion that Mervyn hoped to profit from his association with Welbeck.[19] In his dying words, Welbeck also accuses Mervyn of having preyed upon him in the hope of picking up chances for gain that the master villain might have missed. Although there is nothing concrete to support Welbeck's charges, they do darken the shadow Wortley casts over Mervyn's character.

Another reason for being suspicious of Mervyn is that there are many glaring contradictions in his tale and in his descriptions of his own nature. Throughout his narrative, Mervyn makes great claims for his love of books and his avid reading, and he insinuates that given a chance he would blossom into a man of letters. But while his assertions lead Stevens to become the patron of Mervyn's brief medical education, they will not stand up to scrutiny. His speech is bare of literary references, and the only author he gives evidence of having read is his "darling writer," perhaps Benjamin Franklin, whose "encomiums on rural life" (p. 47) are the foundation of Mervyn's philosophy and ethics.[20] Indeed, a wary reader may ask how much of Mervyn's entire self-description springs from the Franklin model in the Do-Good and Busy-Body essays. Mervyn's claims to learning are dubious at best.

Furthermore, Mervyn's various assertions that he has dreams of living as a Jeffersonian gentleman-farmer, that he has a warm-hearted affection for humanity, and even that he has a romantic nature, all fail to be supported by his actions and too often serve as convenient obfuscations.[21] For example, when Mrs. Althorpe's account of Arthur's youth casts a shadow over his character, Mervyn explains that he had held back details because of his delicate sensibilities: "I cannot look upon the sufferings of those I love without exquisite pain. I cannot steel my heart by the force of reason and by the submission of necessity; and therefore, too frequently employ the cowardly expedient of endeavoring to forget what I cannot remember without agony" (p. 343). Yet he often seems impermeable, as upon the death of Susan Hadwin, whom he abruptly buries without even bothering to awaken Eliza, who chastises him for his callousness. Similarly, he endures other deaths and the sufferings of many close to him and reports the details with cool accuracy, as when he reasons that his father's death "was an event . . . not unfortunate" (p. 393) or when he curtly tells Welbeck of the death of the child that resulted from Welbeck's affair with Clemenza (p. 337). Mervyn also seems to share the cruel indifference the elder Thetford displays toward the cries of a servant girl who begs not to be sent to the public hospital to die, for he remarks that "the rank and education of the young woman, might be some apology for negligence" (p. 159).

Perhaps the most conspicuous contradictions between Mervyn's self-descriptions and his actions stem from his relationship with Eliza Hadwin. His pronouncements about his vulnerability to the charms of women are surely designed to help him win the sympathy of another important listener, Mrs. Stevens. To the doctor's wife, whose name incidentally is also Eliza and who remains one of Arthur's strongest advocates, Mervyn explains how his "romantic and untutored disposition" made him "liable" to being captivated by Eliza who "stole insensibly upon my heart" (p. 124). Yet again, his actions prove that these emotions are much more governable than his rhetorical effusions, for when he calculates the amount of Eliza's inheritance, he concludes that "to foster my passion was to foster a disease destructive of either my integrity or my existence" (p. 125). He then simply stops talking to Eliza and ignores her protests and pleas. Later, when Mr. Hadwin and Susan die and the property appears up for the taking, Mervyn's feelings for Eliza are aroused again, and he urges her to burn the will that appoints Philip Hadwin her guardian, take the loose cash in the house, and run away with him. Next, when Hadwin establishes his claims to the property, Arthur undergoes another "change in my views with regard to my friend" (p. 311). He weighs the girl's depleted fortune against the opportunities for advancement he has found in urban society and decides that Eliza would only hinder his rise in the world.

In view of Brown's well-known support of women's equality, the allusions in this novel to the works of William Godwin, and the sympathy which women readers were likely to feel for Eliza in the ensuing lover's debate, Arthur's self-centered rejection of Eliza serves as another clue to the dubious nature of his character.[22] After Arthur tells Eliza that her immaturity and ignorance would only burden him during his "apprenticeship to fortitude and wisdom" (p. 293), Eliza makes a powerful argument for sharing in his years of learning and experience:

> What angers and distresses me is, that you think me unworthy to partake of your cares and labors; that you regard my company as an obstacle and incumbrance; that assistance and counsel must all proceed from you; and that no scene is fit for me, but what you regard as slothful and inglorious. Have I not the same claim to be wise, and active, and courageous as you are? . . . but you desire it all for yourself. Me, you think poor weak and contemptible; fit for nothing but to spin and churn. Provided I exist, am screened from the weather, have enough to eat and drink, you are satisfied. As to strengthening my mind and enlarging my knowledge, these things are valuable to you, but on me they are thrown away. I deserve not the gift. [p. 296]

The high-mindedness of Eliza's appeal certainly stands in sharp contrast to the pettiness of Mervyn's continued concern with property and finances. After admitting that he "had certainly considered her sex as utterly unfitting her for these scenes and pursuit, to which I had destined myself" (p. 296), Mervyn immediately thinks again of her property and whether marriage to her would compel him to "take up my abode in the woods, to abide forever in one spot, to shackle my curiosity, or limit my excursions" (p. 297). He finally decides against marriage on the grounds that time would probably "unfold qualities in her which I did not at present suspect, and which would evince an incurable difference in our minds" (p. 297). Surely part of the reason that the reversal involved in Arthur's decision to marry Achsa Fielding remains so disturbing to readers is that Eliza emerges as such a strongly sympathetic character in spite of Mervyn's efforts to suppress her with his self-serving rhetoric.

Even when there is no obvious contradiction in Mervyn's assertions, his pious platitudes about his honesty and benevolence and his self-righteous attacks on others are so hollow as to sound nearly comic.[23] As Warner Berthoff has observed, the scene in which Mervyn "stands at the door of a brothel waiting with appropriate trepidation to present himself to some 'supercilious and voluptuous being' suggests an instinct for the comic [in Brown] that would have been worth nourishing." Although Berthoff "does not want to claim too much for Brown as a comic artist manqué," he does believe that the novel comes "close to a kind of laconic social comedy."[24] Indeed, there is much in the novel to suggest the influence of Fielding's *Joseph Andrews* and *Tom Jones*, including the name of Mervyn's unexpected bride.[25]

Yet while there is surely a bit of Blifil in Arthur, the comic dimension of his character is still another mask the reader must penetrate to arrive at a thorough understanding of his motivations and meaning. The strident tone of his sanctimonious utterings, such as his extraordinary condemnation of his revengeful feelings toward a villain named Colvill who raped his sister, put into sharp relief those rare statements of studied self-awareness that reflect the real desperateness of Mervyn's situation in the world. One such remark that has the ring of truth is Arthur's reported statement regarding Betty Lawrence, the servant girl of doubtful virtue who married his aging father: "But think not that I blame Betty. Place me in her situation, and I should have acted just so. I should have formed just such notions of my interest, and pursued it by the same means" (p. 237). This judgment, which may indeed be a prediction of his own marriage, reveals a side of Mervyn that Dr. Stevens chooses not to see.

It is, however, a side of Mervyn that Welbeck believes he does see. Mervyn and Welbeck have much in common—a mutual scorn for manual labor, the law, and the property rights of others. Also, Mervyn claims to have learned much from his master "on the principles of human nature; on the delusiveness of appearance; on the perviousness of fraud; and on the power with which nature has invested human beings over the thoughts and acts of each other" (p. 137). Thus, it is significant that the strongest charges against Mervyn come from the man who knows him most intimately —and that it is Welbeck's conclusion that Mervyn has learned too well. When Arthur self-righteously condemns the imprisoned Welbeck, the dying sharper accuses Mervyn of being the greater villain: "Curses on thy lips, infernal messenger! Chant elsewhere thy rueful ditty! Vanish! if thou wouldst not feel in thy heart fangs red with blood less guilty than thine. . . . you are the author of the scene that you describe" (p. 337). While Welbeck can not be expected to be objective about Mervyn, only he can provide the reader insight into a relationship that Mervyn keeps carefully concealed. Welbeck truly believes that he has been a biter bitten by a villain more artful than himself: "Thy qualities are marvelous. Every new act of thine outstrips the last, and belies the newest calculations. . . . under that innocent guise there lurked a heart treacherous and cruel" (pp. 258–59).

Once the evidence begins to unfold, other aspects of the narrative give hints of Mervyn's duplicity. For example, the many similarities not only between the appearances but also the life stories of Mervyn and Clavering take on new meaning with the recognition that the tale that Clavering recounts of his experience to Arthur's mother is a lie designed to enable him to win asylum, alter his identity, and escape his past. In contrast to his report to her, Clavering did not flee cruel parents in England but doting ones in Philadelphia.[26] Thus, the parallels between these two young men may suggest that, as with Clavering, Mervyn may have fabricated parts of his own history.

Another significant relationship that runs throughout the narrative is Mervyn's connection to a youth named Wallace.

All that can be proved about Wallace from the hard evidence is that he is an ambitious young man who works for the Thetfords and is trying to make his way in the Philadelphia business world so that he may marry Susan Hadwin, Eliza's sister. His plans meet a tragic end when Susan dies of the plague. Wallace meets the same end while searching for her father in the city. But Arthur pieces together fragments of information about Wallace to paint quite a different picture of him in his tale to Stevenses. First, with little grounds for so doing, Mervyn decides that Wallace was the young wag who duped him on his first night in town by telling him he could stay in a room which turned out to be occupied by members of the Thetford family. Also, to support his view of Wallace as villain, Arthur uses a stranger's report that a feverish, dying Wallace made obscene jokes and remarks about women, including his fiancée Susan. Through an accumulation of such hearsay and of surmises that Wallace may have been involved in the corrupt business dealings of the Thetfords, Mervyn completes his character assassination of the youth whose death Arthur says he welcomed.

But Brown clearly spent so much prose upon this complicated subplot because analysis of Mervyn's motives for this attack reveals more about Arthur's character. Mervyn had reason to be jealous of Wallace, whose ambition had enabled him to earn enough money in the city in two years to finance his marriage; Wallace's marriage to Susan would have assured him half of the Hadwin estate. In the context of the novel's important theme of the sexual-financial competition that economic conditions encourage among young men,[27] it is not improbable that Mervyn would use Wallace as a foil in the rhetorical strategy of his narrative: a blackened Wallace, and for that matter a grotesque Welbeck, make a useful contrast to a whitened, angelic Mervyn.

Indeed, to recognize the moral complexity of Mervyn is to understand how similar he is not only to Welbeck but to Brown's other villains as well; comparisons of Mervyn to Ormond, Carwin, and even Wieland are useful for understanding what sets Mervyn apart.[28] Like the others, Mervyn arises from a tragic family situation in which a failure of paternal authority is the key to an unbridled recklessness in the son, and like the others too, he uses the opportunities of an open republican society to escape his background and fabricate a new identity. Willing to use any means to attain his ends, he also possesses the talent for imitating the manners, style, and dress of his social betters, and he has the rhetorical skills needed for persuading or deceiving others.

The difference between Arthur and his destructive and defeated counterparts is that he is able to control his emotions and repress his passions. Without the lust for fame that destroys Welbeck, the irrational obsession of Wieland, the passion for a woman that ruins Ormond, or the unchecked curiosity of Carwin, Mervyn is able to steer a deliberate course among the gaping jaws and ready claws of the new society. Only twice does he lose control of his emotions, and both times he pays for it with physical injury—in the basement of Welbeck's house when he becomes lost in a dark corridor and thinks he is trapped there with the body of Watson and again in Clemenza's bedroom at Mrs. Villars's house. In the first instance, he rushes wildly around the dark passages and crashes into a wall, which leaves him bloody and nearly unconscious. In the second, he becomes so caught up with Clemenza and Mrs. Fielding that he fails to realize that Mrs. Villars intends to shoot him until a bullet grazes his ear. In all his other social interactions, including his relationships with women, Mervyn acts with an icy reserve and calculated restraint for which he is appropriately rewarded in his marriage to Achsa Fielding.

In spite of his protests to the contrary and Stevens's statements in his defense, Arthur is clearly not the simple innocent he pretends to be in Philadelphia. His previous experiences have taught him a great deal: from Betty Lawrence he has learned that the inheritance, the farm, goes to the swift, and from the experiences of his family—including drunkness, wife-beating, rape, and early death—he has learned the dangers of disease, human brutality, and irrationality. He may not be a scholar, but Arthur understands the power of language as his only tool of survival. So successful is he at concealing his deficiencies and creating an appealing identity that the characters who look at him most objectively are the most baffled: Mrs. Althorpe says of him, "take away his jacket and trowsers, and you have as spruce a fellow as ever came from dancing-school or college" (p. 232). Mrs. Wentworth expresses bewilderment: "You may possibly be honest. Such a one as you, with your education and address, may possibly have passed all your life in a hovel; but it is scarcely credible, let me tell you" (p. 363). While Brown's readers may sometimes feel similarly confused, the novel does contain sufficient information about Mervyn's character to allow for an understanding of his psychological composition, which may account for, though perhaps not justify, his chameleonlike response to his world.

Although Mervyn is less innocent than he at first appears, Brown's American society has created great liabilities for him to surmount. Because of the stories about him spread by his old neighbor, Mrs. Althorpe, who testifies against him to Wortley and the Stevenses, he is pursued by a reputation for being lazy, brash, and even cruel. Mrs. Althorpe claims, for example, that he seduced his stepmother and stole his father's savings. The reader never knows if these charges are true. What is certain is that Arthur has no education or marketable skill and no family, friends, or obvious personal talents to help him to survive in the world. Because, according to his report, he had to protect his mother from the drunken rages of his father, he has a skewed attitude toward older men; and because of the recent deaths of his mother and siblings (from

an inherited malady that claimed them before their nineteenth birthdays), he is haunted by dark forebodings of his
own impending end.[29] When he learns late in the narration
that his father died, Mervyn says he now has no traces of a
past; and when he wanders the streets of Philadelphia, after
being tricked by the first person he met and before meeting
Welbeck, he is quite alone.[30]

To survive his desperate situation, Mervyn must be able
to turn every event into an opportunity and be able to mold
himself into a new personality engaging enough to allow him
access to society. In the back of Mervyn's mind hovers
Franklin's maxim that an ambitious man should write something worth reading or do something worth writing about—
Arthur does both. Thus, every judgment the reader makes
about Mervyn must take into consideration the nature of
the society to which he accommodates himself, yet all the
while Brown never lets the reader forget the sordid state of
that society.

The post-Revolutionary society of Philadelphia in the
novel is pervaded by a lack of authority and moral leadership,
symbolized by the city hospital during the plague, where
victims cry for help to the indifferent and jesting attendants.
Disregard for the law is not confined to criminals like
Welbeck but is the rule. Even the good citizen Dr. Stevens
does not think of seeking aid from the authorities in the
death of Watson because he does not trust the legal system.
Stevens has seen his friend Carlton imprisoned for a minor
debt incurred by his father (pp. 262–64) while real villains
walk free, and he understands quite well the nature of the
American legal system, which favors those with wealth and
power.

It is a world of failed fathers and ruined families. The
fathers of Mervyn, Welbeck, and Achsa desert or abandon
their children while those like Mr. Hadwin, Watson, and the
elder Lodi die prematurely from disease, crime, and political

havoc. So fragile are the ties among people that under the pressure of the plague, self-interest quickly prevails over the most intimate of bonds. "Terror had exterminated all the sentiments of nature. Wives were deserted by husbands, and children by parents" (p. 129). At the novel's center, two entire families are destroyed: Mervyn learns the moving story of the deaths of Mary Walpole, her seven daughters, and their adoptive father, Maravegli (pp. 152–54); and he witnesses the removal of the bodies of the younger Thetford, his wife, and child. This latter episode takes on additional significance because on his initial night in the city Mervyn happened to learn that Thetford had put this infant in his wife's bed in what proves to be a doomed effort to replace his deceased first child, save his wife's sanity, and hold his family together.

In this society, ruthless miscreants like the elder Thetford scheme the ruin of their competitors and wait to pick new victims clean, as the innkeepers do to Mervyn on his trip to the city. A wagonload of coffins stands ready to cart off the victims even before they are dead, as the novel's recurrent image of premature burial takes on a poignant social dimension.[31] While Mervyn does meet honest and compassionate men, such as Maravegli and Stevens, as well as two other kindly characters named Medlicote and Estwick, these people are weak and ineffectual. Those like Philip Hadwin and the elder Thetford, who are guided by selfish aims, wield power and authority. In the second part of the novel the scope of this social picture widens into a panorama in which the manipulation of stocks in Frankfort leads to the ruin and suicide of Achsa's father in England, and the maneuverings of Robespierre and Pitt affect the lives of millions. Money, power, and capriciousness even at the highest levels affect the lives of individuals no less fatally than the contagion of the yellow fever.

In the context of this social corruption, Mervyn's most

redeeming characteristic is his revolutionary impulse, as it is in all of Brown's villains. Like Carwin and Ormond especially, Mervyn is an outsider who is disturbed by the cruelty and injustice of the social system and is inclined to want to initiate change. From early in his narrative he expresses shock at the opulence and luxury of the social elite, and he echoes Godwin's *Political Justice* in his observations on the function of inherited wealth: "Wealth has ever been capriciously distributed. The mere physical relation of birth is all that intitles us to the manor or thrones" (p. 57).[32] His first protests against the luxury of the few are motivated by his recognition of his own lowly place on the ladder of wealth, as when he first looks into Welbeck's enclosed garden: "The enclosure was a charming green, which I saw opened into a house of the loftiest and most stately order. . . . My father's dwelling did not equal the height of one story. . . . My heart dictated a comparison between my own condition and that of proprietors of this domain. How wide an impasse was the gulf by which we are separated!" (p. 47).

After his initial reaction, which is to find a way to share this garden, Mervyn undergoes a series of what he calls "revolutions which had taken place in my mind" that lead him to become, temporarily, a social reformer.[33] The high point of his revolutionary fervor occurs when he learns of the cruelty of the public hospital. Mervyn reports Wallace's description of the conditions, and he cries: "O! how poor are the conceptions which are formed, by the fortunate few, of the sufferings to which millions of their fellow beings are condemned" (p. 174). While moved by this heightened awareness of injustice, Mervyn concludes that the problem lies "in the governor of such an institution," and he is ready to "hasten to City-hall . . . to offer myself as a superintendent of the hospital" (pp. 177–79). But experience teaches Arthur to contain his reforming impulses. Unlike Brown's other rebels-turned-criminals, Mervyn is not overwhelmed by frustration and passion. He has learned from the example of Welbeck's ruin that the prudent course for one without resources is to keep up the appearance of honesty, accommodation, and humility. In the wake of Welbeck's misguided course of independence and lust, Mervyn fashions for himself a vocation as the one who would repair the damage done by Welbeck's villainy. Thereby, Mervyn leads a self-serving reform movement that allows one person, himself, to rise from the poverty of the farm to the comforts of his lady's drawing room.[34]

Although it may have disturbed Shelley, Mervyn's failure to become a genuine social reformer should not necessarily lead to a final condemnation of his character. What separates Mervyn from his violent and self-destructive counterparts, Welbeck, Ormond, and Wieland, is that he acts in accord with, and perhaps out of a dim awareness of, his own psychological limitations. In shifting his goals by failing to pursue a romance with Eliza and the promise of a successful life in America that Stevens proposes for him, Mervyn succumbs not only to social restraints but, more importantly, to the formidable obstacles that lie within himself. Though certainly not Brown's most complete psychological study, Mervyn is more complex than he at first appears. His conspicuous Oedipal dream of being stabbed by the fatherlike husband of Achsa usually arouses embarrassment among Brown's post-Freudian readers; however, this scene does serve as an unmistakable signal of the importance of Mervyn's inner life. In fact, in this novel Brown achieves a delicate balance of conscious and unconscious motivations in his central character by presenting his psychological inducements more subtly than in his other works.

Suspicious of the unconscious and of the inner forces that guide him, Mervyn often expresses his bewilderment about what really directs his life. Typically, he asks: "Why, said I as I hasted forward, is my fortune so abundant in unforeseen occurrences? Is every man, who leaves his cottage and the impressions of his infancy behind him, ushered into such a world of revolutions and perils as have trammelled my steps?" (p. 332). While Arthur is not certain of whether he is Everyman or a unique individual, Brown provides the reader with enough detail to understand Mervyn's psychological makeup and the restraints that ultimately prevent him from escaping his particular past. For it is Arthur's unconscious fear of maturity and responsibility that ultimately prevents him from escaping the limitations of his background and achieving a genuine independence of self. In his effort to repress his anxieties, he derides the value of dreams and attributes his decision to marry Achsa to conscious motives such as her wealth and his poverty (pp. 434–35).[35] But ultimately his choice of a wife and a future may not be as conscious as he would like to believe.

Mervyn himself is aware of the impact of some of his family experience upon his nature. He understands that the pattern of early death underlies his bouts of morbid fatalism and that his economic deprivation has made him irrationally jealous of the rich. Still, there are important aspects of his nature of which Arthur is ignorant but Brown's reader aware. His antagonistic relationship with his father has left him with an ambivalent attitude toward other men, especially those in authority over or in competition with him.[36] This tendency partially accounts for his hatred of Wallace and his tormenting of Welbeck and Philip Hadwin. In addition, his special intimacy with his mother left Mervyn with an inclination toward the company of older women, such as Mrs. Wentworth, Mrs. Stevens, and Carlton's sister, which culminates in his marriage to his "new mamma." Through the subsequent stages of Mervyn's development, Brown presents a series of responses that are remarkably consistent with these broad proclivities.

In his relationship with Welbeck, Mervyn alternates between feelings of superiority and defiance toward Welbeck and a yearning to be martyred and victimized by him. Mervyn reveals this tendency to flirt with self-destruction first when he talks about his fascination with the plague. "The rumour [of the plague's devastation] was of a nature to absorb and suspend the whole soul. A certain sublimity is connected with enormous dangers, that imparts to our consternation or our pity, a tincture of the pleasing. . . . I had leisure to conjure up terrific images, and . . . this employment was not enjoined upon me by necessity, but was ardently pursued, and must therefore have been recommended by some nameless charm" (p. 130). Because he is himself obsessed with the knowledge that "seeds of early and lingering death are sewn in my own constitution" (p. 135), he fantasizes about what it might be like to be in the midst of the suffering. Since he had not yet formed his damning opinion of Wallace, he begins to identify with his projection of what he imagines to be the loneliness and desperateness of Susan's fiancé: "My imagination was incessantly pursued by the image of this youth [Wallace], perishing alone, and in obscurity" (p. 134). Thus, Mervyn journeys to the city to save Wallace and is so excited by the risk involved that he stops several people escaping the city to hear of their gruesome experiences: "Hitherto distress had been contemplated at a distance, and through the medium of fancy delighting to be startled by the wonderful, transported by sublimity" (p. 134). While in the city, Mervyn repeatedly and intentionally endangers himself by staying to listen to heartrending tales about the victims such as those told by the kind observers Estwick and Medlicote.

Like the irrational desire to court destruction which Clara Wieland described in herself,[37] Mervyn's underlying hunger for danger explains his prolonged attachment to Welbeck, even against the dictates of reason. Brown makes Mervyn's unconscious motivation explicit in a scene illustrat-

ing the association in Mervyn's mind between Welbeck and
Colvill, the fatherly schoolmaster-turned-rapist who destroyed
Mervyn's sister. As Mervyn lies at the feet of Welbeck who
imitates the voice of Colvill, Arthur expresses the highest
transports of martyrdom. With near delight he imagines
Colvill driving a dagger into his heart, an image that later
springs forth from his unconscious in his dream about
Achsa's husband. This connection in Mervyn's mind between
Welbeck and Colvill only strengthens Mervyn's longing to
provoke his employer's wrath, a tendency evident quite early
in his violation of Welbeck's instructions regarding Mrs.
Wentworth and later when, with the threatening figure of
Welbeck looming above him, the sick and helpless Mervyn
drives the villain into a rage by flaunting the Lodi banknotes
before his eyes. Mervyn's otherwise misguided act of burning
the banknotes may also have been unconsciously motivated
by his desire to defy Welbeck and incur his wrath even at the
risk of losing a potential fortune.[38]

Arthur's description of his feelings during the moments
after this defiant act is a key to understanding his psychological makeup. As he awaited what he thought would be
certain death at the hands of Welbeck, he experienced a
certain self-satisfied pleasure: "all was frenzy and storm in the
countenance and features of Welbeck. Nothing less could be
expected than that the scene would terminate in some
bloody catastrophe. . . . What remained, but to encounter
or endure its consequences with unshrinking firmness?"
(p. 211). Arthur displays a similar combination of self-pity
and calm acceptance of expected punishment in the scenes in
which he incites the anger of Philip Hadwin. This psychological pattern is not surprising in view of Mervyn's curious
position as his mother's protector against his father's drunken
rages: "As to my personal strength, it was nothing; yet my
mother's person was rescued from brutal violence: he was

checked, in the midst of his ferocious career, by a single look or exclamation from me" (p. 344).

The nature of Mervyn's relationship to Welbeck, which finally results in his chastising the criminal and repairing the damage Welbeck has done to a series of women, suggests that Arthur is driven to repeat the ambivalent relationship he had with his father. Thus, to balance the possibility that Mervyn remains close to Welbeck because he himself is either a villain or a fool, Brown provides another possible psychological explanation: that Mervyn's attachment is not completely rational but is also the result of his unconscious desire to recapitulate childhood experiences. His ultimate triumph over this adversary frees him to pass into the next phase of his development, which begins with his rebirth in the arms of Stevens into a world of beneficent fathers and of economic, social, and sexual opportunities.

Under the protection of the benign father figure of Dr. Stevens, Mervyn starts life anew. He begins his romantic relationship with Eliza, his education for a career as a physician, and his role as the benevolent reformer who transforms Welbeck's evil into good. As a conscious self-seeker, Mervyn embraces opportunities to make social contacts, which Welbeck's web of crimes conveniently provides for him. Assured of the love of Eliza and the support and influence of Stevens, Mervyn appears to have shaped a new identity whereby he can be socially useful and personally rewarded for his efforts. In the tone of a young Franklin or Cotton Mather, Mervyn embarks on a vocation of doing good: "My spirits were high, and I saw nothing in the world before me but sunshine and prosperity. I was conscious that my happiness depended not on the revolutions of nature or the caprice of man. All without was, indeed, vicissitude and uncertainty; but within my bosom was a center not to be shaken or removed" (p. 312).

Significantly, it is in this phase of promise that Mervyn takes up the profession of authorship. While it is Stevens who begins the narrative for him, Arthur comes to relish the role of storyteller. Finding that his tale of sufferings and triumph wins him the attention and admiration of others, especially of women like Mrs. Wentworth, Fanny Maurice, who appears in one of the many subplots, and Achsa Fielding, Mervyn never misses an opportunity to repeat his tale and is eager to take up the writing himself when Stevens loses interest.[39]

Mervyn also finds that writing serves for a time as a means of holding his turbulent psychological life under control. In spite of his new career, Mervyn still fears his inner life and tries to repress his unconscious. As he rides in a stagecoach to Baltimore to aid the destitute Watson family, he has a few moments of repose when his "imagination" shows him what he calls "the pictures which my wayward fancy had depicted," but he so distrusts his imagination that he quickly suppresses this experience: "I will not describe my dreams. My proper task is to relate the truth" (p. 371). Later, when he tells Achsa of his Oedipal dream and she is frightened by its implications, he again denies the relevance of unconscious experience to conscious life: "Why surely you place no confidence in dreams" (p. 445). Indeed, he uses his writing as a means of controlling his inner turmoil: "The pen is a pacifyer. It checks the mind's career; it circumscribes her wanderings. It traces out, and compels us to adhere to one path. It ever was my friend. Often it has blunted my vexations; hushed my stormy passions; turned my peevishness to soothing; my fierce revenge to heart-dissolving pity" (p. 414).

But to the disappointment of Stevens and many of Brown's readers, Mervyn does not continue in his promising life as a writer and medical student.[40] Just as in his earlier rejection of Eliza, Arthur abandons this new identity because the conscious attractions of his new life are simply not strong enough to overcome the psychological predispositions that stem from his threatening childhood and financial insecurity. He retreats from potential adulthood into a prolonged, and perhaps permanent, adolescence.

Of course, Brown's depiction of the role of Mervyn's unconscious in his relationship with Achsa is fairly subtle. On the surface, the relationship between Arthur and Achsa has the appearance of a somewhat comic love match in a sentimental romance. Arthur needs money and Achsa wants a husband, and it is difficult to tell who catches whom. While Arthur appears to have cleverly assured himself of Achsa's affection by sitting admiringly at her feet and engaging her in conversation about love, it is she who initiates a Socratic dialogue through which she shows him that he does not really love Eliza—at which point Achsa flushes and, in what is practically an aside to the reader, cries with near delight, "Poor Bess! This will be sad news to thee!" (p. 407). Once she has vanquished her competition, Achsa needs only, according to Dr. Stevens, to arouse Arthur's jealousy. To Arthur's expression of concern about the propriety of his love, Stevens shrewdly assures him: "How quickly would this tranquility vanish, and the true state of your heart be evinced, if a rival should enter the scene and be entertained for preference; then . . . would you be awakened to terror and anguish" (p. 434). Predictably, when Achsa embarks with another youth for the country the next day, Arthur goes into a jealous rage, flies to her, and their love is sealed.

As with so many other aspects of this novel, however, things are more complex than they seem. Besides the obvious Oedipal dream and Arthur's repeated references to his "new mamma," Brown gives even greater emphasis to the psychological importance of the relationship between Arthur and Achsa through the extensive use of the pattern and language of religious conversion to describe Arthur's love. Because Arthur's search for identity, meaning, and authority is so spiritually empty, it is significant that Brown invests Arthur's devotion to Achsa with religious feeling. Describing her attraction as "mystical" (p. 363), Arthur is at a loss to explain "the secret of her power to entrance the soul of the listener and beholder" which "will best account for that zeal almost to idolatry with which she has . . . been regarded by me" (p. 414). When Stevens expresses surprise at the "idolatry which this woman has inspired," Arthur declares that his love is not sexual but spiritual: "Love her I *do* as I love my God; as I love virtue" (p. 431). In response to Stevens's verbal attack upon her as unworthy, Arthur cries out "Hush! Hush! blasphemer!" (p. 432). Like a Puritan asking "what, Lord, may I do to be saved," Arthur pleads with Achsa: "Tell me how I shall serve you? What can I do to make you happier? Poor am I in every thing but zeal, but still I may do something. What—pray tell me what can I do?" (p. 429). He yearns to submit his will completely to hers and become totally dependent upon her authority: "I had vowed to love her and serve her" (p. 414); "I was wax in her hand. Without design and without effort, I was always that form she wished me to assume. My own happiness became a secondary passion. . . . I thought not of myself. I had scarcely a separate or independent existence" (p. 428).

At the culmination of his conversion to the religion of Achsa, Arthur experiences a kind of spiritual crisis, which includes another dream and a night of wandering in the forest. Again, the language Brown uses in both of these episodes strengthens the psychological and religious implications of Mervyn's devotion. The description of the dream is particularly rich in its imagery of psychic turmoil:

> I was roused as by a divine voice that said—Sleep, no more: Mervyn shall sleep no more. . . . What chiefly occupied me was a nameless sort of terror. What shall I compare it to? Methinks, that one falling from a tree, overhanging a torrent, plunged into a whirling eddy, and

gasping and struggling while he sinks to rise no more, could feel just as I did then. . . . I stretched my hand, and caught the arm of a chair. This act called me back to reason, or rather gave my soul an opportunity to roam into a new track equally wild. Was it the abruptness of this vision that thus confounded me! was it a latent error in my moral constitution, which this new conjuncture drew forth into influence? These were all the tokens of a mind lost to itself; bewildered; unhinged; plunged into a drear insanity. [p. 436]

After this opening, he goes on to dream that he seeks Achsa at her house where he finds the door locked (suggestively, this door in his unconscious mind is the only one in the novel which Mervyn cannot open). Then, in the last of Mervyn's symbolic deaths into new life, his Oedipal dream, he imagines himself destroyed by the dagger of Achsa's husband. Mervyn spends the next night actually wandering in the woods. This dream and experience of being lost in the forest also recall an earlier parallel scene in which Mervyn becomes lost on his return to Welbeck. This time, however, he appears to have found an object more worthy of his faith, a protecting mother figure who will provide him psychological asylum and a form of spiritual fulfillment.[41]

While there is much evidence that Arthur's rhetoric of benevolence is never sincere and that he is only seeking the smoothest way to wealth, the psychological development that leads him to marry Achsa belies other less rational motives. While his marriage may represent a financial and social victory, it also symbolizes his ultimate failure to form an independent sense of self and a personal identity. It is also meaningful, that, in marrying his Achsa, Arthur abandons his role as author of his own narrative. The terms in which he casts off this most recent calling suggest a kind of psychic dismemberment: "But why am I indulging in this pen-prattle? The hour she fixed for my return to her is come, and now

take thyself away, quill. Lie there, snug in thy leathern case,
till I call for thee, and that will not be very soon. . . . I *will*
adjure thee, so let *this* be thy last office" (p. 446). This statement of self-abasement underscores the uncertainty of
Mervyn's achievement. The couple's plan to depart America
and Arthur's rather tentative description of anticipated life
with Achsa also raise questions about Arthur's success as an
American hero. He anticipates a rather dull existence: "Our
household . . . should be *thus* composed. Fidelity and skill
and pure morals, should be sought out, and enticed, by
generous recompenses, into our domestic service. Duties
should be light and regular.—Such and such should be our
amusements and employments abroad and at home, and
would not this be true happiness?" (p. 445). The supercilious-
ness of this projected scene and the possible dramatic irony of
Mervyn's question only contribute to the conclusion that in
his struggle for survival Arthur has achieved only a Pyrrhic
victory.[42]

In this view, *Arthur Mervyn* is neither a depiction of
virtue rewarded nor a study of unscrupulous deviousness,
but an anatomy of social and psychological survival which
demands from the reader a systematic character analysis. In
the mercenary world of post-Revolutionary America and
Europe, which Brown depicts in these "Memoirs of the Year
1793," the absence of moral imperatives or shared spiritual
values, symbolized so vividly by the city in plague, makes the
determination of the guilt or innocence of an individual
extremely difficult. Personal and societal revolutions are the
order of the day, and Mervyn's struggle to plot his own
course makes him at once exploitive and open to exploitation.

Just as Stevens needs to believe in Arthur in order to
maintain his faith in humanity, so too does Arthur rely upon
the honesty of Achsa. When he first meets her, he says "Be not
a deceiver, I entreat you. I depend only on your looks and
professions and these may be dissembled" (p. 328). And in-

deed they may, for Arthur has no better grounds for believing this woman whom he meets in a house of prostitution than Stevens has for trusting Mervyn. Achsa's moving tale of her past—a story which perhaps surpasses Arthur's own for sensationalism—may also be a tissue of lies. But Arthur needs to believe her. Arthur is neither a hero nor a villain, for he lacks the force of will to be either. He is one young American who is not prepared to embrace a life of individualism and social freedom with its accompanying risks and responsibilities. Though he can acquire the education and possesses the necessary wit and personality for success, Arthur cannot overcome his psychological limitations, his feelings of inadequacy, insecurity, and dependency. Thus, he retreats from America and from the vision of his future it offers and seeks safety and comfort in the arms of a mother figure who symbolizes, not the American future, but the Judeo-European past.

Between the completion of the first part of *Arthur Mervyn* in early 1799 and the second part in the summer of 1800, Brown continued his startling burst of literary activity with two other major projects. Having won the recognition of the New York intellectuals, he became editor of a new literary journal, the *Monthly Magazine and American Review*. With promises from his friends to submit articles, Brown launched the journal with great optimism. His friends, however, were slow to finish their contributions; and Brown ended up writing most of the pieces himself. Brown's brothers had always advised him to judge his success on the basis of financial gain, and he hoped to impress his merchant-class family by making money from his writing pursuits. After he had bragged to his brothers about this venture, his embarrassment when the magazine failed in December 1800 must have caused him to reconsider a literary career.[43]

In 1799 Brown also completed his fourth major novel, *Edgar Huntly; or, Memoirs of a Sleep-Walker*. Although it is not as intellectually challenging as *Arthur Mervyn* because its central character is not as complex, *Edgar Huntly* is a fascinating book. In it, Brown retreated to some of the Gothic devices he had used in *Wieland*. Huntly is a character tormented by psychological impulses that are often beyond his control, and the mysterious Clithero Edny is a dangerous madman whose motives and actions defy explanation. Brown used the phenomenon of sleepwalking, as he had used ventriloquism and spontaneous combustion in *Wieland*, to achieve thrilling effects.

In *Edgar Huntly*, Brown also manipulated elements of the Indian-captivity narrative with superb results. Borrowing from these narratives which were popular with American readers for over a century, he became the first American novelist to appeal to fears and fantasies about Indians. His use of a wilderness setting and his portraits of struggles between Huntly and his Indian enemies stand at the pivotal point in American literature between the firsthand accounts and the later tales of western adventure and frontier violence. James Fenimore Cooper noted his debt to Brown's innovations. That Brown was more successful in reaching a larger audience with these devices than he had been with his earlier works is acknowledged by the fact that *Edgar Huntly* was his most popular work and went into a second edition in 1801.[44]

After the publication of *Edgar Huntly*, Brown devoted the rest of the year to editing the *Monthly Magazine* and to work on "Stephen Calvert," which was to be the first part of a five-part book that he never completed. (Dunlap later included the Calvert fragment in his biography of Brown.) As the turn of the century was nearing, Brown seemed to alter his direction. He put "Stephen Calvert" aside and took up *Arthur Mervyn* again, completing the second part. Brown's novels were not selling well, his friends were not submitting manuscripts for the magazine as they had promised, and his brothers were strongly urging him to abandon writing and enter business with them. Approaching thirty and unmarried, Brown must have wondered, as had Freneau and Brackenridge before him, if the American republic was capable of supporting its writers and men of letters.

In a letter to Dunlap, Brown made this telling speculation:

> Does it not appear to you, that to give poetry a popular currency and universal reputation, a particular cast of manners and state of civilization is necessary? I have sometimes thought so; but perhaps an error, and the want of popular poems argues only the demerit of those who have already written, or some defect in their works which unfits them for every taste and understanding.[45]

By "poems," Brown meant all imaginative works of serious literary intention. At this point he decided not to abandon his literary efforts, but he did attempt to lessen the philosophical and psychological complexity of his works in order to gain wider popularity among American readers.

It is impossible to gauge the impact of another event in Brown's personal life upon his writing career. About this time he began his long courtship of Elizabeth Linn, the sister of the important Presbyterian minister and writer John Blair Linn. During the four years before their marriage in 1804, Brown met continued resistance from his parents, who forbade his marriage to a non-Quaker, and from Elizabeth and her family, who had doubts about Brown's temperament, his ideas, and his income. Elizabeth may even have agreed with Brown's brothers that her lover's novels were too gloomy and obscure. Whether in response to these influences or not, Brown's philosophical and political views moved during these months toward the conservative attitudes that characterized his political pamphleteering after 1806. And the last two novels that Brown wrote, *Clara Howard; or, The Enthusiasm of Love* and *Jane Talbot: A Novel*, completed before the end of 1801, reflect a significant change in his work.[46]

Lacking the elements that characterized his major works— the supernatural, abnormal psychology, violence, and insanity —these novels contained nothing that would have offended polite readers; and *Jane Talbot* appears almost to represent the resolution of Brown's intellectual conflicts into a compromise between rational skepticism and religious sentiment. For such reasons these works are of less interest to modern readers than are the four major novels. Even in these lesser works, however, there are still hints of the Brown who cannot resist a sly wink at the alert reader and an undercurrent of ironic questioning.

With the publication of *Jane Talbot*, Brown turned his life toward new pursuits. He joined his brothers in their business for a time and tried different kinds of writing. In 1803 he published two important political pamphlets that attracted more public attention than anything he had previously written. In *An Address to the Government of the United States on the Cession of Louisiana to the French*, Brown attacked the policy of the Jefferson administration, which he and his merchant brothers believed to be too soft on France. Shortly thereafter, he followed with *Monroe's Embassy; or, the Conduct of the Government in Relation to Our Claims to the Navigation of the Mississippi*, in which he advocated war as the only way to open the West to American economic interests. Even though Brown's philosophy had moved toward a more conventional view, the inflammatory positions expressed in these pamphlets are still remarkable. Because of these essays, he was suddenly regarded as an important thinker, and his ideas were debated on the floor of Congress.[47] He had achieved status as an intellectual that he could not attain with his novels.

At the end of 1803, Brown felt confident with the new

direction of his career to begin to publish *The Literary Magazine and American Register*, which he edited until 1807. As he introduced this new journal, he looked back over his career and wrote a bitter statement indicating that he felt his years as a novelist in America had been wasted: "I should enjoy a large share of my own respect at the present moment if nothing had ever flowed from my pen, the production of which could be traced to me." While continuing to work on the journal, Brown completed a translation of Volney's *A View of the Soil and Climate of the United States*, in 1804; and in November of that year the respectable editor, translator, and political sage was married to Elizabeth Linn. His parents refused to attend the Presbyterian wedding, and shortly thereafter he was censored by his Quaker meeting in Philadelphia.[48]

In the six years of marriage that followed, Brown was able to support his wife and their four children despite his continually failing health. Between 1807 and 1810 he edited *The American Register, or General Repository of History, Politics, and Science*, a serious semiannual journal, and he began an ambitious work, *A System of General Geography*. He had completed a substantial amount of work on this project, of which only the prospectus survives, when he died of tuberculosis on February 22, 1810.[49]

The career of Charles Brockden Brown is in many ways a reflection of the history of American letters during his time. Like the writers of the 1770s and 1780s who sought ways of appealing to their countrymen and opening their eyes to the truths of their society, Brown had begun his literary life with high hopes of capturing the attention and affecting the minds of the new democratic republic. By the time Brown abandoned fiction, others of that first generation had also ceased their literary efforts.

But despite a lack of response, Brown produced a series of major works that show him to be far ahead of any other

American writer of his time in his themes and in his literary experimentation. His importance as a forerunner of Cooper, Poe, Hawthorne, and Melville has been obscured by literary histories that treat Emerson's *American Scholar* as the start of American letters.

CONCLUSION

Clifford Geertz has said, "Culture is a system of symbols by which man confers significance upon his own experience. . . . At once a product of social interaction, they [the symbols] are to the process of social life as a computer's program is to its operations, the genetic helix to the development of an organism. . . . the symbol system is the information source that, to some measurable extent, gives shape, direction, particularity, and point to an ongoing flow of activity."[1] For the American preachers and poets there had existed before 1776 an available culture. In New England a gradually Americanized English Puritanism provided a rich and complex symbolic language through which artist and social spokesman could articulate a sense of corporate unity and personal identity. The southern and middle colonies possessed a greater mixture of competing cultural influences, as Puritanism gradually intruded to alter the neoclassicism and Anglicanism that had held those colonies closer to the English cultural heritage. Yet in the measured poetry of Richard Lewis of Maryland, the graceful prose of William Byrd of Virginia, and the harmonious preaching of William Smith of Philadelphia, a recognizable symbolic system persisted until the Revolution. Among these writers there remained shared assumptions regarding the relationship between America and England, the differences between the language and forms of contemporary writing and the ancient classics, and the au-

thority to be accorded a writer by his audience. The Revolution left the existing cultures of both the northern and
southern colonies in ruin.

For a brief period of ten to twelve years, all Americans
lived in a new but temporary culture constructed, like the
bivouacs of Washington's army on the move, from fragments
of the old religious rhetoric combined with new political
dreams and economic aspirations. Expressed in newspaper
accounts, broadsides, sermons, and in the "rising glory" poems
and biblical epics, the hasty ideology of Revolutionary ideals
generated enormous military fervor but could hardly sustain
a lasting culture. But as Geertz observes about revolutionary
societies: "Nationalist ideologies built out of symbolic forms
drawn from local tradition—which are, that is, essentialist
—tend, like vernaculars, to be psychologically immediate but
socially isolating; built out of forms implicated in the general
movement of contemporary history—that is, epochalist—they
tend, like *lingua francas*, to be socially deprovincializing but
psychologically forced."[2] While the disparate and previously
divided colonies were indeed deprovincialized between 1774
and 1782 and became politically united, the writers recognized that the amalgam of symbolic language of those years
and the ideology it expressed were psychologically immediate
but socially and artistically contradictory and isolating, even
potentially self-destructive.

The clergy perceived early that the emerging national self-
image stressed competitive and aggressive materialism, and
they rushed to restore religion at the center of the more
complex ideology that would be formed by the Constitutional Conventions and postwar reflections. As experienced
diviners of the hearts of their countrymen and keepers of the
American conscience, the clergy understood the truth of
Geertz's assertion that religion, to succeed, must conquer the
"chaos" which "threatens to break in upon man: at the limits
of his analytical capacities, at the limits of his powers of

endurance, and at the limits of his moral insight. Bafflement, suffering, and a sense of intractable ethical paradox are all, if they become tense enough or are sustained long enough, . . . challenges with which any religion must attempt somehow to cope."[3] When Timothy Dwight declared in 1795 that the student body of Yale was made up of heathens and when he helped to generate the religious awakening that was to sweep America by the 1830s, he was attempting to cope with the bafflement and confusion that Brackenridge, Freneau, Brown, and all thinking men agreed were a threat to the republic. Whether Dwight's approach was beneficial to the nation in the long run is open to debate, but the fact is that he and his clerical brethren responded with the only curative they possessed to diseases of social corruption and moral malaise that wracked the infant nation. In so doing, the ministers acted as genetic engineers of ideology, infusing into the DNA of American culture the molecules of Puritan discipline and perfectionism they had so carefully preserved through the precarious years of the Revolution.

For the literary artists of the new nation, however, the damage to the prewar cultural heritage was even greater, and the repairs demanded extraordinary imagination and creativity. There was no returning to the old forms and symbolic language. The people who made up the potential audience of American literature were no longer English colonials, no longer in awe of classical forms and models, no longer ready to purchase or applaud works of art just because they were produced by English authorities or Whig patriots. In art and literature as in politics, Americans were feeling independent: they would read as they wished and reward what struck their fancy. The writers tried to strike that fancy, but the pursuit of an American audience for literature proved futile. The incipient American ideology and culture would admit religion, but it would not easily absorb the social criticism, the moral challenge, and the aesthetic appeal of serious literature.

Brown, who came to recognize this situation in the 1790s, made the instability of society and the isolation of the artist the material of his writing. The most significant writer of his time, he was really the first to create major American literary works out of the truth that the only position for the artistic imagination in American culture was on the fringe of, or outside, the national ideology, an ideology that would persistently reject the corrective implications of serious American literature. Yet after a brief explosion of creativity, Brown too withdrew. He and his contemporaries stood on the threshold of a new era that was to free the writers of the Romantic movement and permit the imagination to soar to new heights. But the American post-Revolutionary writers, lacking this poetic liberty, were nearly silenced by their conviction that the only way to serve the moral and aesthetic needs of their society was by addressing their readers directly with plain truths.

"Directly" is the key word here because, as Thomas McFarland has argued, the English Romantic poets, whose careers were beginning in the 1790s, also sought to teach moral and aesthetic truths. In place of the dying religious and literary heritage of the Enlightenment, Wordsworth and Coleridge sought to "poeticize philosophy" and to "philosophize poetry"; this desire was "in the air" among the European writers of the early nineteenth century.[4] It was evidently in the air breathed by the confused and uncertain Americans as well, but instead of igniting and feeding a Romantic flame, it settled like the dust of Mount St. Helens upon unpurchased American books and failed magazines. The more our writers tried to speak "directly" to their readers the more resistance they met. Perhaps they would have done better to express their frustrations and yearnings for a new unity through a personal symbolic language, as Emerson, Thoreau, Whitman, Melville, and Hawthorne did four decades later.

The Revolutionary generation possessed the literary keys.

They were finding their way toward more ironic and elusive forms. Their use of the hermit-pilgrim figure symbolized the artist in the new culture as he waited alone in the forest with the wisdom to set men free of their slavish materialism and philosophical bewilderment. The ironic narrators of *Modern Chivalry* and *Arthur Mervyn* prefigure future voices of the American writer, always undercutting their own declarations and forcing the reader to think twice about his and the author's beliefs and values. In a recent review of E. L. Doctorow's *Loon Lake*, Christopher Lehmann-Haupt praises Doctorow for his innovative technique, which provides the reader with two books in one. By "withholding certain information," the narrator puts the reader in the position of accepting one meaning of the novel which is then undermined by a revelation at the end; the reader is forced to go through the novel again to find the new meaning. Lehmann-Haupt remarks: "So in a way it is two books we have to read —the existential adventure we get the first time through, and the tract on history we perceive when we read again knowing the outcome. . . . [The two books] work together to create the portrait of a new kind of American hero—a portrait rich in its psychological dimensions and historical nuance, and subtle in the imagery. . . . it tells us as much about ourselves as Theodore Dreiser did."[5] These words could be written not only about the novels of Doctorow and Dreiser but also about the novels of James, Hawthorne, and Melville. They apply as well to Freneau's "The Lost Sailor" or "The Beauties of Santa Cruz" and to the major works of Brown. The later writers have the advantage of being conscious of a tradition of double meaning and what might be called the technique of "retrospective irony" that stems from the curiously ambivalent, sometimes antagonistic, relationship between the American writer and his audience.

As the early writers first formed these strategies, however, they could not have been aware that their formulations con-

stituted the beginning of a new tradition of American literature. They understood clearly only their disappointments
and frustrations. Perhaps it might have comforted Freneau
or Barlow to have read Friedrich Schiller's description in
1795 of the wound to culture inflicted not only upon America
but upon all those late-eighteenth-century Western societies
that underwent political revolutions: "The simple organization of the first republics . . . [resulted in] a vast number of
lifeless parts. . . . State and Church, law and customs, were
now torn apart; enjoyment was separated from labor, means
from ends, effort from reward. Eternally chained to only one
single little fragment of the whole, man himself grows to be
only a fragment."[6] Perhaps such a universal perception would
have eased Freneau's frustration as he searched for the right
voice to address an audience that no longer cared to read the
lessons of his poems. The more cosmopolitan Barlow seemed
to capture the tragic awareness of Schiller's vision in his last
image of starving ravens picking at the frozen bodies of dead
soldiers in the snows of Russia—a moving symbol of cultural
fragmentation and ruin. While it would be for a later generation of American writers to develop these themes and
devices for fuller artistic expression, the writers of the 1780s
and 1790s provided the primal matter and the first important specimens of American literature.

NOTES

Introduction

1. "Interview," J. Brans, *Southwest Review* 62 (Winter 1977), 11–12, and "Literature and Culture: An Interview with Saul Bellow," *Salmagundi* 30 (Summer 1975), 6.
2. Adams's letter to Jefferson, Feb. 2, 1816, in *The Adams–Jefferson Letters: The Complete Correspondence between Thomas Jefferson and Abigail and John Adams*, ed. Lester J. Cappon (Chapel Hill, 1959), p. 463.
3. Ezra Pound, "The Jefferson–Adams Letters as a Shrine and a Monument," *North American Review* 247 (Winter 1937–38), reprinted in William Cookson, ed., *Selected Prose: 1909–1965* (London, 1968), pp. 118, 126–28.
4. For a recent example, see Henry Nash Smith, *Democracy and the Novel: Popular Resistance to Classic American Writers* (New York, 1978).
5. The best known of such readings is Leslie A. Fiedler, *Love and Death in the American Novel* (New York, 1960; rev. 1966).
6. Even the Norton Anthology includes nothing from Dwight and only Barlow's "Hasty-Pudding"; see Sculley Bradley *et al.*, eds., *The American Tradition in Literature*, 4th ed. (New York, 1977).
7. Warner Berthoff, *A Literature Without Qualities* (Berkeley, 1979), p. 17.
8. Sacvan Bercovitch, *The American Jeremiad* (Madison, Wis., 1979).
9. Henry Steele Commager, *The Empire of Reason: How Europe Imagined and America Realized the Enlightenment* (New York, 1977).
10. Henry F. May, *The Enlightenment in America* (New York, 1976). Interpreters such as Bercovitch have been strongly influenced by theories of symbolic interpretation established through structural

anthropology and best exhibited in the works of Claude Lévi-Strauss, Victor Turner, and Mary Douglas.

11. Leon Howard, "The Late Eighteenth Century: An Age of Contradictions," in *Transitions in American Literary History*, ed. Harry Hayden Clark (Durham, N.C., 1953), pp. 51–89.

12. See Sacvan Bercovitch, "How the Puritans Won the American Revolution," *The Massachusetts Review* 17 (Winter 1976), 597–630.

13. On capitalism and Protestantism see Max Weber, *The Protestant Ethic and the Spirit of Capitalism*, trans. Talcott Parsons (New York, 1958). On sales see William Charvat, *The Profession of Authorship in America, 1800–1870*, ed. Matthew J. Bruccoli (Columbus, O., 1968).

14. An observation made by Yehoshua Arieli, professor of American History at the Hebrew University during a session of a seminar on American culture of the late eighteenth century, National Humanities Center, Research Triangle Park, N.C., Oct. 1979.

15. See Richard Sennett, *The Fall of Public Man: The Social Psychology of Capitalism* (New York, 1978).

I *The Crisis of Authority in the Revolutionary Age*

1. Thomas Jefferson, *The Writings of Thomas Jefferson*, ed. Paul Leicester Ford, 10 vols. (New York: Letterpress edition, 1892–99), I, 9–11.

2. John Adams, *Familial Letters of John Adams and His Wife*, ed. Charles Francis Adams (New York, 1876), p. 50.

3. Samuel Sherwood, *The Church's Flight into the Wilderness: An Address on the Times* (New York, 1776), pp. 11ff.

4. The research of the last decade has provided significant evidence that the leaders of the Revolution were able to tap religious feelings still very much alive in Americans. See Perry Miller, "From the Covenant to the Revival," in *The Shaping of American Religion*, eds. James Ward Smith and A. Leland Jamison (Princeton, 1961), pp. 322–68, and Alan Heimert, *Religion and the American Mind from the Great Awakening to the Revolution* (Cambridge, Mass., 1966), *passim*. For a convenient summary of recent work see Douglas H. Sweet, "Church Vitality and the American Revolution: Historiographical Consensus and Thoughts Towards a New Perspective," *Church History* 45 (1976), 340–57.

5. John Adams to Hezekiah Niles, Feb. 13, 1818, in *Works of John Adams*, ed. Charles F. Adams, 10 vols. (Boston, 1850–56), X, 282–83.

6. *The Rising Glory of America*, in *The Poems of Philip Freneau*, ed. Fred Lewis Pattee, 3 vols. (Princeton, 1902–7), I, 73, 81–83.

7. Kenneth Lockridge, *Literacy in Colonial New England* (New York, 1974), p. 57.

8. *Ibid.*, pp. 92–93.

9. Joseph J. Ellis, *After the Revolution: Profiles in Early American Culture* (New York, 1979), pp. 14, 15. Ellis cites several relevant population studies.

10. On the literary climate of the period see especially Kenneth Silverman, *A Cultural History of the American Revolution* (New York, 1976), *passim*; William Charvat, *The Profession of Authorship in America, 1800–1870*, ed. Matthew J. Bruccoli (Columbus, O., 1968), pp. 5–28; and Ellis, *After the Revolution*, pp. 23–38.

11. See Gordon F. Bigelow, *Rhetoric and American Poetry of the Early National Period* (Gainesville: University of Florida Monographs, 1960), and William L. Hedges, "Toward a Theory of American Literature, 1765–1800," *Early American Literature* 6 (1972), 26–38.

12. On Puritan poetry see Harold S. Jantz, *The First Century of New England Verse* (Worcester, Mass.: American Antiquarian Society, 1944); *Colonial American Poetry*, ed. Kenneth Silverman (New York, 1968); *Seventeenth-Century American Poetry*, ed. Harrison T. Meserole (New York, 1968); Ola Elizabeth Winslow's introduction to her collection of facsimiles, *American Broadside Verse* (New Haven, 1930); and Robert Daly's *God's Altar: The World and the Flesh in Puritan Poetry* (Berkeley, 1978). The southern tradition has been studied by Richard Beale Davis, *The Intellectual Life in the Colonial South, 1585–1763* (Knoxville, Tenn., 1978), and in several other works cited throughout the present study; also by J. A. Leo Lemay, *Men of Letters in Colonial Maryland* (Knoxville, Tenn., 1972). The poems of Mather Byles appeared in the *New England Weekly Journal* and were collected in *Poems on Several Occasions* (Boston, 1744; repr. New York, 1940).

13. Richard Beale Davis, *Literature and Society in Early Virginia: 1608–1840* (Baton Rouge, 1973), p. 148; Davis cites the important critical work on Davies.

14. *Ibid.*, p. 191.

15. "Silence Dogood, No. 6," in the New England *Courant*, June 11, 1722, reprinted in *The Papers of Benjamin Franklin*, ed. Leonard W. Labree, 21 vols. (New Haven, 1959), I, 21–26.

16. On the classical influence, see Richard M. Gummere, *The American Colonial Mind and the Classical Tradition* (Cambridge, Mass.,

1963). In my discussion of Livingston, I am indebted to a paper read by Frank Shuffleton at a meeting of the Northeast Society for Eighteenth-Century Studies, Toronto, Oct. 1979, titled " 'Philosophical Solitude' and the Pastoral Politics of William Livingston."

17. Another poet who followed this moral pastoral tradition in his response to Pomfret is Benjamin Church in his "The Choice."

18. See David D. Hall, *The Faithful Shepherd: A History of the New England Ministry in the Seventeenth Century* (Chapel Hill, 1972), pp. 226–78. On the accommodation of the ministers to change in the eighteenth century see William T. Youngs, Jr., *God's Messengers: Religious Leadership in Colonial New England, 1700–1750* (Baltimore, 1976). Also relevant are the well-known studies of Perry Miller, Alan Heimert, C. C. Goen, Edwin S. Gustad, and Edmund Morgan.

19. Ebenezer Pemberton, *A True Servant of His Generation Characterized* (Boston, 1712), pp. 7–8.

20. For further discussion and references on the relationship between poetry and preaching see my essay "Diversity of Development in the Puritan Elegy and Funeral Sermon: 1660–1750," *Early American Literature* 15 (Fall 1980).

21. Sacvan Bercovitch, *The American Jeremiad* (Madison, Wis., 1978), esp. chaps. 4 and 5.

22. See especially Silverman, *Cultural History*, pp. 9–11, and Ellis, *After the Revolution*, pp. 6–7.

23. On the impact of the Scottish philosophy in America see Terence Martin, *The Instructed Vision: Scottish Common Sense Philosophy and the Origins of American Fiction* (Bloomington, Ind., 1961); Douglas Sloan, *The Scottish Enlightenment and the American College Ideal* (New York, 1971); Herbert W. Schneider, *A History of American Philosophy* (New York, 1963); and Leon Howard, *The Connecticut Wits* (Chicago, 1943).

24. Silverman, *Cultural History*, p. 55.

25. On Kames, see his *Elements of Criticism in Three Volumes* (Edinburgh, 1762), esp. pp. iii–14, 362ff.; on his thought see Ian Simpson Ross, *Lord Kames and the Scotland of His Day* (Oxford, 1972), and Gordon Mackenzie, *Critical Responsiveness: A Study of the Psychological Current in Later Eighteenth-Century English Criticism* (Berkeley, 1949), in particular, chap. 1.

26. For discussions of the relationship between associationism and literary theory in this period, see Martin Kallich, "Association of

Ideas and Critical Theory," *English Literary History* 12 (1945), 301–11; Walter J. Ong, "Psyche and the Geometers: Associationist Critical Theory," in *Rhetoric, Romance, and Technology: Studies in the Interaction of Experience and Culture* (Ithaca, N.Y., 1971), pp. 213–36; and Robert F. Streeter, "Association Psychology and Literary Nationalism in the *North American Review*, 1815–1825," *American Literature* 17 (1945), 243–54.

27. On Godfrey and Evans see Silverman, *Cultural History*, pp. 58–59; on Hopkinson see Paul M. Zall's "introduction" to his edition, *Comical Spirit of Seventy-six: The Humor of Francis Hopkinson* (San Marino, Ca., 1976).

28. John Witherspoon, *Lectures on Moral Philosophy and Eloquence* (Philadelphia, 1810), p. 198.

29. John Witherspoon, *A Serious Inquiry into the Nature and Effects of the Stage* (New York, 1812), pp. 81–82.

30. Freneau's poems on Princeton reveal his attachment to his college training. See "Ode to the Rev. Samuel Stanhope Smith, D.D." in *Poems*, ed. Pattee, III, 244–46, and "Ode on a Remote Perspective View of Princeton College," in *The Last Poems of Philip Freneau*, ed. Lewis Leary (New Brunswick, N.J., 1945), pp. 99–102.

31. See Martin, *Instructed Vision*, pp. 18–19.

32. See Sidney Ahlstrom, *A Religious History of the American People* (New Haven, 1972), pp. 379ff.

33. Important exceptions are those critics who have broken ground in reevaluating the literature of this period: Hedges, "Toward a Theory," 26–38, and his "The Myth of the Republic and the Theory of American Literature," *Prospects* 4 (1979), 101–20; Lewis Leary, *Soundings: Some Early American Writers* (Athens, Ga., 1975); and the many important works of Lewis P. Simpson, especially, *The Man of Letters in New England and the South* (Baton Rouge, 1973). Also useful are the articles of Robert D. Arner that have appeared in *Early American Literature*.

34. George F. Sensabaugh, *Milton in Early America* (Princeton, 1964), p. 176.

35. See especially Ahlstrom, *A Religious History*, pp. 179–80; Edmund S. Morgan, *The Gentle Puritan: A Life of Ezra Stiles, 1727–1795* (New Haven, 1962); Daniel Calhoun, *Professional Lives in America, 1750–1850* (Cambridge, Mass., 1965); Bernard Bailyn, "Religion and Revolution: Three Biographical Studies," *Perspectives in American History* 4 (1970), 87–110; and James W. Schmotter, "The Irony of

Clerical Professionalism: New England's Congregational Ministers and the Great Awakening," *American Quarterly* 31 (Summer 1979), 148–68.

36. Peter Thacher, *Observations upon the Present State of the Clergy of New England, with Strictures upon the Power of Dismissing Them, Usurped by Some Churches* (Boston, 1783), p. 4.

37. *Strictures on the Rev. Mr. Thatcher's [sic] Pamphlet entitled "Observations upon the State of the Clergy in New England" by J.S.—A Layman* (Boston, 1784), pp. 17–18.

38. Moses Welch, "The Relations of Pastor and People," quoted in Calhoun, *Professional Lives*, p. 109, and Richard Beale Davis, "The Early American Lawyer and the Profession of Letters," *Huntington Library Quarterly* 12 (1949), 191–206.

39. Jonathan Boucher, *Reminiscences of an American Loyalist, 1738–1789*, ed. Jonathan Bouchier (New York, 1925; repr. Port Washington, N.Y., 1967), pp. 118–19. A recent study that confirms the emotional appeal Boucher describes is Rhys Isaac, "Preachers and Patriots: Popular Culture and the Revolution in Virginia," in *The American Revolution: Explorations in the History of American Radicalism*, ed. Alfred F. Young (DeKalb, Ill., 1976), pp. 125–56.

40. Douglas H. Sweet, "Toward Sectual Union: Eighteenth-Century Perspectives on Religious Pluralism," paper delivered at the meeting of the Northeast Society for Eighteenth-Century Studies, Toronto, Oct. 1979. For a convenient summary of related issues in the church history of the period, see his "Church Vitality and the American Revolution," 341–57.

41. For a more detailed treatment, see my essay "The Dove and the Serpent: The Clergy in the American Revolution," *American Quarterly* 31 (Summer 1979), 187–203.

42. Among the many studies on the social function of religion during the period, the prominent works are Robert N. Bellah, "Civil Religion in America," in *Religion in America*, eds. Bellah and William G. McLoughlin (Boston, 1968), pp. 3–23; Nathan Hatch, *The Sacred Cause of Liberty: Republican Thought and the Millennium in Revolutionary New England* (New Haven, 1977); Winthrop S. Hudson, ed., *Nationalism and Religion in America: Concepts of American Identity and Mission* (New York, 1970); William Gribbin, *The Churches Militant: The War of 1812 and American Religion* (New Haven, 1973); Conrad Cherry, ed., *God's New Israel: Religious Interpretations of American Destiny* (Englewood Cliffs, N.J., 1971); Martin E. Marty, *Righteous Empire: The*

Protestant Experience in America (New York, 1970); and for a contrasting view, John F. Wilson, *Public Religion in American Culture* (Philadelphia, 1979). I have tried to summarize the major lines of argument in a review of two such recent studies in *Early American Literature* 14 (1979), 128–30.

43. *Select Sermons on Doctrinal and Practical Subjects . . . to which is prefixed a Biographical Sketch of the Author's Life* (Boston, 1808), xv.

44. The most prominent examples of orations that mixed political and religious rhetoric were the Fourth of July sermons. See Robert P. Hay, "Freedom's Jubilee: One Hundred Years of the Fourth of July, 1776–1876" (Ph.D. diss., University of Kentucky, 1967), and his "Providence and the American Past," *Indiana Magazine of History* 65 (1969), 79–101.

45. John Mellen, *The Doctrine of the Cross of Christ; A Discourse Delivered at Wellfleet on Cape-Cod, 13th of April, 1785, at the Ordination of Mr. Levi Whitman* (Plymouth, Mass., 1785), pp. 27–28.

46. Linda K. Kerber cites Washington's *Address* in her *Federalists in Dissent: Imagery and Ideology in Jeffersonian America* (Ithaca, N.Y., 1970), p. 212.

47. As quoted in Silverman, *Cultural History*, p. 485.

48. *Ibid.*, p. 487.

49. *Ibid.*, p. 512.

50. See the several works of Lewis P. Simpson in which he sets forth this argument, especially, "The Symbolism of Literary Alienation in the Revolutionary Age," *Journal of Politics* 38 (1977), 79–100, and *The Man of Letters in New England and the South*, pp. 3–31.

51. In *Soundings*, Lewis Leary asserts that by the end of the eighteenth century "literature was left to women, clergymen, and young men who were too ill for other occupations" (p. 6). But this attitude toward literature was not widespread until the development of a special "sphere" of women's activity, which Nancy Cott has detailed in her *The Bonds of Womanhood: "Women's Sphere" in New England, 1780–1835* (New Haven, 1977); see also Ann Douglas, *The Feminization of American Culture* (New York, 1977).

52. Recent historical and anthropological studies of the crisis of authority in this period have explored the complex responses to the struggle for power in the new society. See, for example, Hannah Arendt, "What Was Authority?" in *Authority*, ed. Carl J. Friedrich (Cambridge, Mass., 1958); Edwin G. Burrows and Michael Wallace,

"The American Revolution: The Ideology and Psychology of National Liberation," *Perspectives in American History* 6 (1972), 167–306; and Rhys Isaac's three studies, "Order and Growth, Authority and Meaning in Colonial New England," *American Historical Review* 76 (1971), 728–37; "Preachers and Patriots," pp. 125–56, and "Ethnographic Method—an Action Approach," paper delivered at the Atlantic History and Culture Seminar, Newberry Library, Oct. 1977. Underlying such studies is a wealth of research on the anthropology of rhetoric and culture and the social function of metaphor led by seminal works of Clifford Geertz, Victor Turner, Jürgen Habermas, Paul Ricoeur, Claude Lévi-Strauss, Mary Douglas, and Hayden White.

53. The use of the hermit figure stems not only from classics and the English Augustans but from a biblical wisdom tradition, which Wesley Kort has examined in his manuscript on the wisdom tradition in American literature, and which he has shared with me.

54. In "Hawthorne and His Mosses," reprinted in *The Portable Melville*, ed. Jay Leyda (New York, 1952), p. 408.

55. John Blair Linn, *The Powers of Genius* (Philadelphia, 1802), p. 13.

56. "Advertisement of the Author" for Elijah Fitch, *The Beauties of Religion: A Poem Addressed to Youth* (Providence, 1789), p. 3.

57. "Advertisement" for *Sky-Walk*, Brown's lost novel, in Philadelphia's *Weekly Magazine*, Mar. 17, 1798, reprinted in *The Rhapsodist and Other Uncollected Writings*, ed. Harry R. Warfel (New York, 1943), pp. 135–36.

58. "Cento," in *The Literary Magazine and American Register* 4 (Philadelphia, 1805), 8. See also G. Harrison Orians, "Censure of Fiction in American Romances and Magazines, 1789–1810," *Publications of the Modern Language Association* 52 (1937), 195–224.

59. William Hill Brown, *The Power of Sympathy* (Boston, 1789; repr. Boston, 1961), p. 1.

60. Freneau's intellectual struggles are detailed in Chapter IV; see also Nelson F. Adkins, *Philip Freneau and the Cosmic Enigma: The Religious and Philosophical Speculations of an American Poet* (New York, 1949).

61. Joseph S. Buckminster, "On the Dangers and Duties of the Men of Letters," *The Monthly Anthology* 7 (Sept. 1809), 148.

62. James Kirke Paulding, "National Literature," *Salmagundi*, 2d ser., in *The American Literary Revolution*, ed. Robert E. Spiller (New York, 1967), p. 385. In his review of American letters Samuel

Lorenzo Knapp also looked for a time "when the long neglected works of our country shall take their proper place," in his *Lectures on American Literature* (New York, 1829), p. 169.

II   *Timothy Dwight*

1. The most balanced study of Dwight is Kenneth Silverman's excellent Twayne series volume, *Timothy Dwight* (New York, 1969). The standard biography is Charles E. Cuningham, *Timothy Dwight, 1752–1817: A Biography* (New York, 1942). An essential study is Leon Howard's *The Connecticut Wits* (Chicago, 1943); less useful because slanted against Dwight is Vernon Lewis Parrington, *Main Currents in American Thought*. Vol. I, *The Colonial Mind* (New York, 1927), pp. 364–74.

2. Silverman attributes Dwight's adjustments more to his intellectual and emotional attachment to the Puritan alternations between "birthday or doomsday," as reflected in the fears and hopes of the Puritan jeremiad.

3. On Dwight's career as an educator, see also William B. Sprague, "Life of Timothy Dwight," in *The Library of American Biography*, ed. Jared Sparks (Boston, 1845), and "Memoir of the Life of President Dwight," in Dwight's *Theology; Explained and Defended*, 5 vols. (Middletown, Conn., 1818–19), I, v–lxxi. See also Benjamin Silliman, *A Sketch of the Life and Character of President Dwight* (New Haven, 1817).

4. Adolf G. Koch examines Dwight's involvement in these religious-political controversies in *Republican Religion* (New York, 1933). On Dwight's politics see Richard J. Purcell, *Connecticut in Transition: 1775–1818* (Washington, D.C., 1918; repr. Middletown, Conn., 1963); and Joseph Haroutunian, *Piety Versus Moralism: The Passing of the New England Theology* (New York, 1932). On Dwight's magazine activities, see Robert Edson Lee, "Timothy Dwight and the Boston *Palladium*," *New England Quarterly* 35 (1962), 229–39; and Lyn Richardson, *Early American Magazines, 1741–1789* (New York, 1931).

5. On Dwight's role in the religious revival there is disagreement: those who stress his role as the key leader are Lyman Beecher, *Autobiography* (Cambridge, 1961); Ralph Henry Gabriel, *Religion and Learning at Yale* (New Haven, 1958); and S. G. Goodrich, *Recollections of a Lifetime* (New York, 1857). Edmund S. Morgan,

"Ezra Stiles and Timothy Dwight," *Proceedings of the Massachusetts Historical Society* 72 (1963), 229–39, argues that Dwight must share the credit with other religious leaders.

6. On British reviews of Dwight's writing, see William B. Cairns, *British Criticism of American Writings, 1783–1815* (Madison, Wis., 1918), and Silverman, *Dwight*, pp. 41–44.

7. *The Friend*, Nos. I–VI, appeared in *American Museum* 5 (Jan.-June 1789) and 6 (July-Dec. 1789), 5:69–71, 220–22, 445–57, 564–67; 6:154–56, 283–86. Although Dwight began composing these essays in 1786, they did not appear until 1789; see Silverman, *Dwight*, pp. 43, 49–50.

8. See, for example, David Minter, *The Interpreted Design as a Structural Principle in American Prose* (New Haven, 1969).

9. On the theme of the confidence man in American writing see Richard B. Hauck, *A Cheerful Nihilism: Confidence and "the Absurd" in American Humorous Fiction* (Bloomington, Ind., 1971); Susan Kuhlmann, *Knave, Fool, and Genius: The Confidence Man as He Appears in Nineteenth Century American Writing* (Chapel Hill, 1973); and Warwick Wadlington, *The Confidence Game in American Literature* (Princeton, 1975).

10. Silverman, *Dwight*, p. 43. For a discussion of *The Triumph* see Lewis Leary, "The Author of *The Triumph of Infidelity*," *New England Quarterly* 35 (1963), 101–17; Jack Stillinger, "Dwight's *Triumph of Infidelity*: Text and Interpretations," *Studies in Bibliography* 15 (1962), 159–66; and Silverman, *Dwight*, pp. 92–94.

11. All references to Dwight's major poems are to the Scholars' Facsimiles and Reprints text of *The Major Poems of Timothy Dwight with a Dissertation on the History of Eloquence and Poetry of the Bible,* eds. William J. McTaggart and William K. Bottorff (Gainesville, Fla., 1969). On Dwight's intellectual trials at the time he composed *The Triumph* see Howard, *Connecticut Wits*, pp. 206–38.

12. For an analysis of *Greenfield Hill*, see Silverman, *Dwight*, pp. 52–79, and John Griffith, "*The Columbiad* and *Greenfield Hill*: History, Poetry, and Ideology in the Late Eighteenth Century," *Early American Literature* 10 (1975–76), 235–50. My colleague Thomas P. Roche has made the interesting observation that the poem is really not pastoral but is modeled on Ben Jonson's "To Penhurst" and John Denham's "Cooper's Hill."

13. On Dwight's adherence to an emerging Protestant ethic, see A.

Whitney Griswold, "Three Puritans on Prosperity," *New England Quarterly* 7 (1934), 475–93.

14. On the personal internalization of the guilt for failure in American social history see Martha Banta, *Failure and Success in America: A Literary Debate* (Princeton, 1978).

15. On the larger shift in ideology of which Dwight's intellectual fusion is a prime example and for which it is an important force see Sacvan Bercovitch, *The American Jeremiad* (Madison, Wis., 1979).

16. Philip J. Greven has traced the cultural evolution Dwight's argument illustrates in his *The Protestant Temperament: Patterns of Child-rearing, Religious Experience, and the Self in Early America* (New York, 1977).

17. See also Silverman, *Dwight*, p. 57.

18. *Remarks on the Review of Inchiquin's Letters* (Boston, 1815), p. 14.

19. *Travels; In New-England and New York*, 4 vols. (New Haven, 1821–22), I, 1. Dwight's inclination toward travel literature is only one of several ways in which he anticipates Thoreau.

III *Joel Barlow*

1. James Woodress, *A Yankee's Odyssey: The Life of Joel Barlow* (New York, 1958), p. 86.

2. This view of Barlow has persisted from his time to ours as evidenced in Samuel Miller, *A Brief Retrospective of the Eighteenth Century*, 2 vols. (New York, 1803), II, 167–232, and H. A. Beers, *The Connecticut Wits and Other Essays* (New Haven, 1920); for stress upon distinguishing traits see Lewis P. Simpson, "The Satiric Mode: The Early National Wits," in *The Comic Imagination in American Literature*, ed. Louis D. Rubin, Jr. (New Brunswick, N.J., 1973), pp. 49–61.

3. On "The Hasty-Pudding" see Theodore Grider, "Joel Barlow's 'The Hasty Pudding': A Study in American Neo-Classicism," *British Association for American Studies Bulletin*, n.s., No. 11 (1965), 35–42; and Robert D. Arner, "The Smooth and Emblematic Song: Joel Barlow's 'The Hasty Pudding,'" *Early American Literature* 7 (1972), 76–91. Critics who have examined Barlow's major works in their historical context are Roy Harvey Pearce, *The Continuity of American Poetry* (Princeton, 1961); Arthur L. Ford, *Joel Barlow* (New York, 1971); Leon Howard, *The Connecticut*

Wits (Chicago, 1943), and *The Vision of Joel Barlow* (Los Angeles, 1937).

4. Quoted in Woodress, *A Yankee's Odyssey*, p. 52.

5. *Ibid.*, p. 51.

6. *The Works of Joel Barlow in Two Volumes*, eds. William K. Bottorff and Arthur L. Ford (Gainesville, Fla., 1970), I, 5. All references to "The Prospect of Peace" are to Volume I of this work.

7. On Barlow's early development see Theodore A. Zunder, *The Early Days of Joel Barlow, A Connecticut Wit* (New Haven, 1934); also useful is Charles B. Todd, *Life and Letters of Joel Barlow* (New York and London, 1886), and Joseph L. Blau, "Joel Barlow, Enlightened Religionist," *Journal of the History of Ideas* 10 (1949), 430–44.

8. Besides the works of Woodress and Howard, there have been a number of studies of Barlow's intellectual crisis. See M. R. Adams, "Joel Barlow, Political Romanticist," *American Literature* 9 (1937), 113–53; Merton A. Christensen, "Deism in Joel Barlow's Early Work: Heterodox Passages in *The Vision of Columbus*," *American Literature* 27 (1956), 509–20; Victor C. Miller, *Joel Barlow: Revolutionist, London, 1791–92* (Hamburg, 1932); Kenneth R. Ball, "A Great Society: The Social and Political Thought of Joel Barlow," (Ph.D. diss., University of Wisconsin, 1967); and Vernon Lewis Parrington, *Main Currents in American Thought*, Vol. I, *The Colonial Mind* (New York, 1927), 387–95.

9. All references to Barlow's *The Vision* and *The Columbiad* are to the Scholars' Facsimiles and Reprints texts in *The Works of Joel Barlow in Two Volumes*, eds. Bottorff and Ford, Vol. II.

10. For a provocative view of Barlow as a modern myth-maker and national designer see Cecelia Tichi, *New World, New Earth: Environmental Reform in American Literature from the Puritans through Whitman* (New Haven, 1979), chap. 4; on Barlow's use of myth see Robert D. Richardson, Jr., "The Enlightenment View of Myth and Joel Barlow's *Vision of Columbus*," *Early American Literature* 13 (1978), 34–44.

11. Barlow quotes Richard Price's "Observations on the Importance of the American Revolution" and anticipates that a "happy state of human affairs will take place [in America] before the final consummation of all things" (footnote, p. 341).

12. See, for example, Witherspoon's *Lectures on Moral Philosophy and Eloquence* (Philadelphia, 1810), pp. 197–302. For discussion of this moral argument for modern poetry see Terence Martin, *The In-*

structed Vision: Scottish Common Sense Philosophy and the Origins of American Fiction (Bloomington, Ind., 1961), *passim*.

13. John Dos Passos praised Barlow's blend of political philosophy and critical theory in his "Citizen Joel Barlow of the Republic and of the World," in *The Ground We Stand On* (New York, 1941), pp. 256–80.

14. On Barlow's experience in Europe and his political writings, see P. H. Boyton, "Joel Barlow Advises the Privileged Orders," *New England Quarterly* 12 (1939), 477–99; Milton Cantor, "Joel Barlow: Lawyer and Legal Philosopher," *American Quarterly* 10 (1958), 165–74 and "The Life of Joel Barlow," (Ph.D. diss., Columbia University, 1964); Robert F. Durden, "Joel Barlow in the French Revolution," *William and Mary Quarterly* 8 (1951), 327–54; Miller, *Joel Barlow: Revolutionist*; and Woodress, *A Yankee's Odyssey*, pp. 115ff.

15. A view shared by Howard, *Connecticut Wits*, pp. 309–13; and Woodress, *A Yankee's Odyssey*, pp. 248–78; and Lewis Leary "The Man of Letters as Citizen: Joel Barlow," paper presented at the National Humanities Center, Research Triangle Park, N.C., spring 1979, and to be included in a memorial volume in honor of Charles Frankel. I am grateful to Professor Leary for allowing me to read a typescript of this essay.

16. Tichi sees the roots of Barlow's systematic utopianism in the perfectionism of New England Puritanism, *New World, New Earth*, esp. pp. 137ff.

17. Howard stresses Barlow's belief in the perfectibility of all people in *The Vision of Joel Barlow*, pp. 11–12; in "Citizen: Joel Barlow," Leary says of Barlow: "through all his life, he was a religious person, and his religion was that of universal love" (p. 3).

18. Ford summarizes the criticism of this work in *Joel Barlow*, chap. 3, pp. 83–84.

19. Woodress, *A Yankee's Odyssey*, pp. 269–78.

20. On Barlow's political experiences abroad see Irving Bryant, "Joel Barlow, Madison's Stubborn Minister," *William and Mary Quarterly* 15 (1958), 438–51; Joseph Dorfman, "Joel Barlow: Trafficker in Trade and Letters," *Political Science Quarterly* 59 (1944), 83–100; and Leon Howard, "Joel Barlow and Napoleon," *Huntington Library Quarterly* 2 (1938), 37–51.

21. "Advice to a Raven in Russia" has been reprinted in Woodress, *A Yankee's Odyssey*, pp. 338–39, and in Ford, *Joel Barlow*, pp. 103–5. For commentary on the poem see James F. Tanner, "The

'Triple Ban' and Joel Barlow's 'Advice to a Raven in Russia,' "
Early American Literature 12 (1977), 294–95.

IV *Philip Freneau*

1. The standard biography of Freneau is Lewis Leary's *That Rascal Freneau: A Study in Literary Failure* (New Brunswick, N.J., 1941); also useful are Mary S. Austin, *Philip Freneau* (New York, 1901); Jacob Axelrad, *Philip Freneau: Champion of Democracy* (Austin, Tex., 1967); Philip M. Marsh, *Philip Freneau: Poet and Journalist* (Minneapolis, 1967). Brief but valuable introductions can be found in Fred Lewis Pattee, "Life of Philip Freneau," in his edition, *The Poems of Philip Freneau*, 3 vols. (Princeton, 1902–7), I, xii–cxii, and Mary W. Bowden's Twayne series volume, *Philip Freneau* (Boston, 1976).

2. On Freneau's religious and philosophical ideas, see Nelson F. Adkins, *Philip Freneau and the Cosmic Enigma: The Religious and Philosophical Speculations of an American Poet* (New York, 1949).

3. Freneau's notebook in the Freneau Collection, Rutgers University Library, New Brunswick, N.J., p. 49; also cited in Leary, *That Rascal*, p. 49.

4. On Freneau's religious and philosophical speculations, Adkins serves as a corrective to Leary's slighting of Freneau as a serious thinker. Leary's emphasis is upon Freneau's political activities and his role as an editor and public poet.

5. While most of Freneau's critics have focused on one aspect of his career—his pre-Romanticism, his political journalism, or his role in the Revolution—a balanced examination is Philip M. Marsh, *The Works of Philip Freneau: A Critical Study* (Metuchen, N.J., 1968). On other aspects of Freneau's poetic achievement see Harry Hayden Clark, "What Made Freneau the Father of American Poetry?" *Studies in Philology* 26 (1929), 1–22, and "The Literary Influences of Philip Freneau," *Studies in Philology* 22 (1925), 1–33; see also William L. Andrews, "Philip Freneau and Francis Hopkinson," in *American Literature, 1764–1789: The Revolutionary Years*, ed. Everett H. Emerson (Madison, Wis., 1977), pp. 127–44, and Ruth W. Brown, "Classical Echoes in the Poetry of Philip Freneau," *The Classical Journal* 45 (1949–50), 29–34.

6. In *That Rascal*, Leary stresses Freneau's tendency to want to escape; however, Freneau's declarations of retreat are often rhetorical

devices, as Richard C. Vitzthum has demonstrated in his study of Freneau's use of land and sea imagery, *Land and Sea: The Lyric Poetry of Philip Freneau* (Minneapolis, 1978); see also William D. Andrews, "Goldsmith and Freneau in 'The American Village,'" *Early American Literature* 5 (1971), 14–23, whose excellent analysis of a single poem illustrates the interplay of Freneau's personal feeling and use of literary convention.

7. Moses Coit Tyler, *The Literary History of the American Revolution: 1763–1783*, 2 vols. (New York, 1898), I, 173.

8. See Leary, *That Rascal*, chaps. 6 and 7, and "Philip Freneau," in *Major Writers of Early American Literature*, ed. Everett Emerson (Madison, Wis., 1972), pp. 245–71; also see Edwin H. Cady, "Philip Freneau as Archetypal American Poet," in *Literature and Ideas in America: Essays in Memory of Harry Hayden Clark* (Athens, O., 1975), esp. pp. 6–7.

9. William L. Hedges notes this ambivalence in "The Myth of the Republic and the Theory of American Literature," *Prospects* 4 (1979), 113–14.

10. Cf. Leary, *That Rascal*, who stresses Freneau's overriding political ambition.

11. "To a New-England Poet," in *The Last Poems of Philip Freneau*, ed. Lewis Leary (New Brunswick, N.J., 1945), p. 112.

12. *Poems*, II, 297. All references to Freneau's poems will be to the Pattee edition.

13. In *The Prose of Philip Freneau*, ed. Philip M. Marsh (New Brunswick, N.J., 1955), pp. 297, 368. Unless otherwise noted, references to Freneau's prose will be to this volume.

14. Vernon Lewis Parrington stresses these aspects of Freneau's career and works in *Main Currents in American Thought*, Vol. I, *The Colonial Mind* (New York, 1927), 374–87; Leary and Cady agree with Axelrad that "it was his [Freneau's] weakness as a poet that he stopped too low to conquer the readers to whom he addresses his poems," *Philip Freneau*, p. 149.

15. A more sympathetic reading of Freneau's compromise is Laurence B. Holland's "Philip Freneau: Poet in the New Nation," in Laurence B. Holland, Nathaniel Burt, and A. Walton Litz, *The Literary Heritage of New Jersey* (Princeton, 1964), 3–41, and Carol A. Kyle, "That Poet Freneau: A Study of the Imagistic Success of 'The Pictures of Columbus,'" *Early American Literature* 9 (1974), 62–70.

16. On the revision of "The Beauties of Santa Cruz," see Vitzthum,

Land and Sea, pp. 35–37, 77–81; also see Jane Donahue Eberwein, "Freneau's 'The Beauties of Santa Cruz,'" *Early American Literature* 12 (1977), 271–76, who argues that Freneau was not an "an escapist in 1776."

17. On the distinctions between the 1779 version of "The House of Night" and the 1786 poem see G. Ferris Cronkite, "Freneau's 'The House of Night,'" *Cornell Library Journal* 8 (1969), 3–19, and Vitzthum, *Land and Sea*, pp. 73–76. See also Lewis Leary's sensitive reading of Freneau's "The House of Night," which demonstrates how he has modified his opinion of Freneau's literary achievement, in "The Dream Visions of Philip Freneau," *Early American Literature* 11 (1976), 156–71; also see his essay "Philip Freneau," in *Soundings: Some Early American Writers* (Athens, Ga., 1975), pp. 131–60.

18. Besides Franklin and Fielding, Freneau was aware, of course, of the use of such personae in classical and biblical literature, as well as in modern English prose essays.

19. On Freneau as a prose writer see Harry Hayden Clark, "What Made Freneau the Father of American Prose?" *Transactions of the Wisconsin Academy of Sciences, Arts and Letters* 25 (1930), 39–50; Frank Smith, "Philip Freneau and the Time-Piece and Literary Companion," *American Literature* 4 (1932), 270–87; Marsh, *A Critical Study*, and his introduction to *The Prose Works*.

20. Adkins, *Cosmic Enigma*, p. 14.

21. On Freneau's use of Tomo Cheeki, see Leary, *That Rascal*, pp. 260–65, 323–24, 459–64.

22. Studies that place Freneau's individual struggle in the context of contemporary English literary history, are Paul Fussell, *The Rhetorical World of Augustin Humanism: Ethics and Imagery from Swift to Burke* (Oxford, 1965); Chester F. Chapin, *Personification in Eighteenth-Century English Poetry* (New York, 1955); and Patricia Meyer Spacks, *The Poetry of Vision: Five Eighteenth-Century Poets* (Cambridge, Mass., 1967).

23. Cf. Leary, "Dream Visions," pp. 158–59.

24. Clifford Geertz, *The Interpretation of Cultures* (New York, 1973), p. 242.

25. See Pattee's footnote to the poem in *Poems*, III, 28.

V *Hugh Henry Brackenridge*

1. The standard biography is Claude M. Newlin, *The Life and Writings of Hugh Henry Brackenridge* (Princeton, 1932); the best recent study is Daniel Marder's Twayne series volume, *Hugh Henry Brackenridg* (New York, 1967).

2. On Brackenridge's eccentricities and his career as a judge and civic leader, see Leland D. Baldwin, *Pittsburgh: The Story of a City* (Pittsburgh, 1938), and William W. Edel, *Bulwark of Liberty* (Carlisle, Pa., 1950), pp. 124ff.

3. H. M. Brackenridge, "Biographical Notice of H. H. Brackenridge, Late of the Supreme Court of Pennsylvania," *Southern Literary Messenger* 8 (1842), 1–19, reprinted in *Modern Chivalry* (Philadelphia, 1865), pp. 152–53. Another useful record by the author's son Henry is *Recollections of Persons and Places in the West* (Philadelphia, 1834).

4. *Father Bombo's Pilgrimage to Mecca, 1770* has been edited and has an introduction by Michael Davitt Bell (Princeton, 1975). On Brackenridge's college years, see also Martha Conners, "Hugh Henry Brackenridge at Princeton University, 1768–1771," *Western Pennsylvania Historical Magazine* 10 (1927), 146–62.

5. "Preface," from the *United States Magazine* 1 (1779), reprinted in *A Hugh Henry Brackenridge Reader, 1770–1815,* ed. Daniel Marder (Pittsburgh, 1970), pp. 70–71.

6. "To the Inhabitants of Westmoreland County," *Pittsburgh Gazette,* Apr. 28, 1787.

7. Details appear in Henry Marie Brackenridge's account, *History of the Western Insurrection in Western Pennsylvania, Commonly Called the Whiskey Insurrection 1794* (Pittsburgh, 1859); cf. William Findley's critical view of Brackenridge in *History of the Insurrection in Four Western Counties of Pennsylvania* (Philadelphia, 1796); see also an account of the anger of the federal troops toward Brackenridge as they marched to Pittsburgh in "The Library," *Pennsylvania Magazine* 71 (1947), 44–67.

8. *Modern Chivalry,* ed. Claude M. Newlin (New York, 1937), p. 471: all references are to this edition. On Brackenridge's debt to Cervantes, see Lewis Leary, *Soundings: Some Early American Writers* (Athens, Ga., 1975), pp. 161–74; John R. Henrickson, "The Influence of *Don Quixote* on *Modern Chivalry*" (Ph.D. diss., Florida State University, 1959); and Joseph H. Harkey, "The Don

Quixote of the Frontier: Brackenridge's *Modern Chivalry*," *Early American Literature* 8 (1973), 193–203.

9. Arthur Hobson Quinn, *American Fiction: An Historical and Critical Survey* (New York, 1934), p. 11.

10. Leary stresses the fact that "sedition laws made plain speech dangerous" as the reason for Brackenridge's detachment from his observations (*Soundings*, p. 169). But this argument is not borne out by Brackenridge's willingness to express unpopular ideas in print under his own name on many occasions; his motives for employing narrative masks are more complex and literary. H. M. Brackenridge insisted that "whatever satirical freedom may be discovered in his works, is aimed at certain professors of religion, and not at religion itself, of which he always speaks with respect—frequently referring to the Scriptures, of which he was a perfect master," "Biographical Notice," pp. 155–56.

11. *Incidents of the Insurrection on Western Pennsylvania in the Year 1794*, 4 vols. (Philadelphia, 1795), I, 71.

12. Constance Rourke, *American Humor: A Study of National Character* (New York, 1931), *passim*; an appreciation of this socially unifying impulse in Brackenridge is apparent in Leary, *Soundings*, pp. 171–72, and Vernon Lewis Parrington, *Main Currents in American Thought*, Vol. I, *The Colonial Mind* (New York, 1927), pp. 395–400.

13. This narrative fragment appeared in installments of the *United States Magazine* from January through July 1779 and has been reprinted in the *Brackenridge Reader*, ed. Marder, pp. 78–92. All page references in text for material quoted from Brackenridge works are to this edition.

14. While the devices of the dream and the mysterious hermit in the forest have a long literary history, Marder also feels that in manner and tone, Brackenridge's use of these devices anticipates Poe; see his *Brackenridge*, pp. 76–77.

15. See especially Newlin, *Life and Writings*, pp. 58–70, and Marder, *Brackenridge*, pp. 31–38.

16. H. M. Brackenridge, "Biographical Notice," pp. 17–18; cited also in Newlin, *Life and Writings*, pp. 53–54.

17. For a humorous account of this incident and details of his second marriage, see John Pope, *A Tour Through the Southern and Western Territories of the United States of North America* (Richmond, 1792), pp. 14–16, also summarized in Marder, *Brackenridge*, pp. 48–49.

18. See especially, Wendy Martin's excellent "The Rogue and the Rational Man: Hugh Henry Brackenridge's Study of a Con Man in *Modern Chivalry*," *Early American Literature* 8 (1973), 179–92; David H. Hirsch, *Reality and Idea in the Early American Novel* (The Hague, 1971), pp. 193–203; Lewis Leary's "Introduction" to his edition of an abridged *Modern Chivalry* (New Haven, 1965), pp. 7–19; and Michael T. Gilmore, "Eighteenth-Century Oppositional Ideology and Hugh Henry Brackenridge's *Modern Chivalry*," *Early American Literature* 13 (1978), 181–92.

19. Newlin's text provides exact reproductions of the first editions of the various parts and has been checked against the revised edition of 1815.

20. Marder and Leary are inclined to dismiss Part II; see *Brackenridge Reader*, ed. Marder, p. 152, and Leary's "Introduction." However, Wendy Martin treats the entire novel as a unit and thereby discovers that "Brackenridge is the first American novelist to focus on the theme of the alienated artist in a democracy" ("Rogue and Rational Man," p. 189).

21. On the importance of the popular poetry of the English satirist John Walcott (Peter Pindar), see Chapter IV, and *Peter Pindar's Poems*, ed. Paul M. Zall (Columbia, S.C., 1972).

VI   Charles Brockden Brown

1. William Charvat, *The Profession of Authorship in America, 1800–1870*, ed. Matthew J. Bruccoli (Columbus, O., 1968), p. 24.

2. The standard biography is Harry R. Warfel, *Charles Brockden Brown: American Gothic Novelist* (Gainesville, Fla., 1949); also useful are David Lee Clark, *Charles Brockden Brown: Pioneer Voice of America* (Durham, N.C., 1952); William Dunlap, *The Life of Charles Brockden Brown; Together with Selections from the Rarest of His Printed Works, from His Original Letters, and from His Manuscripts Before Unpublished*, 2 vols. (Philadelphia, 1815), and Dunlap's abridgment, *Memoirs of Charles Brockden Brown, the American Novelist* (London, 1822); William H. Prescott, "Life of Charles Brockden Brown," in *The Library of American Biography*, ed. Jared Sparks (New York, 1834); and Donald A. Ringe's Twayne series volume, *Charles Brockden Brown* (New York, 1966).

3. Quoted in Warfel, *Brown*, p. 29.

4. Reprinted in *The Rhapsodist and Other Uncollected Writing*, ed. Harry R. Warfel (New York, 1943).

5. Quoted in Warfel, *Brown*, p. 29.
6. Quoted in *ibid.*, pp. 10–11.
7. See a recent edition of *Alcuin: A Dialogue*, ed. Lee Edwards (Northampton, Mass., 1970).
8. Quoted in Dunlap, *Life of Charles Brockden Brown*, I, 25. On the intellectual context of Brown's fiction, see Kenneth Bernard, "Charles Brockden Brown and the Sublime," *The Personalist* 45 (1964), 235–49; Warner B. Berthoff, " 'A Lesson in Concealment': Brockden Brown's Method in Fiction," *Philological Quarterly* 37 (1958), 45–57; Richard Chase, *The American Novel and Its Traditions* (New York, 1957); Alexander Cowie, *The Rise of the American Novel* (New York, 1951); Leslie A. Fiedler, *Love and Death in the American Novel* (New York, 1960; rev. 1966); Arthur Kimball, *Rational Fictions: A Study of Charles Brockden Brown* (McMinnville, Ore., 1968); David H. Hirsch, "Charles Brockden Brown as a Novelist of Ideas," in his *Reality and Idea in the Early American Novel* (The Hague, 1971), pp. 74–100; Arthur Hobson Quinn, *American Fiction: An Historical and Critical Survey* (New York, 1936); Martin S. Vilas, *Charles Brockden Brown: A Study of Early American Fiction* (Burlington, Vt., 1904); Lulu Rumsey Wiley, *The Sources and Influence of the Novels of Charles Brockden Brown* (New York, 1950); Lillie Deming Losche, *The Early American Novel* (New York, 1907); William L. Hedges, "Charles Brockden Brown and the Culture of Contradictions," *Early American Literature* 9 (1974), 107–42; Michael Davitt Bell, *The Development of American Romance: The Sacrifice of Relation* (Chicago, 1980), pp. 3–61; and Bernard Rosenthal's "Introduction" to his edition, *Critical Essays on Charles Brockden Brown* (Boston, 1981), pp. 1–21.
9. "Walstein's School of History," in *The Monthly Magazine and American Review* 1 (1799), 409, reprinted in *The Rhapsodist and Other Uncollected Writing*, p. 153.
10. In *The Rhapsodist and Other Uncollected Writing*, p. 136.
11. *Ibid.*
12. I have examined the careers of Huntly and Ormond in "Charles Brockden Brown," in Leonard Unger, ed., *American Writers: A Collection of Literary Biographies* (New York, 1979), Supplement I, Part I, pp. 124–49; see also John Cleman, "Ambiguous Evil: A Study of the Villains and Heroes in Charles Brockden Brown's Major Novels," *Early American Literature* 10 (1975), 190–219.
13. All references to *Wieland* are to the recent definitive edition of Sydney J. Krause and S. W. Reid (Kent, O., 1977), p. 6. For the

best commentaries on *Wieland*, see Krause's useful introduction to
his edition and Larzer Ziff, "A Reading of *Wieland*," *Publications
of the Modern Language Association* 87 (1962), 51–57; Warner
Berthoff, "The Literary Career of Charles Brockden Brown," (Ph.D.
diss., Harvard University, 1954), chap. 5; and Michael Davitt Bell,
" 'The Double-Tongued Deceiver': Sincerity and Duplicity in the
Novels of Charles Brockden Brown," *Early American Literature* 9
(1974), 143–63, reprinted in *Early American Literature: A Collection
of Critical Essays*, ed. Michael T. Gilmore (Englewood Cliffs, N.J.,
1980), p. 157. See also Paul Witherington, "Image and Idea in
Wieland and *Edgar Huntly*," in a special Brown issue of *The Serif*
3 (1966), 19–26; Ringe, *Brown*, pp. 25–48; Chase, *American Novel*,
pp. 29–35; William M. Manly, "The Importance of Point of View
in Brockden Brown's *Wieland*," *American Literature* 35 (1963),
311–21; David Brion Davis, *Homicide in American Fiction, 1798–
1860* (Ithaca, N.Y., 1957); George Snell, *The Shapers of American
Fiction, 1798–1947* (New York, 1947); and Robert Hemenway,
"Fiction in the Age of Jefferson: The Early American Novel as
Intellectual Document," *Midcontinent American Studies Journal* 9
(1966), 91–102.

14. A modern edition of *Carwin* has been published with *Wieland*, see
Krause and Reid, pp. 245–310, and in *Three Early American
Novels*, ed. William S. Kable (Columbus, O., 1970), pp. 131–90;
see Kable's introduction to "Memoirs of Carwin," pp. 10–12.

15. Quoted in Warfel, *Brown*, pp. 175–76.

16. All references to *Arthur Mervyn* are to the definitive Bicentennial
edition, *Arthur Mervyn or Memoirs of the Year 1793* (Kent, O.,
1980). There is considerable disagreement about whether the second
part should be considered as part of a single novel in two parts:
both David Lee Clark, *Pioneer Voice*, pp. 179ff., and R.W.B. Lewis,
*The American Adam: Innocence, Tragedy and Tradition in the
Nineteenth Century* (Chicago, 1955), pp. 94–98, practically ignore
the second part. For discussion of this, see J. W. Reid, "Textual
Essay," Bicentennial edition of *Arthur Mervyn*, pp. 476–489; Ringe,
Brown, pp. 24, 65–66; and Warfel, *Brown*, pp. 145, 243. On the
structure of the novel see Kenneth Bernard, "*Arthur Mervyn*: The
Ordeal of Innocence," *Texas Studies in Literature and Language* 6
(1965), 441–59. I believe that Bernard errs in seeing Stevens as a
"negligible factor" in the novel (p. 442).

17. Dunlap called the change "as unsuspected as disgusting," in *Life
of Charles Brockden Brown*, II, 40. It was reported that Shelley

was "extremely displeased"—see *Peacock's Memoirs of Shelley*, ed.
H.F.B. Brett-Smith (London, 1909), pp. 35ff. For more recent
comment on these attitudes, see Warner Berthoff, "Adventures of a
Young Man: An Approach to Charles Brockden Brown," *American
Quarterly* 9 (1957), 421–54, and Ringe, *Brown*, p. 77.

18. Compare the sympathetic interpretations of Mervyn in Lewis,
American Adam, pp. 97ff., and Henry Petter, *The Early American
Novel* (Columbus, O., 1971), pp. 337ff., with those inclined to view
the novel as presenting an ironic condemnation of his character:
Bell, " 'The Double-Tongued Deceiver,' " esp. pp. 155–58, and
Berthoff, "Adventures of a Young Man," pp. 421–54. A good
summary of the criticism on the novel is Norman S. Grabo's
"Historical Essay" in the Bicentennial edition of *Arthur Mervyn*,
pp. 447–75.

19. The misappropriation of money and goods is a central theme of the
novel discussed by James H. Justus in "Arthur Mervyn, American,"
American Literature 42 (1970), 304–24. Just as Arthur intrudes
into rooms he also insinuates himself into the lives of others who
can help him financially (see Ringe, *Brown*, p. 77).

20. Both Hedges, "Culture of Contradictions," pp. 23, 136–38, and
Justus, "Arthur Mervyn," pp. 306–22, have noted the thematic
importance of Franklin. Also, pertinent perhaps to Mervyn's
career is Franklin's *Reasons for Preferring an Old Mistress to a
Young One* (Philadelphia, 1745), where he recommends that young
men marry older women. While Franklin's *Autobiography* had not
yet been published, its existence and content were known among
Philadelphia intellectuals who had read the section completed
before 1789 and had urged Franklin to print it. See Mary E.
Rucher, "Benjamin Franklin," in *American Literature, 1764–1789:
The Revolutionary Years*, ed. Everett H. Emerson (Madison, Wis.,
1977), pp. 105–25. During the 1790s Franklin was seen by some as
a master of self-promotion; see Richard D. Miles, "The American
Image of Benjamin Franklin," *American Quarterly* 9 (1957), 118ff.
Brown's well-known admiration of Franklin (Warfel, *Brown*, pp.
32–33, and Clark, *Pioneer Voice*, p. 242) would not preclude his
ironic use of the Franklin image or moral teachings.

21. Mervyn's language is filled with national-agrarian rhetoric: he seeks
"asylum"; he wants a life of "competence"; the city offers only
"pollution." He is so convincing that Vernon Lewis Parrington
praised the work as an illustration of Jeffersonian dogma; see his
Main Currents in American Thought, Vol. 2, *The Romantic*

Revolution in America (New York, 1927), p. 190. A germane study
is Charles C. Cole, Jr., "Brockden Brown and the Jefferson
Administration," *Pennsylvania Magazine of History and Biography*
72 (July 1948), 253–63, which traces Brown's shift from a Jeffersonian to a Federalist philosophy. Mervyn changes his mind on the
question of the city vs. the country, and he abandons the Jeffersonian themes and catchwords as he gravitates toward Achsa.
Justus sees this shift as an awakening ("Arthur Mervyn," pp.
309–13), while Ringe (*Brown*, pp. 70–85) views it as possibly ironic.

22. See Brown's *Alcuin*. The influence of Godwin's *Caleb Williams*
(1794) upon *Arthur Mervyn* has been frequently discussed, as in
Bernard, "Ordeal of Innocence," pp. 456–59, and Bell, " 'The
Double-Tongued Deceiver,' " pp. 155–56.

23. In "Culture of Contradictions," pp. 135–38, Hedges explains this
false ring as the result of Arthur's alternating among available
cultural styles of discourse, which include those of Jonathan Edwards, John Woolman, and Franklin.

24. Berthoff, "Introduction" to his edition of *Arthur Mervyn* (New
York, 1962), p. xviii; also see Hedges, "Culture of Contradictions,"
p. 123.

25. Bernard, "Ordeal of Innocence," p. 444, notes a similarity between
Mervyn and Joseph Andrews.

26. This conclusion can be drawn from the various reports about
Clavering: the version Clavering gave to the Mervyns (p. 30); the
tale Mrs. Wentworth tells about Clavering (pp. 67–68); the version
told to Stevens by Wortley and his friends (pp. 250–51); and
Mervyn's account to Mrs. Wentworth (pp. 356–57). The only
conclusion is that on his suicidal path Clavering deceived the
Mervyns as well as his friends and relatives. Bernard has also
noticed similarities between Mervyn and Clavering, in "Ordeal of
Innocence," p. 459.

27. This theme also underlies Achsa's "shocking tale" about her early
life and disastrous first marriage which she related to Arthur (pp.
416–26) and is illustrated in the fate of Wortley whose plans and
years of labor to save money for marriage are thwarted by Welbeck's
financial schemes (p. 227). In his essay "Walstein's School of
History," Brown stresses the close connection between property and
sex in relation to human happiness. See *The Rhapsodist and Other
Uncollected Writing*, p. 152.

28. Bernard, "Ordeal of Innocence," p. 457, views Welbeck and
Mervyn as complementary opposites; Hedges, "Culture of Con-

tradictions," pp. 127–29, and Petter, *Early American Novel*, pp. 334–35, see the two drawn together to torment one another; and Patrick Bracaccio sees them as doubles in "Studied Ambiguities: *Arthur Mervyn* and the Problem of the Unreliable Narrator," *American Literature* 42 (1970), 21.

29. The suicides in the novel include Mervyn's sister, Clavering, and Achsa's father; Welbeck supposedly makes several attempts.

30. Mervyn is most terrified when he is alone, whether wandering the streets during the plague (pp. 128–46), trapped in Welbeck's basement (pp. 110–13), hiding in Welbeck's attic (p. 211–13), or lost in the forest (p. 79 and again p. 440). One thinks of Huck Finn's suicidal feelings when alone on a still Sunday morning, or of Ishmael on the mast, and of other American characters for whom the combination of freedom and uncertain identity proves nearly self-destructive. On such isolation and torment, see Hedges, "Culture of Contradictions," pp. 138–39.

31. In addition to the episode in which Arthur himself is placed in a coffin while still alive (p. 149), there are suggestions that the young Thetford is still alive when carried in a coffin from his home (p. 140), and that Watson is still alive when Welbeck and Mervyn bury him (p. 110). There is also a hint that Mervyn might have rushed Susan Hadwin to her grave prematurely (pp. 280–81). Also important is the recurrent image of the destruction of the family, which Brown may have intended as a challenge to the standard projection of family solidarity in the popular sentimental novel. On the latter see Terence Martin, "Social Institutions in the Early American Novel," *American Quarterly* 9 (1957), esp. 77–80.

32. See Godwin on property, *Political Justice*, ed. H. S. Salt (London, 1890), chaps. 1, 2.

33. The frequent repetition of this phrase and Mervyn's awareness of being in a world of political revolutions and, in Stevens's phrase, "mercantile anxieties and revolutions" (p. 227), suggests a relationship between individual and corporate turmoils. On the function of social and political ideas in the novel, see David H. Hirsch, "Charles Brockden Brown as a Novelist of Ideas," *Books at Brown* 20 (1965), 165–84, and Hedges, "Culture of Contradictions," *passim*.

34. On Mervyn's exploitation of Welbeck's sins, see Berthoff, "Introduction," p. xvii, and Ringe, *Brown*, p. 75.

35. On Mervyn's unconscious motives see Bracaccio, "Unreliable Narrator," pp. 22–27. On the function of the irrational in Brown in general, see Kimball, *Rational Fictions*, and his "Savages and

Savagism: Brockden Brown's Dramatic Irony," *Studies in Romanticism* 6 (1967), 214–15.

36. Hedges also notes a suggested father-son relationship between Welbeck and Mervyn ("Culture of Contradictions," p. 127).

37. Clara makes similar comments about the lure of death in *Wieland*, p. 234. She also shares Mervyn's attitude toward the emotionally pacifying effect of writing, pp. 221, 228.

38. There are no rational grounds for Mervyn's revealing his possession of the money or for his burning of it after hearing Welbeck's transparent story. But as Welbeck goes into a rage, Mervyn is clearly the ready martyr.

39. Although Brown does make one error by having Arthur refer to Stevens as a third party when he is supposedly the audience of the narrative (see Bernard, "Ordeal of Innocence," p. 442), the shift of Arthur to writer-narrator emphasizes his break with Stevens and highlights his new role as Arthur-author.

40. For commentary on the importance of Mervyn's calling as a writer, see Bell " 'The Double-Tongued Deceiver,' " pp. 158–60, and Paul Witherington, "Benevolence and the 'Utmost Stretch': Charles Brockden Brown's Narrative Dilemma," *Criticism* 14 (1972), 175–91.

41. This language suggests that Mervyn's spiritual emptiness and moral confusion lead him, and others like Welbeck and Stevens, to invest a religiouslike faith in objects and other persons.

42. In Arthur's closing comment about his future "happiness" are the seeds of future satires on American expectations, such as Edward Albee's *American Dream*, in which a young man like Arthur brings "satisfaction" to his new parents. The play closes with Grandma's ironic observation: "So, let's leave things as they are right now . . . while everybody's happy . . . or while everybody's got what he thinks he wants" (*The American Dream* and *The Zoo Story* (New York, 1961) p. 127).

43. Warfel, *Brown*, pp. 166–75.

44. *Ibid.,* p. 154.

45. Quoted in *ibid.,* p. 54.

46. For discussion of these novels see Ringe, *Brown*, pp. 112–29.

47. See Warfel, *Brown*, pp. 203–19, and Warner Berthoff, "Brockden Brown: The Politics of the Man of Letters," *The Serif* 3 (1966), 3–10.

48. "The Editors' Address to the Public," *The Literary Magazine and American Register* 1 (1803), 4. On the church's censorship of Brown, see Warfel, *Brown*, p. 227.

49. Warfel describes the years of his declining health, in *Brown*, pp. 228–37.

Conclusion

1. Clifford Geertz, *The Interpretation of Culture* (New York, 1973), p. 250.
2. *Ibid.*, pp. 242–43.
3. *Ibid.*, p. 100.
4. Thomas McFarland, *Romanticism and the Forms of Ruin: Wordsworth, Coleridge, and Modalities of Fragmentation* (Princeton, 1981), p. 47.
5. *New York Times*, Sept. 12, 1980, p. C-21.
6. Friedrich von Schiller, quoted in McFarland, *Romanticism and the Forms of Ruin*, p. 11.

SELECT BIBLIOGRAPHY

Not included below are the standard histories and anthologies covering the period, the well-known primary writings and collected works of the major writers presented, or works already cited in the notes. There is an abundance of primary and secondary material relating to the various subjects discussed in this book, but limitations of space allow for a listing of only those works that I found most important in formulating my ideas and developing my approach.

Primary Sources

Beattie, James. *Elements of Moral Science.* Philadelphia, 1792–94.

———. *Essays on Poetry and Music.* London, 1776.

———. *Evidences of the Christian Religion.* Dublin, 1786.

Blair, Hugh. *A Critical Dissertation on the Poems of Ossian, the Son of Fingal.* London, 1763.

Brown, John. *The History of the Rise and Progress of Poetry, Through Its Several Species.* Newcastle, Eng., 1764.

Byles, Mather. *Poems on Several Occasions.* 1744; reprinted New York, 1960.

Campbell, George. *The Philosophy of Rhetoric,* ed. Lloyd F. Bitzer. Carbondale, 1963.

Dennie, Joseph. *The Lay Preacher,* ed. John E. Hall. Philadelphia, 1817.

Fithian, Philip Vickers. *Journal,* eds. John Rogers Williams, Robert G. Albion, and Leonidas Dodson. 2 vols. Princeton, 1900–34.

Kames, Henry Home, Lord. *Loose Hints upon Education Chiefly Concerning the Culture of the Heart.* Edinburgh, 1781.

Kettel, Samuel, ed. *Specimens of American Poetry, with Critical and Biographical Notices.* 3 vols. Boston, 1829.

Loeth, Robert. *Lectures on the Sacred Poetry of the Hebrews,* trans. G. Gregory. First published in Latin in England in 1753; Boston, 1815.

Ramsay, David. *History of the American Revolution.* London, 1791.

Smith, Elihu Hubbard, ed. *American Poems* (1793). Reprinted with introduction and notes by William K. Bottorff. Gainesville, Fla., 1966.

Wheatley, Phyllis. *The Poems of Phyllis Wheatley,* ed. Julian D. Mason. Chapel Hill, 1966.

Williams, William. *Mr. Penrose: The Journal of Penrose, Seaman,* ed. David H. Dickason. Bloomington, 1969.

Secondary Sources

Adair, Douglass. *Fame and the Founding Fathers,* ed. Trevor Colbourn. New York, 1974.

Addison, Daniel Dulany. *The Clergy in American Life and Letters.* London, 1900.

Albanese, Catherine L. *Sons of the Fathers: The Civil Religion of the American Revolution.* Philadelphia, 1976.

Aldridge, Alfred Owen, ed. *The Ibero-American Enlightenment.* Urbana, 1971.

Appleby, Joyce Oldham. "The Social Origins of American Revolutionary Ideology." *Journal of American History* 64 (1978), 935–58.

Arendt, Hannah. *On Revolution.* New York, 1979.

Arieli, Yehoshua. *Individualism and Nationalism in American Ideology.* Cambridge, Mass., 1964.

Bailyn, Bernard. *Education in the Forming of American Society: Needs and Opportunities for Study.* Chapel Hill, 1960.

———. *The Ideological Origins of the American Revolution.* Cambridge, Mass., 1967.

———. *The Ordeal of Thomas Hutchinson.* Cambridge, Mass., 1974.

———. "Political Experience and Enlightenment Ideas in Eighteenth-Century America." *American Historical Review* 67 (1961–62), 339–51.

———, ed. *Pamphlets of the American Revolution, 1750–1776.* Cambridge, Mass., 1965.

Baldwin, Alice M. *The New England Clergy and the American Revolution.* Durham, 1928.

Bates, Mary Dexter. "A Study of American Verse from 1783 to 1799." Ph.D. dissertation, Brown University, 1954.

Bell, David V. J. *Power, Influence, and Authority: An Essay in Political Linguistics.* New York, 1975.

Bellah, Robert N. *The Broken Covenant: American Civil Religion in Time of Trial.* New York, 1975.

Bercovitch, Sacvan. *The Puritan Origins of the American Self.* New Haven, 1975.

Berens, John F. *Providence and Patriotism in Early America, 1640–1815.* Charlottesville, 1978.

Berk, Stephen E. *Calvinism versus Democracy: Timothy Dwight and the Origins of American Evangelical Orthodoxy.* Hamden, Conn., 1974.

Berman, Harold J. "The Interaction of Law and Religion." *Capital University Law Review* 8 (1979), 345–56.

———. *The Interaction of Law and Religion.* Nashville, 1974.

Berthoff, Rowland T. *An Unsettled People: Social Order and Disorder in American History.* New York, 1971.

Billias, George A., ed. *Law and Authority in Colonial America: Selected Essays.* Barre, Mass., 1965.

Boorstin, Daniel J. *The Americans: The Colonial Experience.* New York, 1958.

———. *The Americans: The National Experience.* New York, 1965.

Boys, Richard C. "The Beginnings of the American Poetical Miscellany, 1714–1800." *American Literature* 42 (1945), 243–54.

Breen, Timothy H. *The Character of the Good Ruler: A Study of Puritan Political Ideas in New England, 1630–1730.* New Haven, 1970.

Bridenbaugh, Carl. *Mitre and Sceptre: Transatlantic Faiths, Ideas, Personalities, and Politics, 1689–1775.* New York, 1962.

Brooks, Van Wyck. *The World of Washington Irving.* New York, 1944.

Brown, Herbert Ross. *The Sentimental Novel in America, 1789–1860.* Durham, 1940.

Buel, Richard. *Securing the Revolution: Ideology in American Politics, 1789–1815.* Ithaca, 1972.

Bushman, Richard L. *From Puritan to Yankee: Character and the Social Order in Connecticut, 1690–1765.* Cambridge, Mass., 1967.

Butt, John Everett. *The Oxford History of English Literature: The Mid-Eighteenth Century,* ed. and completed by Geoffrey Carnall. Oxford, 1979.

Cady, Edwin H., ed. *Literature of the Early Republic*. New York, 1969.

Carroll, Peter N., ed. *Religion and the Coming of the American Revolution*. Waltham, Mass., 1970.

Charvat, William. *The Origins of American Critical Thought, 1810–1835*. Philadelphia, 1936; reissued New York, 1968.

Cherry, Conrad. *Nature and Religious Imagination: From Edwards to Bushnell*. Philadelphia, 1980.

Colbourn, Trevor H. *The Lamp of Experience: Whig History and the Intellectual Origins of the American Revolution*. Chapel Hill, 1965.

———, ed. *Fame and the Founding Fathers*. New York, 1974.

Cowing, Cedric B. *The Great Awakening and the American Revolution: Colonial Thought in the 18th Century*. Chicago, 1971.

Craven, Wesley Frank. *The Legend of the Founding Fathers*. New York, 1956.

Cronin, James E. "Elihu Hubbard Smith and the New York Friendly Club, 1795–1798." *Publications of the Modern Language Association* 64 (1949), 471–79.

Crowley, J. E. *This Sheba, Self: The Conceptualization of Economic Life in Eighteenth-Century America*. Baltimore, 1974.

Davidson, Philip. *Propaganda and the American Revolution, 1763–1783*. Chapel Hill, 1941.

Davis, David Brion. *The Problem of Slavery in the Age of Revolution, 1770–1823*. Ithaca, 1975.

Davis, Richard Beale. "The Colonial Virginia Satirist: Mid-Eighteenth Century Commentaries on Politics, Religion, and Society." *Transactions of the American Philosophical Society*, n.s., 57 (1967), 5–74.

———. *Intellectual Life of Jefferson's Virginia, 1790–1830*. Chapel Hill, 1964.

Dexter, Franklin B. *Biographical Sketches of the Graduates of Yale College with Annals of the College History*. 6 vols. New York, 1885–1912.

Douglas, Mary, ed. *Rules and Meanings: The Anthropology of Everyday Knowledge*. London, 1973.

Downey, James. *The Eighteenth Century Pulpit: A Study of the Sermons of Butler, Berkeley, Secker, Sterne, Whitefield and Wesley*. Oxford, 1969.

Emerson, Everett H., ed. *American Literature, 1764–1789*. Madison, 1977.

———, ed. *Major Writers of Early American Literature*. Madison, 1972.

Ernst, Joseph A. *Money and Politics in America, 1755–1775: A Study in the Currency Act of 1764 and the Political Economy of Revolution.* Chapel Hill, 1973.

Fiering, Norman. *Moral Philosophy of Seventeenth-Century Harvard: A Discipline in Transition.* Chapel Hill, 1981.

Fischer, David Hackett. *The Revolution of American Conservatism: The Federalist Party in the Era of Jeffersonian Democracy.* New York, 1965.

Foner, Eric. *Tom Paine and Revolutionary America.* New York, 1976.

Fox, Dixon Ryan, and John Allen Krout. *The Completion of Independence, 1790–1830.* New York, 1944.

Free, William J. *The Columbian Magazine and American Literary Nationalism.* The Hague, 1968.

Friedman, Lawrence J. *Inventors of the Promised Land.* New York, 1975.

Fritz, Paul Samuel, and David Williams, eds. *The Triumph of Culture: 18th Century Perspectives.* Toronto, 1972.

Gay, Peter. *The Enlightenment: An Interpretation.* 2 vols. New York, 1966.

Gelpi, Albert J. *The Tenth Muse: The Psyche of the American Poet.* Cambridge, Mass., 1975.

Gipson, Lawrence Henry. *The Coming of the Revolution, 1763–1775.* New York, 1954.

Gohdes, Clarence L. F., ed. *Essays on American Literature in Honor of Jay B. Hubbell.* Durham, 1967.

Gombrich, E. H., Julian Hochberg, and Max Black. *Art, Perception and Reality.* Baltimore, 1972.

Graff, Gerald. *Literature Against Itself: Literary Ideas in Modern Society.* Chicago, 1979.

Granger, Bruce. *American Essay Serials from Franklin to Irving.* Knoxville, 1978.

———. *Political Satire in the American Revolution, 1763–1783.* Ithaca, 1960.

Greene, Evarts B. *The Revolutionary Generation, 1763–1790.* New York, 1943.

Greene, Jack P. "Search for Identity: An Interpretation of the Meaning of Selected Patterns of Social Response in Eighteenth-Century America." *Journal of Social History* 3 (1970), 189–220.

———. "An Uneasy Connection: An Analysis of the Precondition of the American Revolution." In *Essays on the American Revolution,* eds. Stephen G. Kurtz and James H. Hutson. Chapel Hill, 1973.

———, ed. *The Ambiguity of the American Revolution.* New York, 1968.

Gunn, Giles B. *The Interpretation of Otherness: Literature, Religion, and the American Imagination.* New York, 1979.

Guthrie, Warren. "The Development of Rhetorical Theory in America, 1635–1850." *Speech Monographs* 8 (1946), 14–22.

Habermas, Jürgen. *Communication and the Evolution of Society,* trans. Thomas McCarthy. Boston, 1979.

——. *Knowledge and Human Interests,* trans. Jeremy J. Shapiro. Boston, 1971.

Harris, Neil. *The Artist in American Society: The Formative Years, 1790–1860.* New York, 1966.

Hartz, Louis. *The Liberal Tradition in America: An Interpretation of American Political Thought since the Revolution.* New York, 1955.

Hedges, William L. *Washington Irving: An American Study, 1802–1832.* Baltimore, 1965.

Henderson, Harry B., III. *Versions of the Past: The Historical Imagination in American Fiction.* New York, 1974.

Hofstadter, Richard. *America at 1750: A Social Portrait.* New York, 1971.

——. *Anti-intellectualism in American Life.* New York, 1963.

——. *The Paranoid Style in American Politics, and Other Essays.* New York, 1965.

Hovenkamp, Herbert. *Science and Religion in America, 1800–1860.* Philadelphia, 1978.

Howard, Leon. *Literature and the American Tradition.* Garden City, N.Y., 1960.

Howe, Irving. *Decline of the New.* New York, 1970.

Howe, Mark De Wolfe. *The Garden and the Wilderness: Religion and Government in American Constitutional History.* Chicago, 1965.

Howell, Wilbur Samuel. *Eighteenth-Century British Logic and Rhetoric.* Princeton, 1971.

Isaac, Rhys. "Dramatizing the Ideology of Revolution: Popular Mobilization in Virginia, 1774 to 1776." *William & Mary Quarterly* 33 (July 1976), 357–85.

Israel, Calvin, ed. *Discoveries and Considerations: Essays on Early American Literature and Aesthetics Presented to Harold Jantz.* Albany, 1976.

Jacobson, Norman. "Knowledge, Tradition, and Authority: A Note on the American Experience." In *Authority,* ed. Carl J. Friedrich. Cambridge, Mass., 1958.

Jameson, Frederic. *The Political Unconscious: Narrative as a Socially Symbolic Act.* Ithaca, 1981.

Jedrey, Christopher. *The World of John Cleaveland: Family and*

Community in Eighteenth-Century New England. New York, 1979.

Jehlen, Myra. "New World Epics: The Novel and the Middle Class in America." *Salmagundi* 36 (1977), 49–68.

Jones, Howard Mumford. *Belief and Disbelief in American Literature*. Chicago, 1967.

―――. "The Drift to Liberalism in the American Eighteenth Century." In *Authority and the Individual*. Cambridge, Mass., 1937.

Jordan, Winthrop D. "Familial Politics: Thomas Paine and the Killing of the King, 1776." *Journal of American History* 60 (1973), 294–308.

Joyce, Lester D. *Church and Clergy in the American Revolution: A Study in Group Behavior*. New York, 1966.

Kammen, Michael G. *People of Paradox: An Inquiry Concerning the Origins of American Civilization*. New York, 1972.

―――. *A Season of Youth: The American Revolution and the Historical Imagination*. New York, 1978.

Kerber, Linda K. *Women in the Republic: Intellect and Ideology in Revolutionary America*. Chapel Hill, 1980.

Ketcham, Ralph L. *From Colony to Country: The Revolution in American Thought, 1750–1820*. New York, 1974.

Knollenberg, Bernhard. *Growth of the American Revolution: 1766–1775*. New York, 1975.

Koch, Adrienne. *Power, Morals, and the Founding Fathers: Essays in the Interpretation of the American Enlightenment*. Ithaca, 1961.

―――, ed. *The American Enlightenment: The Shaping of the American Experiment and a Free Society*. New York, 1965.

Kohn, Hans. *American Nationalism: An Interpretive Essay*. New York, 1961.

―――. *The Idea of Nationalism: A Study in Its Origins and Background*. New York, 1967.

Krout, John Allen, and Dixon Ryan Fox. *The Completion of Independence, 1790–1830*. New York, 1944.

Leary, Lewis. "Thomas Day on American Poetry, in 1786." *Modern Language Notes* 61 (1946), 464–66.

Leder, Lawrence H., ed. *The Meaning of the American Revolution*. Chicago, 1969.

Lowance, Mason I. *The Language of Canaan: Metaphor and Symbol in New England from the Puritans to the Transcendentalists*. Cambridge, Mass., 1980.

Lynen, John F. *The Design of the Present: Essays on Time and Form in American Literature*. New Haven, 1969.

Magliola, Robert R. *Phenomenology and Literature: An Introduction.* West Lafayette, Ind., 1977.

Maier, Pauline. *From Resistance to Revolution: Colonial Radicals and the Development of American Opposition to Britain, 1765–1776.* New York, 1972.

Main, Jackson Turner. *The Social Structure of Revolutionary America.* Princeton, 1965.

Martin, Jay. "William Dunlap: The Documentary Vision." In *Theater und Drama in Amerika: Aspekte und Interpretationen,* eds. Edgar Lohner and Rudolf Hass. Berlin, 1978.

Mazlish, Bruce. "Leadership in the American Revolution: The Psychological Dimension." In *Leadership in the American Revolution.* Washington, D.C., 1974.

McCaughey, Elizabeth P. *From Loyalist to Founding Father: The Political Odyssey of William Samuel Johnson.* New York, 1980.

McCleur, J. F. "The Republic and the Millennium." In *The Religion of the Republic,* ed. Elwyn A. Smith. Philadelphia, 1971.

McLoughlin, William G. "The Role of Religion in the American Revolution: Liberty of Conscience and Cultural Cohesion in the New Nation." In *Essays on the American Revolution,* eds. Stephen G. Kurtz and James H. Hutson. Chapel Hill, 1973.

Meserve, Walter J. *An Emerging Entertainment: The Drama of the American People to 1828.* Bloomington, 1977.

Meyer, Donald H. *The Democratic Enlightenment.* New York, 1976.

Middlekauff, Robert. "The Ritualization of the American Revolution." In *The Development of an American Culture,* eds. Stanley Coben and Lorman Ratner. Englewood Cliffs, N.J., 1970.

Miller, John C. *The Federalist Era, 1789–1801.* New York, 1960.

Miller, Lillian B. *Patrons and Patriotism: The Encouragement of the Fine Arts in the United States, 1790–1860.* Chicago, 1966.

Miller, Perry. "From Edwards to Emerson." In *Errand into the Wilderness.* Cambridge, Mass., 1956.

Monk, Samuel H. *The Sublime: A Study of Critical Theories in XVIII-Century England.* 1935; reprinted Ann Arbor, 1960.

Mooij, J. J. A. *A Study of Metaphor: On the Nature of Metaphorical Expressions, with Special Reference to Their Reference.* Amsterdam, 1976.

Moore, Frank. *Diary of the American Revolution: From Newspapers and Original Documents.* 2 vols. New York, 1860.

Morgan, Edmund S. "The American Revolution Considered as an

Intellectual Movement." In *Paths of American Thought*, eds. Arthur M. Schlesinger, Jr., and Morton White. Boston, 1963.

———. "The Puritan Ethic and the American Revolution." *William & Mary Quarterly*, 3d ser., 24 (1967), 3–43.

———, and Helen M. Morgan. *The Stamp Act Crisis: Prologue to Revolution*. Chapel Hill, 1953.

Morris, Wright. *The Territory Ahead*. New York, 1958.

Murray, Jain H. *The Puritan Hope: A Study in Revival and the Interpretation of Prophecy*. London, 1971.

Murrin, John M. "Review Essay." *History and Theory* 11 (1972), 236–75.

Nagel, Paul C. *One Nation Indivisible: The Union in American Thought, 1776–1861*. New York, 1964.

———. *This Sacred Trust: American Nationality, 1798–1898*. New York, 1971.

Nash, Gary B. *Class and Society in Early America*. Englewood Cliffs, N.J., 1970.

———. *The Urban Crucible: Social Change, Political Consciousness, and the Origins of the American Revolution*. Cambridge, Mass., 1979.

Needham, H. A., ed. *Taste and Criticism in the Eighteenth Century: A Selection of Texts Illustrating the Evolution of Taste and the Development of Critical Theory*. London, 1952.

Neil, J. Meredith. *Toward a National Taste: America's Quest for Aesthetic Independence*. Honolulu, 1975.

Niebuhr, H. Richard, and Daniel D. Williams, eds. *The Ministry in Historical Perspectives*. New York, 1956.

Nye, Russel B. *American Literary History, 1607–1830*. New York, 1970.

———. *The Cultural Life of the New Nation, 1776–1830*. New York, 1960.

———. *This Almost Chosen People: Essays in the History of American Ideas*. East Lansing, 1966.

Patterson, Samuel White. *The Spirit of the American Revolution as Revealed in the Poetry of the Period: A Study of American Patriotic Verse from 1760 to 1783*. Boston, 1915.

Peyre, Henri. *Literature and Sincerity*. New Haven, 1963.

Pickering, James H., ed. *The World Turned Upside Down: Prose and Poetry of the American Revolution*. Port Washington, N.Y., 1975.

Plumb, H. J. "The Public, Literature and the Arts in the 18th Century." In *The Triumph of Culture: 18th Century Perspectives*, eds. Paul Fritz and David Williams. Toronto, 1972.

Pocock, J. G. A. *Politics, Language and Time: Essays on Political Thought and History.* New York, 1971.

———. "Virtue and Commerce in the Eighteenth Century." *Journal of Interdisciplinary History* 3 (1972–73), 125–34.

Pole, J. R. *Political Representation in England and the Origins of the American Republic.* London, 1966.

Porte, Joel. *Representative Man: Ralph Waldo Emerson in His Time.* New York, 1979.

———. *The Romance in America: Studies in Cooper, Poe, Hawthorne, Melville and James.* Middletown, 1969.

Potter, David M. *People of Plenty: Economic Abundance and the American Character.* Chicago, 1954.

———, and Gordon L. Thomas, eds. *The Colonial Idiom.* Carbondale, 1970.

Purcell, James S., Jr. "Literature Culture in North Carolina Before 1820." Ph.D. dissertation, Duke University, 1950.

Rathbun, John W. "The Historical Sense in American Associationist Literature Criticism." *Philological Quarterly* 44 (1961), 553–68.

Richardson, Robert D. *Myth and Literature in the American Renaissance.* Bloomington, 1978.

Ricoeur, Paul. *The Rule of Metaphor: Multi-disciplinary Studies of the Creation of Meaning in Language,* trans. Robert Czerny. Toronto, 1977.

Robbins, Caroline. *The Eighteenth-Century Commonwealthman: Studies in the Transmission, Development and Circumstance of English Liberal Thought from the Restoration of Charles II until the War with the Thirteen Colonies.* Cambridge, Mass., 1959.

Rorty, Richard. *Philosophy and the Mirror of Nature.* Princeton, 1979.

Rossiter, Clinton L. *The American Quest, 1790–1860: An Emerging Nation in Search of Identity, Unity, and Modernity.* New York, 1971.

———. *Seedtime of the Republic: The Origin of the American Tradition of Political Liberty.* New York, 1953.

Ruland, Richard. *The Native Muse.* New York, 1972.

Sachs, William S., and Ari Hoogenboom. *The Enterprising Colonials: Society on the Eve of the Revolution.* Chicago, 1965.

Sanford, Charles L. *The Quest for Paradise: Europe and the American Moral Imagination.* Urbana, 1961.

Sapir, J. David, and J. Christopher Crocker, eds. *The Social Use of Metaphor: Essays on the Anthropology of Rhetoric.* Philadelphia, 1977.

Schlesinger, Arthur M. *Prelude to Independence: The Newspaper War on Britain, 1764–1776.* New York, 1958.

Shahan, Robert W., and Kenneth R. Merrill. *American Philosophy from Edwards to Quine.* Norman, Okla., 1977.

Shaw, Peter. *American Patriots and the Rituals of Revolution.* Cambridge, Mass., 1980.

———. *The Character of John Adams.* Chapel Hill, 1976.

Shy, John W. *Toward Lexington: The Role of the British Army in the Coming of the American Revolution.* Princeton, 1965.

———, ed. *The American Revolution.* Northbrook, Ill., 1973.

Sibley, John L., and Clifford K. Shipton, eds. *Biographical Sketches of Graduates of Harvard University in Cambridge, Massachusetts.* 17 vols. Cambridge, Mass., 1873–1975.

Simpson, Lewis P. "Federalism and the Crisis of Literary Order." *American Literature* 32 (1960), 254–66.

———. "Literary Ecumenicalism of the American Enlightenment." In *The Ibero-American Enlightenment,* ed. A. Owen Aldridge. Urbana, 1971.

———. "The Printer as a Man of Letters: Franklin and the Symbolism of the Third Realm." In *The Oldest Revolutionary: Essays on Benjamin Franklin,* ed. J. A. Leo Lemay. Philadelphia, 1976.

———, ed. *The Federalist Literary Mind.* Baton Rouge, 1962.

Slotkin, Richard. *Regeneration Through Violence: The Mythology of the American Frontier, 1600–1860.* Middletown, 1973.

Smith, James Ward, and A. Leland Jamison. *Religion in American Life.* 4 vols. Princeton, 1961.

Smith-Rosenberg, Carroll. *Religion and the Rise of the American City: The New York City Mission Movement, 1812–1870.* Ithaca, 1971.

Spencer, Benjamin. *The Quest for Nationality: An American Literary Campaign.* Syracuse, 1957.

Spengemann, William C. *The Adventurous Muse: The Poetics of American Fiction, 1789–1900.* New Haven, 1977.

Sprague, William B. *Annals of the American Pulpit.* 9 vols. New York, 1859.

Stein, Roger B. "Copley's *Watson and the Shark* and Aesthetics in the 1770s." In *Discoveries and Considerations: Essays on Early American Literature and Aesthetics,* ed. Calvin Israel. New York, 1976.

———. "Pulled Out of the Bay: American Fiction in the Eighteenth Century." *Studies in American Fiction* 2 (Spring 1974), 13–36.

———. *Seascape and the American Imagination.* New York, 1975.

Stineback, David C. *Shifting World: Social Change and Nostalgia in the American Novel.* Lewisburg, Pa., 1976.

Strout, Cushing. *The New Heavens and New Earth: Political Religion in America.* New York, 1973.

Takaki, Ronald T. *Iron Cages: Race and Culture in Nineteenth-Century America.* New York, 1979.

Turner, Victor. *Dramas, Fields, and Metaphors: Symbolic Action in Human Society.* Ithaca, 1974.

Tuveson, Ernest Lee. *The Imagination as a Means of Grace: Locke and the Aesthetics of Romanticism.* Berkeley, 1960.

———. *Redeemer Nation: The Idea of America's Millennial Role.* Chicago, 1968.

Van Alstyne, Richard W. *Genesis of American Nationalism.* Waltham, Mass., 1970.

Walton, Craig. "Hume and Jefferson on the Uses of History." In *Philosophy and the Civilizing Arts: Essays Presented to Herbert W. Schneider,* eds. Craig Walton and John P. Anton. Athens, Ohio, 1974.

Waltzer, Michael. "On the Role of Symbolism in Political Thought." *Political Science Quarterly* 82 (1967), 191–204.

———. "Puritanism as a Revolutionary Ideology." In *New Perspectives on the American Past,* eds. Stanley N. Katz and Stanley I. Kutler. Boston, 1969.

Weber, Max. *The Protestant Ethic and the Spirit of Capitalism,* trans. Talcott Parsons. New York, 1950.

Weis, Frederick Lewis. *The Colonial Clergy and the Colonial Churches of New England.* Lancaster, Mass., 1936.

Wertenbaker, Thomas J. *The Founding of American Civilization: The Middle Colonies.* New York, 1938.

White, Hayden V. *Metahistory: The Historical Imagination in Nineteenth-Century Europe.* Baltimore, 1973.

Wiebe, Robert H. *The Segmented Society: An Introduction to the Meaning of America.* New York, 1975.

Williams, Raymond. *Culture and Society, 1780–1950.* New York, 1966.

Wills, Garry. *Inventing America: Jefferson's Declaration of Independence.* Garden City, N.Y., 1978.

Wood, Gordon S. *The Creation of the American Republic, 1776–1787.* New York, 1969.

———. "The Democratization of Mind in the American Revolution." In *Leadership in the American Revolution.* Washington, D.C., 1974.

———. "Rhetoric and Reality in the American Revolution." *William & Mary Quarterly* 23 (1966), 3–32.

Wright, Louis B. *The Cultural Life of the American Colonies: 1607–1763.* New York, 1957.

Wright, Lyle H. *American Fiction, 1774–1850: A Contribution Toward a Bibliography.* 2nd rev. ed. San Marino, 1969.

Ziff, Larzer. *Literary Democracy: The Declaration of Cultural Independence in America.* New York, 1981.

———. *Puritanism in America: New Culture in a New World.* New York, 1973.

Zuckerman, Michael. "The Fabrication of Identity in Early America." *William & Mary Quarterly*, 3d ser., 34 (1977), 183–214.

INDEX